THE ELEGANT WEDDING AND THE BUDGET-SAVVY ❧ BRIDE ❧

How to Have the Wedding of Your Dreams for Half the Price

DEBORAH MCCOY

A PLUME BOOK

PLUME
Published by the Penguin Group
Penguin Putnam Inc., 375 Hudson Street, New York, New York 10014, U.S.A.
Penguin Books Ltd, 27 Wrights Lane, London W8 5TZ, England
Penguin Books Australia Ltd, Ringwood, Victoria, Australia
Penguin Books Canada Ltd, 10 Alcorn Avenue, Toronto, Ontario, Canada M4V 3B2
Penguin Books (N.Z.) Ltd, 182–190 Wairau Road, Auckland 10, New Zealand

Penguin Books Ltd, Registered Offices: Harmondsworth, Middlesex, England

First published by Plume, a member of Penguin Putnam Inc.

First Printing, January, 1999
10   9   8   7   6   5   4   3   2   1

Photos provided by Roberts Photographics, Inc., Boca Raton, Florida.

Ⓟ REGISTERED TRADEMARK — MARCA REGISTRADA

LIBRARY OF CONGRESS CATALOGING-IN-PUBLICATION DATA:
McCoy, Deborah.
    The elegant wedding and the budget-savvy bride : how to have the wedding of your dreams
for half the price / Deborah McCoy.
        p.   cm.
    Includes bibliographical references.
    ISBN 0-452-27850-3
    1. Weddings—United States—Planning.   2. Consumer education—United States.
I. Title.
HQ745.M38   1999
395.2'2—dc21   98-29062
                                                                                CIP

Printed in the United States of America
Set in Goudy and Opti-Franco Light
Designed by Eve L. Kirch

BOOKS ARE AVAILABLE AT QUANTITY DISCOUNTS WHEN USED TO PROMOTE PRODUCTS OR SER-
VICES. FOR INFORMATION PLEASE WRITE TO PREMIUM MARKETING DIVISION, PENGUIN PUTNAM
INC., 375 HUDSON STREET, NEW YORK, NEW YORK 10014.

For Dino,
forever my love . . .

For Millie and Donald,
always in my heart . . .

I love you because you
Are helping me to make
Of the lumber of my life
Not a tavern
But a temple;
Out of the works of my every day
Not a reproach
But a song.
                    —From "Love"
                    Roy Croft

CONTENTS

INTRODUCTION

My name is Deborah McCoy and I'm in the wedding business. I work with brides six days a week to help them plan the elegant weddings of their dreams; it's not easy.

The story of my entry into this business is funny, now that I look back on it, and I think it's worth retelling, since I'm sure that many of you, unless you educate yourselves, will suffer the same kind of trials and tribulations that I did. In Florida, when we face adversity, we say that we're up to our you-know-what in alligators, and that's how I felt when planning my stepdaughter's wedding. It was the first wedding I had planned, I wasn't in the business, and I didn't know the first thing about weddings. I had no idea what an arduous task it was to plan one, nor did I realize the trauma that could occur if something went amiss. (It's sort of akin to taking a swim in quicksand.) Now, after years of experience, my favorite bit of advice to brides is: *Be careful how you plan.* If something goes wrong, you can't throw another wedding next weekend.

When my stepdaughter decided to marry, I sat down and made up a budget, based on what I *thought* the cost would be. It was an effort in futility. I hadn't shopped, surveyed the market, or gotten any estimates, and when I did, my budget and my dreams for her wedding went down the drain. Had I been logical and practical in my approach, I would have done my homework and formulated a workable, realistic budget. But when the estimates started to roll in, I felt like jumping from the nearest bridge. Being on a limited budget, it was necessary to put on my thinking cap and come up with a solution to my problem.

At the time, Elva's (my business) was a custom fashion design house in Boca Raton, Florida, and we made very upscale for very upscale women. My wed my stepdaughter was her wedding g piece, and veils, which we designed and made. (We also made the bridesmaids' dresses). Because of my business, I was able to get the invitations at cost.

The wedding was held in December, near Christmas, and after visiting a few florists, I could not believe the prices they were asking for poinsettia centerpieces and bridal party flowers. It was astronomical. I decided to save some money by finding a freelancer to do the job and began calling wholesale floral companies to ask for referrals. I was finally given a name, but in hindsight, I can't believe I acted so irrationally. Here I was, entrusting the beauty of my stepdaughter's wedding to a man I didn't know, *just to save a few bucks?* Fortunately, he was a talented florist. (One of the most talented I've ever come across. His name is Tim Berry. He later became my partner in our floral business.) The flowers for the wedding turned out magnificently, and I paid one-fourth the cost. Don't ever do this; I was lucky!)

I missed the boat on the band, however, hiring a less-than-rocking group. They were passable, but I should have bit the bullet and spent the money. When it comes to entertainment, it's critical to find a great DJ, band, orchestra, or even a one-man band (if you're having a small wedding). *The entertainment makes the party.*

We hosted the reception at the finest resort in Boca Raton, and we were "had." Because so many of our family were light drinkers or teetotalers, we were advised by the catering director to buy the liquor based on consumption (by the drink). *Big* mistake! We selected a moderately priced wine to be served with dinner and had a four-hour open bar. At the end of the evening, we were handed a liquor bill that was close to $5,000. We were in total shock; there were only ninety people attending the wedding, which meant, based on the per-drink cost and the cost of the wine, everyone drank approximately eight drinks and consumed a bottle of wine. When I alerted the catering director to this ridiculous discrepancy, her response, in effect, was, "You signed the contract, you pay." We did; we had no choice. (Had I known then what I know now, things would have been *very* different.)

My stepdaughter's wedding was my entry into this business. Afterward, I got calls ("Could you do my wedding?") and from there, Elva's evolved into a full-service bridal salon. But I was also determined to make the business an information resource center for brides. I studied everything I could about all facets of wedding planning. Tim and I opened a wedding-floral business, and I began to learn about flowers and design. I studied etiquette and learned how to write invitations correctly. I began to work with catering directors and photographers and videographers. I was determined to become a master of my trade.

After a few years, it became obvious to me that brides wanted a realistic approach to wedding planning. The days of Dad picking up the tab were fading fast, and the questions from my clients' mouths were much different from the What should I serve at my bridesmaids' luncheon? types of questions that dominated old-fashioned bridal books. The women I worked with asked hard-hitting, rational questions: How do I protect myself with a contract? How do I know the band I hire will be the same one that will show? How do I buy liquor so I don't get ripped off?

I decided to write a book, and my husband thought I had lost my mind. For hours, I'd sit at the computer and spill out page after page, which he'd trash, and then I'd start all over again. When we thought I had something worthwhile, I called an associate in the wedding business, Pam Roth, and told her of my idea. The first word out of her mouth was, "Jimmy."

In case you don't know "Jimmy's" identity,

he is none other than that incredibly talented bridal gown designer, *Demetrios*. He is a household name among brides and is recognized for the diversity of his designs (from sheer, simple elegance to the traditionally ornate), their quality, and their more-than-affordable price point. He is also the publisher of the national bridal magazine, *For the Bride*. When he heard of my proposal, he suggested that I come to New York, and the rest is history.

The result of this meeting was *For the Bride*, my first book, which has been critically acclaimed as the most "comprehensive book on the subject to date." The book received great reviews, coast-to-coast, and because of it, I appeared on *The Sally Jessy Raphael Show* as her bridal expert.

The book opened many doors. I became Demetrios's etiquette columnist and a feature article writer for his magazine. Next, I became a feature article writer for the nationally published *Wedding Pages* and took over their Internet *FAQS*. In the meantime, I became intrigued with the Internet myself and decided to go online. I wanted my web site (www. debmccoy.com) to be informative, fun, and helpful; it is. Bell Atlantic voted it one of the best, and I think it's a great wedding resource. Please come and visit.

My online experience, however, didn't stop there and recently expanded when Denis Reggie, a famous celebrity photographer, introduced me to *The Knot*. It is considered the finest, most comprehensive wedding research center online for brides. Accessed through AOL and the World Wide Web, it can provide you with at-your-fingertips information from wedding gowns to the latest wedding trends and services. It is so popular that *The Knot* reaches hundreds of thousands of brides- and grooms-to-be, per month. I am very happy to say that I will be contributing to *The Knot* as a guest expert. Watch for me and look for more information about *The Knot* and how it

can be of service to you, throughout the chapters of this book. (See appendix I for more information.)

In the interim, my business got bigger and bigger. Elva's currently stocks gowns that retail from $500 to $5,000 and the diversity in their price point keeps me in touch with women from all socioeconomic backgrounds. I also offer consulting programs that start at $500, because it's important to me that I be affordable to all brides.

When I made up my mind to write *The Elegant Wedding and the Budget-Savvy Bride*, it was because I began to realize that weddings (and their price) had gotten out of hand. Common sense seemed to be a long-gone commodity. Good taste seemed to be making its exit, too, and the money spent was mind-boggling. I figured it was time to put on the brakes.

The result has been a total learning experience for me. I never realized the endless possibilities that are open to the bride who displays ingenuity and initiative. Not only can she have an elegant wedding and save money, she can have a wedding that would make even a princess proud.

Let me give you an example. When I began to write the chapter on wedding cakes, I was stymied. What could I say to the budget-conscious bride? Buy a second-rate cake from your supermarket? Hardly. But then I did some research and determined that anyone with half a brain can make a cake and make it terrific!

For the best, most accurate information, I went to the experts for help: Sylvia Weinstock, Rose Levy Beranbaum, Ron Ben-Israel, and Jane Stacey. Betty Baird, a phenomenal local baker (she baked Loni Anderson and Burt Reynolds's wedding cake), gave me a terrific recipe and taught me how to tier a cake. (All of the experts' information is passed on to you in "The Wedding Cake" chapter and in appendix II.)

I'm not a baker, but I tackled the problem

with gusto. For several weekends, I made different cakes (my husband gained five pounds and insisted we take them to the store to give to our clients). It took time, but I proved to myself that if I could do it, anyone could. Then I tackled the problem of frosting and decorating, not with pastry bags and piped do-dads, but by frosting the cakes smooth and decorating *around* them, simply and elegantly. (None of the cakes featured in this book take longer than forty-five minutes to decorate.) The result: There's no reason why you can't make your own delectable, beautiful cake and save hundreds of dollars in the process!

It was the same when I tackled the problems of photography and videography. To get the best usually means spending thousands of dollars, but I wanted the experts to tell me what a bride should know, and the best way for her to save money. My experience with Denis Reggie, Monte Zucker, Roy Chapman, and Tim Roberts (who first got me interested in photography) was a total education. All of their invaluable information and advice is passed on to you in this book.

When it came to decorating and creating elegant tables (the factor with the power to make your guests think they're dining at The Ritz), I used my ingenuity and all my years of experience with flowers, designing centerpieces and, believe it or not, my experience with fabric and fashion. I knew that a bride could easily create elegant, inexpensive, *non-floral* centerpieces and then create incomparable accents (table runners and napkin stuffers) to go along with them that would make her tables "sing" with elegance.

Brides often give me the excuse that they don't have the time to shop, research, and plan their wedding the way they should. I say bologna! If you schedule your free time properly and wisely your time will be well spent and you will reap the rewards. I work six days a week in my bridal salon while also working as a wedding consultant and writing for *The Wedding Pages*, in addition to the time I spend on the Internet answering countless *FAQs*. When I wrote this book, I scheduled a different wedding component every weekend and dedicated myself to researching it. (There were also many components that I implemented and created myself.) If I can do it, you can do it.

The point is: *If you use your common sense, budget your time and money wisely, and show some initiative, you can save money.* And I don't mean a few hundred dollars. You can do it for thousands less than the average cost of a traditional wedding!

Good Luck—and have fun!
All the best,

Deb McCoy

Chapter One

THE TEN COMMANDMENTS OF ELEGANT WEDDING PLANNING

. . . to seek elegance rather than luxury, and refinement rather than fashion; to be worthy, not respectable, and wealthy, not rich; to study hard, think quietly, talk gently, act frankly . . . to bear all cheerfully, do all bravely, await occasions, hurry never. . . . This is to be my symphony.
—William Henry Channing, My *Symphony*

I decided to write this book after years of working with brides who wanted an elegant (synonym: expensive) wedding, but could not afford it. Hogwash! Elegance does not relate to money, but to a state of mind. Contrary to popular belief, the words elegant and expensive are *not* synonyms. Every bride can have an elegant wedding; the one she's always dreamed about. But she has to use her common sense, be practical, use her ingenuity, and make a commitment to give her *elegant* wedding the time and attention it deserves and requires.

Today, the majority of engaged couples pay for their own wedding. And if you're one of them, I will tell you that it's very easy to get into trouble if you don't budget wisely. The idea is to *spend only what you can afford*—and not go into debt. Being in debt is no way to begin married life. That's *Commandment One*.

The photographer I work with was once hired by a bride who was so immersed in her-self and her wedding that she forgot one important factor: She could not afford what she planned. After the reception, her husband wrote a bad check to a very prestigious hotel in Palm Beach. The hotel had him arrested and thrown in jail. When the photographer called the bride to make an appointment to see her proofs, the woman said that she couldn't because her husband was ". . . on vacation." Some vacation! Don't let this happen to you.

Commandment Two: Educate yourself. The more you know about the vendors, goods, and services you'll need, the better off you'll be. No one will pull the wool over your eyes. Study all the books and information you can find. My first book, *For the Bride*, is an excellent re-source and thoroughly discusses all facets of wedding planning, in-depth, first step to last.

You must also study weddings—past and present. What makes some elegant and ⟨…⟩ not? What are the little touches th⟨…⟩

them special? What's the look that *you* want to achieve? The only way you will glean this information, come to logical conclusions, and set attainable goals for yourself, is by learning about weddings. It's important to study and research bridal magazines and wedding books; go to the library and bookstores.

Learn about etiquette. This is *Commandment Three.* It's very important. You cannot have true elegance without proper etiquette; they go hand in hand.

A wedding is not a time "to have it your way." The precepts that guide a fast food restaurant chain should not be applied to your wedding. Etiquette, over the years, has been modified to adapt to our fast-paced lifestyle, but its tried-and-true rules and standards (that guarantee success) should never be ignored. As I tell my clients: If you want to break the rules, know what the rules are. Then make an educated decision.

The word *etiquette* is French, literal translation: *ticket.* And maybe it is. A ticket to a more gracious lifestyle, to more perfect speech and better manners, and to perfecting our own style within the realm of good taste. It's also interesting to note that the synonym of the word etiquette is *decorum.* Decorum relates to the way we act, the way we behave—to living our life with courtesy toward others and with a sense of propriety; it is a lifestyle.

We lightly interpret the meaning of the word etiquette to apply to the proper crossing of t's and dotting of i's. Etiquette and decorum— *and they are one and the same*—mean that we must exhibit decency and civility in everything we do. It's far more complex than how to implement the proper wording on a wedding invitation.

Commandment Four: Read the contract, including the fine print (and learn to adapt it). What is it about a wedding that makes people so trusting? The romance? The idea that nothing can go wrong—to me!? A feeling of complete,

blind faith in the vendor? I have no idea . . . But I do know this: The majority of brides, grooms, and their families sign contracts without reading them—let alone reading the fine print. *This is the worst mistake you can make.*

Your contract is your only recourse should something go amiss. To ignore it, or slough it off, is like committing a mortal sin in Wedding World. Let me give you an example. A couple once approached me for help. They hired a video company that promised them the ultimate wedding video: completely edited, special effects, music of their choice, the addition of baby and honeymoon pictures, etc. But after the wedding, the company called the couple to say that all those extras they *thought* were included, would cost hundreds of dollars more. The couple was devastated.

The first thing I did was examine their contract. It said nothing about the added extras. The couple was caught dead to rights. They could not afford the additional expense and ended up with an unedited tape of their wedding. They paid way too much for a raw tape. They were had!

If their contract had been specific, however, and included—*in writing*—all of the things that they were promised, they would have had no problem with this vendor. He would have done what the contract specified.

Commandent Five: Contracts can also be modified. They are not written by God or etched in stone. If the cancellation policy states, for example, that you lose your deposit if *you* cancel the wedding, ask if you can *adapt* it: "In the event of cancellation, the deposit is completely refundable, provided that the vendor books another event on the same date and at the same time of day. If not, and the wedding is canceled two months or more in advance of the date of the affair (which gives the vendor time to book another event), the deposit may be applied to another party or occasion, if reserved within one year of the date of this contract." (The changes you make to your contracts depend on your negotiating skills; it's always better to get your money back, if possible.)

The "party" or "occasion" mentioned above doesn't necessarily mean another wedding. You may decide to have a birthday or anniversary party or a family reunion at the property. The point is, you don't lose the money! (Cancellation policies on all contracts should be adapted, except for ones that apply to custom orders, such as wedding gowns, bridesmaids' dresses, or invitations.)

Part II of this commandment also relates to a contract. It's called a *receipt*. *Always get a receipt and make sure it's specific!* Don't walk out of a bridal shop, for example, with a receipt that says: White wedding gown, size 10. Or, you may end up with a white wedding gown in a size 10, but not the one you thought you ordered. Once again, you have no legal recourse if your receipt isn't specific. *Your receipt is your contract.* Use it to protect yourself. (This rule applies to all vendors, not just bridal shops.)

Commandment Six: More does not mean better—and more costs money! Elegant weddings are not vulgar, crass, or overdone. They are subtle, tasteful, and beautiful.

Many brides like to feature large or life-size portraits of themselves (in their bridal attire) at their wedding. Others place monitors around the reception room that run videos of their love story. This is vulgar. A wedding is not supposed to convey a message to the guests that says, "I'm Queen For A Day," or, "Look At Me!" A wedding is a life celebration for *all* to enjoy.

One of my brides, who spent a fortune on these portraits and videos (against my advice), ended up with a cash bar and a cocktail hour that featured one platter of cheese and crackers. The wedding was late afternoon and everyone was starving.

I attended her wedding. The topic on most of the guests' lips was her egomania, not the beauty or elegance of her wedding. The thousands she spent on portraits and videos should have been spent on her guests and her reception.

UNDERSTANDING ELEGANCE

The word *elegant* is also French and is defined as richness and grace, confined by the restraints of propriety and good taste. Elegance has nothing to do with bridal portraits and videos, but has everything to do with how you are perceived as a hostess, and ultimately as a human being.

The bride and groom in the example above could have hosted a reception memorable for its hospitality and goodwill. Their guests could have left the celebration with wonderful complimentary words on their lips about the graciousness of their hosts, the terrific food, and how beautiful the bride looked. But this bride chose to glorify herself instead.

Elegance is a state of mind. It's a way of life that culminates—for better or for worse—at a wedding. How well you use it and how well you apply it is up to you.

Commandment Seven: Guests are the central players. It's my opinion (based on my experience) that brides, grooms, and their families, with more and more frequency, are discounting the role that guests play at the celebration. A wedding is *not* The Bride's Day, as it has unfortunately become. It is a very special day, for all who are invited, to celebrate with the bride and groom and their families, to share their joy and their love. Guests should be the bride and groom's top priority.

Commandment Eight: Don't forget the step-parents—include everyone. In the United States today, the *blended* family has replaced the traditional family. For that reason, most of us have stepparents and stepfamilies and all the joy—or problems—that may go along with them.

Weddings are a time of happiness, family togetherness, and inclusion. No matter what kind of relationship you have with your stepparents or stepfamilies, it's time to put your personal feelings aside. Don't take any actions that could hurt a family member (and stepparents are members of your family). Don't make plans, for example, that include certain immediate family members and exclude others. At a wedding, everyone is equal. Be sure that *all* parents (and grandparents) are represented in some way; even a corsage or boutonniere will do. You'll be glad you did.

Commandment Nine: Apply common courtesy to every aspect of planning your wedding. Always put yourself in the other person's shoes. Let me give you an example. If you were invited to a dinner party and you were seated across the room from your husband, how happy would you be? Not very. So why do brides and grooms insist on seating their bridal party members at their table without their dates or spouses? The result is an empty bridal table whose members are busy visiting their companions, who are seated elsewhere. It's only common courtesy to seat people with their dates or spouses—people who will make them feel happy and relaxed.

And finally, *Commandment 10: Be pleasant and kind.* Nothing turns me off like a bride who walks into my store with a scowl on her face. It certainly doesn't give me the impetus to be overly helpful, although I try my best to be.

Most vendors and service people try to be as affable and as helpful as possible with their wedding clients; after all, it's their livelihood. In the same vein, you should be just as pleasant when you meet with them.

The customer has the option (and the advantage) of going elsewhere if he or she doesn't like the attitude of the vendor. However, the vendor doesn't have that latitude. He can't say to the client, "You're miserable and I'd prefer not doing business with you." Although, many times, he'd like to.

A wedding vendor's reputation, for good or ill, spreads like wildfire in this business, but there's a flip side to this coin. Wedding World is a small planet that's composed of a network of wedding vendors and professionals; they talk often and, many times, share the same clients. For that reason, don't ever think that your attitude and deeds are above scrutiny or notice. The vendors I work with appreciate kind, caring customers and will break their back to please them. But a client's bad deeds or attitude may not go without retribution. Let me give you some examples.

Recently, the photographer I work with called to thank me for referring a bride, who was so pleasant and kind, he felt it deserved a call. I agreed; she was the same with me. Because this woman had been so considerate, I know that both of us (and the other vendors she hired) did our best to give her exemplary service. We made her feel like a princess, and rightfully so. On top of it, the photographer will probably give her a free portrait and I gave her wedding jewelry to complement her gown. *Kindness is rewarded.*

On the other hand, I once worked with a young woman who had a very mean-spirited mother (who was paying the tab). The mother tried to control her daughter, and made her life miserable.

My friend, the catering director at the country club where the reception was being held, said this woman was making her life unbearable. She called her twenty times a day trying to reduce the price and was abrasive (she also didn't like the way she treated her daughter). My friend became so incensed with this woman that she charged her *excessively.* She made her pay for white-glove service, valet parking, and cake cutting (items that normally were part of the package deal), and anything else she could think of. This ugly woman, who wanted so much to pay less paid *more*—and she never knew it.

Ralph Waldo Emerson said, "Character is higher than intellect." And Henry James, when his nephew asked him what he ought to do in life, answered, "Three things in human life are important. The first is to be kind. The second is to be kind. And the third is to be kind." Truer words were never spoken. Apply them to every aspect of your life and every facet of planning your wedding and things may turn out better and more economical—*and more elegant*—than you ever expected!

Chapter Two

GOOD TASTE

...let us be very strange and well bred: Let us be as strange as if we had been married a great while; and as well bred as if we were not married at all.
—William Congreve, *The Way of the World*, 1700

Elegance is defined as . . . richness and grace, confined by the restraints of propriety and good taste. *Memorize* this definition and *apply* it to every aspect of planning your wedding!

Take it to heart, literally, and I guarantee that you will have the elegant wedding of your dreams, within the boundaries of your budget.

EDUCATE YOURSELF

Good taste is learned and acquired. While some people seem to come by it naturally, others have to work harder to achieve it. Either way, it's a goal. That's why it's so important to study weddings—*past and present*—and to understand proper etiquette. These are the building blocks to elegance.

Bridal magazines are more than bridal gown catalogs (believe it or not). They also feature weddings. By studying them, you can begin to formulate ideas for your wedding. If the flowers, for instance, that are pictured in a photo strike you as garish, make a mental note; *That's*

not what I want. If, on the other hand, you see a photo of a gold-and-white color scheme that appeals to you, make a note and cut the picture out of the magazine. Put it in your notebook. (More about this later in this chapter.) *The more pictures a vendor sees, the more insight he'll have into the type of wedding you want to have.*

Bridal books are also very important. Take the time to go to different bookstores to make an evaluation before you purchase. Check the authors' credentials. Are they in the business? Or are they editors? It's best to buy the books of people *who plan weddings for a living,* and not the books of people who only write about them.

Go to your public, university, or college library. Many times you'll find wedding books that are out of print, and they are invaluable sources of information. It's great to look at weddings throughout the decades. Their beauty, elegance, subtlety, and sophistication might surprise you and give you some terrific ideas.

The more you study and research, the more you'll learn. You'll be able to come to grips with your wedding. You'll be able to discern what's tasteful and what isn't. You'll establish the look you want to have and the color scheme that's best for you. You'll be able to establish goals and see them logically through to their fruition. The more you know, the easier wedding planning will become.

Taste and Its Tangible By-product

Being tasteful has a positive, tangible by-product; *it will save you money*. No one needs a headpiece composed of white electric twinkle lights (yes, this really happened; the crown kept shorting out as the bride made her way up the aisle). It cost a fortune, but was it tasteful? Was it necessary?

Do you need life-size portraits of yourself to decorate the reception site? Or video monitors (featuring you and your husband) positioned about the room to greet your guests? Are they tasteful? Are they essential? Do they make you a better hostess?

Do you need cocktail napkins inscribed with your names and the date of your wedding? Doesn't the caterer furnish them? Are they im-

perative? Are they the epitome of good taste? Will your guests even notice them?

The items in the preceding examples cost, collectively, thousands of dollars. They are frivolous and expensive and unnecessary. Do they make a wedding elegant? Hardly. Do they make you a better hostess? *No.* And just think what could have been done with the money: a phenomenal band to keep the guests entertained (and dancing); beautiful centerpieces to make your tables unforgettable; or a fabulous cocktail hour, loaded with plenty of good food and drink to start the evening with a bang! Do these items make a wedding elegant and memorable? *Yes!* Do they make you the hostess with the mostest? *Yes!*

Coming to Grips with Your Goals

Once you study and research weddings, you should begin to picture yours in your imagination. This is critical. You must have a broad idea of what you want before you interview and hire anyone to implement your ideas. *The more specific you are with a vendor, the better off you'll be.* You'll know (and they'll know) if they're able to execute your ideas.

Write down your goals. Under each subheading in your notebook make notes. Detail the kind of ceremony, flowers, invitations, and reception you want to have. Include the photos you've cut from magazines. *Determine what you want.* Once you do, you're on your way to achieving your goal.

It's my job to teach you how to achieve that

goal, *within the confines of propriety and good taste and within the boundaries of your budget!* It's also up to the vendor(s) to advise you on the best way to implement your ideas, and if those ideas are feasible.

Tradition and Good Taste

Tradition is that timeless bridge to our history, to our very being. It ties the old to the new and connects us to our past. It's the reason why, after centuries, a bride carries " . . . something old, something new, something borrowed, something blue . . . and wears a penny in her shoe." It's the reason we eat wedding cake and throw birdseed. (See how tradition gets modified?) It's the reason a bride carries flowers and walks on an aisle runner. Tradition makes weddings meaningful. Where would we be without it?

Don't shortcut tradition. For example, don't put return-address stickers on your wedding invitation envelopes when all it takes is the *time* to write them. Don't have a dessert reception or a cash bar. Don't skip centerpieces when you can make them. Don't use silk flowers for your bridal bouquet and your bridal party flowers. Good quality silks aren't cheaper than fresh; they can't capture the beauty and uniqueness of fresh flowers, and they're unnecessary if you budget wisely.

Tradition is a part of our heritage and culture. When you plan your wedding, think of it and of all the beautiful customs that make weddings meaningful and special. Think in terms of how you plan to uphold tradition, or how you plan to modify it. But don't let it go by the wayside.

Let's not forget the purpose of a wedding: *To celebrate.* Recently, I saw a post on the Internet's wedding newsgroups about dancing: "Should we have dancing—or not?" Some said that neither they nor their immediate families were dancers, so what was the point of having music? Many said that they'd rather skip the dancing to give their guests the opportunity to talk and get to know one another; after all, loud music is distracting. Others said they were going to feature four hours of chamber music.

Allow me to respond. One, a wedding reception is not a coffee klatch. I can't imagine people, elegantly dressed, sitting at a table talking for one to two hours, let alone three to four. Two, the music should be distracting. It should make you want to jump up and dance! And three, four hours of chamber music might give one a headache. (Due to the different ages and tastes of wedding guests, it's best to play a mix of music.)

Once again, this is an example of the bride and groom exercising their personal wants and neglecting their guests. They might wish their guests to sit at a table and talk the night away, or listen to an evening of chamber music, but their guests might have a different idea. Don't expect them to sit all night and be bored on your account. Didn't they attend your wedding with the idea of making merry?

Don't forget, you're the hosts! Some budget-conscious brides and grooms opt for cash bars (guests pay for their own liquor) and dessert receptions (what you see is what you get—dessert) in an effort to keep the cost down.

The wedding reception is the first party that a bride and groom host as husband and wife. Responsible, gracious hosts make sure their guests are their first priority.

If you issued a formal invitation, inviting people to your home at six o'clock in the evening, would you serve them a plate of pastries and charge them for their drinks? Would you blame your guests if they left early to get a tuna salad platter? Or left because they were insulted? Wouldn't you be? A wedding is no different. If you issue an invitation to your wedding, you are asking your families and friends to be your *guests*; they are not paying participants. A wedding is a celebration that you're hosting. It's up to *you* to impart good food, good drink (not necessarily alcohol), and lots of goodwill to your guests.

I've seen many posts about dessert receptions on the Internet's wedding newsgroups. One bride said that her guests left early to go to Denny's: they were starving; she was heartbroken. Another said that she felt a dessert reception wasn't appropriate because her relatives and friends, who lived out of town, were making an expensive trip in her honor. She was right. (Not only are guests expected to pay for travel and lodging, they're also expected to bring a gift. And what about the shower gift they may have given? Or the engagement gift?) A wedding, besides uniting two people in holy matrimony, is also a venue for the bride and groom to show their guests their appreciation for all they've done for them.

Cash bars and dessert receptions are *not* the way to achieve elegance or to impress wedding guests with your hospitality and graciousness. If you budget wisely and plan well, there's no reason to have either. Be savvy, educate yourself, and take the time to properly structure and budget for that elegant wedding and reception of your dreams. With a little effort, you can do it affordably—and economically!

THE MEMORIES—FROM WHOSE PERSPECTIVE?

Because the bride, groom, and their families seem to find themselves in a wedding day daze, it's important to appoint a *guardian*—someone to look past the fantasy. This precautionary measure can have a direct effect on the success of your wedding and your guests' perceptions of it. Let me give you an example. Many times, a bride and her mom will visit me after the wedding. They coo and awe over all the details, everything couldn't have been more perfect! Then I run into her bridesmaid, who has a different story to tell: "It was awful. Everyone was starving. It took them an hour to serve the first course after the salad. It was so bad that people were pounding on the tables. I don't know how Sue could have missed it." Or, "They only had one bartender for one hundred fifty people. We spent the entire cocktail hour in line to get one drink. Mary was having her pictures taken. She didn't have a clue."

It's so important to appoint a close family member (who's not a part of the bridal party) to oversee the affair. He or she should be introduced to your catering director ahead of time and to the captain or maître d' who will be running the affair. The staff must know that they will answer to the guardian at the reception, and that their wishes are to be respected.

While you might think your wedding day was a fantasy come true, your guests may not be so lucky. It's important that your families and friends share your fairy-tale feeling. After all is said and done, what kind of a wedding did you have if your guests have nothing good to say about it?

Good food, good drink, dancing, family, friends, a beautiful bride and a handsome groom, a sense of well-being, plenty, and lots of love. These are the things that make for a tasteful, memorable, *elegant* wedding.

It's Time to Make a Notebook!

Make a notebook from a loose-leaf binder and divide it into subheadings: florists, caterers, bridal shops, consultants, etc.

Keep your estimates and any and all information you gather in your notebook. Buy clear plastic envelopes that seal and are made exclusively for three-ring binders. Place one under each subheading. (You can find them at drugstores or office stationery stores and outlets.) Do not, however, keep contracts in a binder. After they're signed, take them home and put them in a safe place.

Chapter Three

Continuity

But love me for love's sake, that evermore
Thou mayst love on, through love's eternity.
—Elizabeth Barrett Browning, *Sonnets from the Portuguese*

Elegance from beginning to end is called *continuity* and it's amazing that every time I look up the definition of a wedding-related word, it has a French origin. Etiquette, elegance, and now, continuity. Could it be that the French have the edge? When it comes to social graces, perhaps they have.

Continuity simply means being continuous, exhibiting a continuous flow. *This is a concept that must be applied to your wedding.* All the parts must connect, from one to the next, to produce an elegant "whole" called a wedding.

Establish Formality

Weddings are either formal, semiformal, or informal. The first step is to decide which you prefer. Correlate each wedding type to your personality and decide on the one that makes you and your families the most comfortable. In other words, if you're laid-back people, have an informal wedding. Or, if you want to put on the ritz, have a semiformal affair (a formal wedding would be too rigid). Your goal is for your families to feel comfortable, relaxed, and happy. That's hard to accomplish if your father

has never worn a tux or your mom a long, imposing gown.

Once you decide, the idea is to extend the *theme of formality* all the way through, from the invitations to the garter toss. This is where continuity comes into play. Don't mix the formal with the informal, or the semiformal with the formal. This breaks the connection (or continuity)—and the elegance.

Elegance, however, is not confined to the realm of the formal or semiformal wedding and can be achieved even in the most informal of settings. Let's say that you decide to have a spaghetti dinner reception at the home of your aunt (who has the room to comfortably handle fifty guests).

You choose to have the cocktail hour on the porch, which is decorated with colorful electric paper lanterns, strung from one end to the other. The servers, dressed as Italian waiters, pass Campari and soda in glasses (and wine and beer). They serve *bruschetta* (baked Italian bread slices, smothered with sauce, onions, basil, and cheese) and marinated eggplant and mushrooms. Platters of Italian cheeses and crackers and fresh fruit grace the end tables (covered with crisp, white rented tablecloths), which are placed strategically around the room. A violinist, dressed like a gypsy, plays lively Italian tunes on his fiddle, and people begin to get in the mood!

After an hour of mingling and light hors d'oeuvres and drink, dinner is served in the dining room. Six rented tables are covered in classic Italian red-and-white checked cloths. Red-and-white checked napkins are fanned in the water glasses and quaint white wooden chairs (also rented) surround the tables. The room looks like an intimate Italian restaurant. A bottle of Chianti, stuffed with a burning candle and surrounded by fresh, polished, brightly colored fruit (which sits on a bed of ferns), serves as a centerpiece for each table. The lights are dimmed, and the violinist plays soft, romantic dinner music.

Dinner starts with cold *antipasti*, which has been placed on each table. Afterward, a salad of fresh tomato, basil, and buffalo-mozzarella, drizzled with olive oil, is served. Then come steaming bowls of spaghetti and meatballs, along with plenty of hot, fresh garlic bread, topped off by hearty glasses of deep red Chianti. The meal ends with a sweet, but light, Italian ice and fresh fruit. The wedding cake, a Sicilian cake with chocolate frosting (which the bride and groom have made) will make its appearance later. Everyone then returns to the porch, where the violinist is joined by a guitarist (who also sings) and a keyboard player. The room has been cleared, the bar is opened, and the dancing and the party begin!

Elegant, *yes!* Everyone feels great. The food and drink were superb. The entertainment different and made-for-merriment. The ambiance—festive and romantic. And the host and hostess were tops! Who could ask for more?

Expensive, *no!* A caterer was hired who handled the food, the rentals, and the staff. The choice of food was inexpensive, cooked to perfection, and filling. And the presentation was flawless. The bride and groom were able to buy their own liquor, and their friends and family did the decorating. They had fun making their own wedding cake, and they were proud of it! They employed a three-piece band and everyone danced! And the best part: No one had to worry about clean up. That was the caterer's responsibility.

THE ELEGANCE INDEX

The following chart analyzes each wedding type and its components. An X is marked under the appropriate response for either the formal, semiformal or informal wedding. Study the index and make sure you conform to its standards. You may deviate in one or two places—that's okay, but the less you deviate, the more elegant—and continuous—your wedding will be.

THE ELEGANCE INDEX
The Essentials for Your Formal, Semiformal, and Informal Wedding

F = Formal   SF = Semiformal   Inf = Informal   EE = Extraneous Extra

The Essentials:	F	SF	Inf	EE
The Engagement:				
a. Ring	x	x	x	x
b. Photos for newspaper				x
c. Announcement				x
d. Party				x
The Ceremony:				
a. Officiant	x	x	x	
b. Bridal-party flowers	x	x	x	
c. Music	x	x		
d. Flowers/decorations for site	x	x		
e. Guest books				x
f. Wedding programs				x
The Reception:				
a. Ample food and drink	x	x	x	
b. Flowers/decorations	x	x		
c. Entertainment	x	x		
d. Favors for guests				x
e. Valet parking	x	x		
Bridal Attire:				
a. Gown:				
Designer, plain/elegant, chapel or no train	x	x		
Traditional, fancy, heavy beading, long train	x			
Not too fancy, moderate beading, chapel train		x		
Elegant day dress or suit		x	x	
Simple day dress or suit			x	
b. Headpiece:				
With cathedral veil	x			
With fingertip veil	x	x		
With shoulder-length veil	x	x		
Headpiece with tulle, but no veil			x	x
Headpiece alone			x	
Bridesmaids' Attire:				
Dresses or suits, long, fancy or elegant, plain	x	x		
Tea-length dresses or suits, fancy or elegant, plain	x	x		

(Continued)

The Essentials:	F	SF	Inf	EE
Street-length or midcalf dress or suit		x	x	
Floral print		x	x	
A simple day dress or business suit			x	

Formal Wear for Groom and His Bridal Party:

	F	SF	Inf	EE
Tuxedos	x	x		
Tails (for evening affairs, only)	x			
Dinner jackets (in tropical climates or in summer)	x	x		
Cutaways and strollers (daytime, only)		x		
Business suits			x	

Mothers' Attire:

	F	SF	Inf	EE
Attractive day dress or suit			x	
Elegant day dress, suit, street-length or midcalf		x		
Elegant tea-length or midcalf dress or suit, or simple cocktail dress		x		
Beaded or glitzy long or tea-length dress or suit, or fancy cocktail dress	x			

Guests' Attire:

Women:	F	SF	Inf	EE
Attractive day dress or suit			x	
Elegant day dress or suit		x		
Elegant tea-length or midcalf dress or suit or simple cocktail dress		x		
Fancy long or tea-length dress or suit, or fancy cocktail dress	x			
Men:				
Business suits		x	x	
Tuxedos	x	x		
Dinner jackets (in tropical climates or in summer)	x	x		

Gifts:

	F	SF	Inf	EE
a. For the bridal party	x	x	x	
b. For the hosts	x	x	x	
c. That the bride and groom give each other	x	x	x	x

Rehearsal Dinner:

	F	SF	Inf	EE
	x	x		
a. Flowers and decorations				x
b. Invitations				x

Photography and/or Video

	F	SF	Inf	EE
	x	x	x	

(Continued)

The Essentials:	F	SF	Inf	EE
Invitations and Accessories:				
a. For ceremony and reception	x	x		
b. Printed napkins, matches, etc.				x
Rented Transportation				x
Wedding Rings	x	x	x	x
Wedding Cake	x	x	x	
Honeymoon	x	x	x	x
Wedding Photos or Article for Newspaper	x			x

HOW TO USE THE INDEX

The elegance index is based on the *basics* you need for your particular wedding type. To see if your wedding flows—or has continuity—see how many items connect under each subheading. If your wedding is semiformal, for example, you should be able to connect the Xs (under the column **SF**) in a straight line, from the top of the page to the bottom. As mentioned, you may have a couple of deviations, however, if your line runs repeatedly amuck, it's best to change your wedding type. You're planning a different type of wedding than you think you are.

Under Wedding Rings, all four categories are checked. This is because you don't need a ring to be engaged or to be married, however, it's become so much a part of our tradition that I can't imagine a bride (or groom) without them. The same with a honeymoon and the gifts that the bride and groom give each other. Of course, they're extraneous expenses, but I firmly believe that anyone who goes through the rigors of planning a wedding should have a honeymoon; it's a must! As far as the gifts you give each other? Sure, they're thoughtful and nice, but could the money be better spent on the honeymoon (which in itself is a gift to the bride and groom)?

I've also listed engagement and wedding photos and announcements for newspapers as extraneous expenses. Many experts frown on engagement announcements that specify wedding dates, since many a burglar has robbed a house while the family attends the wedding. These announcements are also expensive. Many big city newspapers (and others not so big) demand big bucks to put engagement and wedding announcements in their newspapers. I think it's money better spent on you!

For the etiquette obsessed, however, announce your formal wedding. According to that old-time etiquette: A woman's name should appear in print three times: when she's born, when she's married, and when she dies.

The index should also be utilized to keep your mind-set simple. If you wonder if you need a particular item, check the index. If you can't find it, you probably don't need it.

Use the index as your reference. Adapt it to your needs. You may want entertainment at your informal wedding, for example, or to send less formal invitations to your formal rehearsal dinner. That's fine. Or, you may decide you want a limousine, even if it's an extraneous expense. *The idea of the index is to give you the basics.* If you want to embellish or change them, that's up to you.

Chapter Four

The Double Budget and Tips for Successful Shopping and Saving Money

A hundred dollars wasted is more costly than one thousand dollars well spent. —An old proverb

A stitch in time saves nine. —An old proverb

Part I: The Basics

Time — Your Enemy or Your Friend?

Don't plan your wedding in a rush. It's the worst thing you can do. Recently, a bride and her family came into my store. It was February and they were planning an April wedding. The bride did not have time to order a gown; her choices were limited to what she could buy off-the-rack. She ended up with a second-rate photographer (the one she wanted was reserved). The videographer she called was already taken. There were no bands available; she settled for a DJ. Her mother said that she had no idea that wedding planning was so complicated or so time consuming.

Planning a wedding in haste means settling for second best. It also puts undue stress on the bride, groom, and their families. It prevents them from properly shopping and researching each vendor they plan on using, and they in turn may hustle them to sign on that dotted line. That's dangerous! Time is their enemy.

If you properly schedule your time, however, you'll be less stressed. You'll easily be able to shop and research each vendor, and you'll have the time to check their references. You won't be pushed to sign a contract. You'll educate yourself and discover what's available in the marketplace. Armed with this knowledge, you'll be able to negotiate the best price you can. Time is your friend.

Allocating Time

To achieve a truly elegant wedding affordably, with all those special touches that make it exceptional, you're going to need lots more time than the person who has unlimited resources. But I firmly believe that you can do it—*just as elegantly*—for a lot less and in better taste.

The key is to make the most of your free time. Every weekend and free evening should be spent researching a different vendor. Each should be shopped, studied, and ultimately reserved. If you're lucky enough to have a mom or a sister who has some free time, let them do some scouting for you. It will eliminate unsuitable vendors and save your precious time and effort for more important tasks.

After you read this book, decide on the ideas that you'll implement on your own. Let's assume that you and your groom choose to make your own wedding cake (No kidding! Read chapter 18, "The Wedding Cake"). You may need a weekend (two days) to practice and a weekend (two days) to make the actual cake. Since the cake will freeze well for two months, you should schedule the weekends to make the actual cake eight weeks prior to the wedding date. (You can make the practice cake anytime. Just pencil the time into your schedule.)

In this book, I offer many new cost-saving ideas that will take time and effort to implement. I suggest making your own invitations. They are stunning and unique and inexpensive to do, but they require much more of a commitment than running down to the local stationery store and ordering from a catalog.

Proper time-budgeting will save you stress and prevent you from making mistakes. By giving yourself lots of time and structuring it well, you'll be able to easily prepare for that elegant wedding and make your dreams come true!

The Double-Budget Bonanza

By now you should realize that there are two wedding-planning budgets, both of equal importance. One is your financial budget. The other is your time-budget (or how well and efficiently you allocate your time). If you plan both with equal fervor and dedication, you will find yourself on the right wedding track, emotionally, physically, and financially. Your goal is to formulate both budgets realistically and to take the time to implement them, down to the last detail. If you stick to your budgets, I guarantee that you'll reap a bride's bonanza! (In the next chapter, I'm going to teach you how to set priorities, how to properly schedule your time, and how to book vendors.)

Referrals—Gather Them Now!

Ask recently married friends, relatives, and business associates for the names of places and vendors they used for their wedding and if they were happy with the results. You'll start to notice that the same names keep popping up over and over, for better or for worse. Stay away from vendors with shoddy reputations. Shop only those vendors who come with good references.

When Tim Berry and I opened Floral Concepts (our wedding floral business), we worked for very little money. We wanted to get our name out into the marketplace and generate clients. We started with small weddings, photographed our work, and created an album to show our prospective customers. One day, I asked one of my brides and her parents if we could compete for her flowers. They had already interviewed a well-known florist and were happy with the results, but they gave me a chance.

Her wedding was an upscale affair and after reviewing the job, I gave them an estimate that was 40 percent less. They did not jump at my offer. They explained they were more comfortable with the other florist, who was established and familiar with the reception site. I countered by saying that our talent and the quality of our flowers equaled his, and that we had also done weddings at the property (although not nearly as many). I asked them to take a look at our work. Afterward, they booked us.

We worked very hard and the flowers were magnificent. The bride cried when she saw her bouquet and the reception room was awesome. Her parents couldn't thank us enough. On the following Monday, the bride's father dropped by and left me a card (I thought it was a thank you note). In it were five one-hundred-dollar bills.

Our flowers were tops, and we didn't charge anywhere near what the big guys did. Brides who were lucky enough to find us (most were referred to us, or came through my bridal shop), reaped a bonanza. Don't be afraid to open your mouth and ask for referrals from recently married friends, relatives, and business associates. *They are your greatest wedding resource.*

SHOPPING: THE SECRET TO SUCCESS

Every week, it seems a bride walks into my store and says, "*Oh no!* There's my dress and it's three hundred dollars cheaper! I didn't know your store was here." You didn't? That's because you didn't research or shop or ask questions. I run a major ad in the Yellow Pages in my local phone directory and in all the phone directories in the surrounding towns. I also advertise heavily in the national bridal magazines. Most of my business comes from these ads and from brides who refer me to their friends.

Don't be a bride who spends $300 more than she has to (for any wedding item). Isn't that money better spent on an extra day or two at a romantic honeymoon lair? Take the time to research and shop *before* you purchase. *It will save you money.* That's the crux of successful, economical wedding planning.

THE RULES FOR SUCCESSFUL SHOPPING

Ralph Nader, the distinguished consumer advocate, suggests following this checklist (from the introduction to *The Frugal Shopper Checklist Book*) before shopping. He entitled it 10 WAYS TO SHAFT YOURSELF AS A CONSUMER[1]:

1. Buy before you think
2. Buy before you read
3. Buy before you ask questions
4. Buy before you can afford to buy
5. Buy before you see through the seller's smile and smooth tongue
6. Buy before you comparison shop
7. Buy when you are tired or hungry
8. Buy when you are rushed
9. Buy to dote on your child or because your child demands the product
10. Buy just to keep up with your friends or neighbors

When it comes to successful wedding shopping, I don't think a more appropriate checklist was ever devised. Read it a few times and keep Mr. Nader's words in mind.

I'm going to take the liberty of adding one more item to the checklist:

11. Buy because you're influenced by and/or confused by your friends' or families' tastes or wants

Don't take your bridal party or a group of relatives with you when you shop. What they want for you and your wedding and what you want for you and your wedding, may be two entirely different things. It's also confusing. When you shop take your mom or one trusted friend, and stay focused.

Recently, a bride walked into my store with four of her bridesmaids. The gown the bride loved, they didn't. They made her try on twenty different gowns, disregarding the dress their friend had her heart set on. Finally, in desperation, she said, "Let's go out for lunch and discuss this." She came back two hours later, *sans* bridesmaids. "What happened?" I inquired. "I fired them" was her answer. "They had no right to try to influence me. It's my wedding and I love that dress; it's the one I want."

It's also unfair to the vendor. Don't clutter a shop (especially a small one) with unnecessary people who take up room or who address the vendor with confusing, irrelevant suggestions or input. It's bewildering. Who's the vendor to listen to? The bride, or her friends or relatives?

HURDLES ON THE TRACK TO SUCCESS

Everyone wants the best for their wedding, but there are two obstacles that may stand in your way. One, you may not know what the best is. And two, you may be too blinded by price to shop for excellence. These obstacles, if not overcome, can lead to disaster, and they are easily surmounted. One, you must read and study bridal magazines and wedding books to teach yourself to recognize quality goods, services, and vendors. And two, you must research and shop the marketplace.

When it comes to wedding planning, *shopping is a learning experience*. When interviewing vendors, it's best to take lots of notes (even concepts you don't like may appeal to you later) and ask lots of questions. You will soon see the distinctions between vendors and their

capabilities. You'll also discover what makes some mundane and others exceptional, and the impact they can have on your wedding, your memories, and your wallet. You should question the vendor as to why he or she is more expensive than their competition, and the differences in their experience, expertise, style, equipment, etc.

A DANGEROUS LIAISON

If you only shop to get the best price, you're shopping with tunnel vision and nothing could be more dangerous. You'll see nothing but dollar signs and excellence will fall by the wayside. It's limiting and self-defeating.

That's why it's critical to shop vendors in all price ranges. It's the greatest wedding education you can give yourself. If you study, shop, and research as hard as you should, you may even stumble upon a pot of gold at the end of your wedding rainbow, but don't think it's by chance; you'll have earned it.

THE FIVE QUESTIONS

These Five Questions Will Save the Day—and the Budget! It's easy to become immersed—and to go broke—when planning a wedding. For that reason, *don't be rushed to sign on that dotted line!* After you interview vendors, take your notes home to make an analysis. Think of the vendor's suggestions and ideas and question them. Is it necessary, for example, to have pew bows for the ceremony? Can I live without them? Do they really enhance the look of my ceremony site? Is it possible that I could make them myself, or that one of my family or friends could? How much money can I save?

Get in the habit of asking yourself The Five Questions. They will keep you in focus and your budget in line:

1. Are the vendors' ideas/suggestions right for me?
2. If they are, can I afford them?
3. Who should implement them? (Can I do it myself—or are they above my level of expertise?)
4. How much money can I save?
5. Will they make me a better hostess? (Are they necessary to achieve elegance?)

Make copies of the Vendor Suggestions sheets (entitled Part 1 and Part 2) at the end of this chapter. Put copies of both in your notebook under the appropriate vendor heading. Take them with you when you shop. Use as many as you need.

Fill out Part 1 when interviewing vendors. Fill out Part 2 when you get home, to analyze their ideas and suggestions while they're still fresh in your mind. *Start to formulate ideas and to draw conclusions about your wedding.*

Before you make a decision, ask yourself The Five Questions. It's the same precaution that you take when you count to ten before you blow your top.

Part II: Controllable Factors that Equal Big $avings

Secrets to Cutting the Budget

The factors that will have the most impact in terms of saving money are the guest list, the bridal party, extraneous extras, and the selection of your wedding date. The first three factors must be strictly controlled; the last is a matter of preference (but one that can save you big bucks).

The Guest List

The more people you invite to your wedding and reception, the greater the cost. Obviously, if you're trying to be economical and have an elegant wedding, you'll make it small—one hundred people or less. This is my suggestion, but not for the obvious reason.

I find large weddings to be impersonal and cold. So many people are invited from so many different facets of the bride's and groom's lives that it makes fraternization difficult. There are two different families, two different sets of friends, friends of two sets of parents, business associates of the families' and of the bride's and groom's, cohorts from work, and acquaintances. It's a mishmash that doesn't blend well in the few short hours called a wedding.

Guests at large affairs are politely seated with their family or friends. Intimidated by the large crowd and their surroundings, most find it difficult to get up, walk to another table, and say, "Hi, I'm Suzy Smith from Ontario. Who are you?"

Small affairs, however, lend themselves to intimacy, and these are my favorite weddings. The room is usually small, and the ten to twelve tables that fill it foster camaraderie. Everyone is up and talking or dancing with one another. Everyone feels close (because they are) and open to conversation and mingling. The bride and groom can easily cavort among their guests. They don't feel pressed to make the rounds of tables to thank their friends and families for attending (at a large wedding, this may take an hour or more of valuable reception time). The bride and groom who host a small wedding can enjoy it and can mix, mingle, dance, and party with *all* their guests!

Besides the social advantage, there's a big money-saving bonanza to be reaped by a small guest list. You won't need hundreds of invitations. Your food and liquor costs will be less.

You won't need as many centerpieces and/or decorations. And a band (with fewer musicians) will work just fine! It's amazing how a smaller guest list can reduce reception costs, exponentially.

Control your guest list to obtain the greatest savings. To learn how to regulate it properly, see chapter 15, "Invitations." It is one of the most critical chapters in this book.

THE OTHER FACTOR—ELEGANCE!

Many of my brides say, "I'm not serving chicken or hosting a beer and wine reception. If I had two hundred people, that's what I'd be stuck with. I want ice sculptures, filet of beef, good wine with dinner, and an exceptional cake. Therefore, I'm only inviting eighty guests. I want it to be elegant."

Elegance is a prime reason to keep the guest list small. You can afford to do so much more, and do it well, when you're paying for less people. It's also the best way to save money (and to have a more elegant wedding) than you ever thought possible.

CONTROLLING THE BRIDAL PARTY

The formality of the wedding no longer dictates the size of the bridal party. At one time, formal weddings required at least four bridesmaids and corresponding groomsmen. Those days are long gone.

Large bridal parties result in unnecessary expenses and, many times, unwarranted headaches and stress. Let me explain. Let's say that you're planning on five bridesmaids and five groomsmen, that's only ten people, after all. No, it's not! You can't invite your bridal party without their dates or spouses. That means twenty people. These people are sure bets to attend. (It's not like saying: We'll invite Aunt Mary and Uncle Harry who live in Oshkosh, but they won't show!) If you invite a total of one hundred guests, and twenty comprise your bridal party and *their* guests, you've just spent one-fifth of your allotment. Is that your intention?

Five bridesmaids and five groomsmen mean five bouquets and boutonnieres. It also means twenty people will attend the cocktail hour and twenty people will occupy two to three tables at the reception (depending on the seating arrangements). It also means additional centerpieces. And it all translates into one thing: *Money* that could have been better spent! I personally feel that two attendants (for each side) is plenty. Relatives and close friends can be appointed to usher (they would have been invited anyhow) and seat guests.

But there's another reason for controlling the size of your bridal party: *stress.* Nothing can make a bride more emotional and harried than out-of-control bridesmaids. And it only takes one bad apple to spoil the barrel. Fights don't normally break out if the bridal party is small, but the larger it is, the greater the chance for discord. I've seen out-and-out fights, resulting in a maid resigning or the bride dismissing her. It's gotten to the point that I require the bride to sign on the dotted line to be responsible for the payment of her bridesmaids' dresses (should they drop out for whatever reason); I've been stuck with so many gowns.

Don't let yourself in for this kind of stress. It's so unnecessary. The people in your wedding party must be your closest friends or family, not acquaintances. Keep your bridal party small for your own peace of mind and to keep your pocketbook in check.

AVOID THE HOLIDAY TRAP

Holidays spell M-O-N-E-Y and vendors want more of it on holidays (or holiday weekends). To avoid this money pit, schedule the wedding three weeks after or three weeks before the holiday. But money isn't the only problem: service and quality also suffer during holidays, the busiest times of the year for clubs, restaurants, florists, bands, orchestras, DJs, etc. If you want TLC for your wedding and reception, skip the holidays.

Good Negotiating Skills a Must

Reception sites are most open to negotiation. Let's say that you have two possibilities in mind. Club A is more expensive than Club B (and you prefer it). But Club B is making you an offer you can't refuse. They've proposed an entree upgrade, more extensive hors d'oeuvres, and thrown in a wedding cake. What should you do? Go back to Club A. Tell the catering director about Club B's proposal. If they want your business, they'll meet or even beat their offer. *It's all in how well you negotiate.* Once terms are agreed upon, get them in writing.

You might try to negotiate with your band or orchestra leader or DJ, but chances are your efforts will be for naught. Most times, they'll have a waiting list for their services, unless you agree to an off-day or off-season reception.

The Many Advantages of Off-Day and Off-Season Receptions

Most brides in the United States marry in the summer and most prefer Saturday night. These are premium times and caterers charge accordingly. Why play into their hands? To save *big* money, book your wedding on an off-day or on an off-month. Many times, caterers have trouble reserving Friday night, Saturday afternoon, Sunday afternoon, and Sunday night. Couple this with an off-season month, for example, April or November, and you should reap big savings. (Don't take a chance on the winter months or Mother Nature may fool you!) In the caterer's mind, it's better to book

business at a discount than to have no business at all. A discount may include a 10 percent decrease across the board or an entree upgrade or a champagne toast. It's all in how well you negotiate.

You should also obtain savings from the photographer, videographer, limousine company (should you choose to have one), and entertainment. Once again, your savings depend on your negotiating skills and how well you know the marketplace. You must be able to say, "I really like and appreciate your work. But considering my reception is on Sunday, I was hoping that we could negotiate a better price. Vendor B is willing, although I'd much rather do business with you." All they can say is no.

Control Those Extraneous Extras—and Save Big Bucks

In each chapter in this book, you will find ways to save money, where to focus your attention, and what's skippable—or those things that are extraneous and unnecessary to elegant wedding planning. *You must eliminate the skippables from your budget.* Collectively, they can cost thousands of dollars. These can include matches, cocktail napkins, wedding programs, menus, unnecessary wedding photos, favors, and limousines. The point is: Put your money where it counts—*focus on the priorities!*

I once attended a wedding where the bride (and groom) were wine connoisseurs. During their sit-down dinner, they had a different wine served with each course, from the appetizer to the dessert. I have never seen so much wine, and I noticed that many people refused it; it was just too much. The problem: The bride and groom sacrificed the cocktail hour for this inordinate offering of wine.

Their wedding was late in the afternoon. It was after six when the guests arrived at the reception and everyone was starving. Sparkling wine (with strawberries in the glasses) was passed to the guests, and so were hors d'oeuvres, but there weren't enough waiters to adequately serve the large crowd. Every time one came out of the kitchen with a tray of food or drink, the guests nearest the door pounced on him like vultures. Those of us not near the door were lucky to receive one hors d'oeuvre and a glass of wine. There was much grumbling and complaining. This is not the key to elegant, successful wedding planning.

The solution to the problem was simple. People at a wedding don't need to be served a different wine with each course. The bride and groom should have spent the money on the cocktail hour. Everyone would have been happy, full, and in good spirits.

Moral of the Story: Use your common sense! It's one of the best resources you've got!

VENDOR SUGGESTIONS, PART 1

Vendor name: _____

Address: _____

Phone number: _____

Suggestions, ideas, and estimated cost: _____

_____

_____

_____

_____

_____

_____

_____

_____

_____

_____

_____

_____

_____

_____

_____

VENDOR SUGGESTIONS, PART 2

Vendor name: _____

Analysis (Which ideas are right for me? Will they enhance the look of my wedding? Can I

afford it? Are they necessary? Will they make me a better hostess?):

_____

_____

_____

_____

_____

_____

Implementation (Is it best for the vendor to implement the ideas? Or can I do it myself, or

have friends or family do it? How much can I save?):

_____

_____

_____

_____

_____

_____

Chapter Five

PRECAUTIONS, PRIORITIES, SHOPPING, AND BUDGETING

Where Should You Spend Your Time and Those Hard-Earned Dollars?

Qui plus despent qua li nafiert sans colp ferir a mort se fiert. (He who spends more than he has kills himself without striking a blow.)

—From a twelfth-century ring inscription

THE FIRST PRECAUTION—AND EXPENDITURE

Wedding cancellation insurance is now available. It's not expensive and its basic coverage protects your deposits and your wedding attire. It also covers your gifts and wedding photos, if damaged, and offers liability coverage for the wedding and reception. It's a good investment.

This insurance may also be upgraded to meet your particular needs. It does not cover you, however, should you decide to call off the nuptials. (For more information, see appendix I.)

THE SECOND PRECAUTION: A WEDDING CONSULTANT

Have you ever planned a wedding before? If you haven't, think about hiring a consultant, one who does the job full-time and plans weddings for a living. These people are invaluable, not only for their expertise but for the money, aggravation, time, and effort they can save you.

One of my best tales is of the bride who planned her wedding outside, at an ocean club. I begged her to change her mind, but she

was unflappable. The morning of the wedding, a terrible gale blew. The tent, which was put up that morning, was ripped from its hinges and sailed into the ocean. The bride's mother called me, hysterical. It was Sunday morning. The wedding was at six that evening.

I immediately called my wholesale nursery and ordered extra trees, potted plants, and flowers. I then called the florist and told him that plans had changed and that we were moving inside. I also told him to bring lots of tulle to drape the ceiling and extra hands to help. We changed one of the ugliest rooms I had ever seen into a wonderland. Ficus trees, twinkling with little white lights, framed the room. Elegant palms, which surrounded the *chuppa* (Jewish wedding canopy), were also lit and basket after basket of potted plants and flowers graced the floor, from one end of the room to the other. The ceiling was draped in billowing white tulle. When the bride saw it, her tears turned to smiles. Had she not had me, however, the outcome would not have been so happy. Wedding vendors are impossible to contact on weekends. What could she have done, on her own, to save the day?

When a bride hires me as her consultant, I save her money. Dresses and invitations, for example, are discounted to my clients. When I send her to a vendor, I'm sure of the outcome. If an estimate comes in that's overbudget, I know what to cut, without sacrificing quality or elegance. And, I know what has to be in her contracts to protect her interest. I'm well worth my fee.

In my opinion, a bride who hosts a traditional wedding, including a ceremony, a reception, and all that goes with it, needs a consultant. It may be the best, most cost-effective, and money-saving decision she can make. The option is hers. (For information about how to contact a consultant in your town, see appendix I.)

Part I: Setting Priorities

Once you get your priorities straight, you'll be able to properly structure your time and your finances. You'll know how and where to spend your money and the components that require your utmost attention emotionally, physically, and financially. You'll be on your way to stress-free, happy wedding planning.

To properly set priorities, you must ask yourself three questions:

1. *How can I make my ceremony as meaningful as possible?*
2. *How can I make my reception as successful as it can be?*
3. *How can I ensure that my memories will be lasting and significant?*

Part II: The Components

SHOPPING FOR THE TANGIBLES

There are two types of wedding components. The first I call the *tangibles*, for example: engagement and wedding rings, gowns, tuxes, invitations, and ceremony and reception sites. The secret here is to shop for *value, service, and comfort*. Let's discuss each component and their importance:

• *Engagement rings*. You must study and learn about diamonds before your purchase a ring. They are standardized according to ideals established by the Gemological Institute of America and other prestigious gem labs. Once you know and understand how diamonds are graded, you can walk into any store and *shop price.* For example: I want a diamond with acceptable depth and table percentages; a girdle that's cut to medium thickness; a culet that's small; and a diamond that exhibits good polish and symmetry. I want the stone to be a VS with a color grade of H, I, or J, with minimal fluorescence. I would like a round (brilliant) diamond, and its carat weight to be approximately 0.75. Once you have a basic understanding of diamonds, you can shop till you drop for the best price. No one will pull the wool over your eyes. (For more information, see chapter 7, "The Engagement Ring.")

• *Ceremony and Reception Sites.* Unless you're marrying at your church or temple, shopping for a ceremony and reception site means shopping tenaciously for the right place that provides the right ambiance at the right price. (For more information, see chapter 8, "The Ceremony.") Booking a reception site (to get the best deal) requires good negotiating skill and an attention to detail. (For more information, see chapter 9, "The Reception.")

• *Wedding Gowns and Bridesmaids' Dresses.* Shopping for the best price is easy when searching for the right gown and dresses for your maids. *But let me caution you.* While most brides say shopping for their gown is the most enjoyable part of wedding planning, it can also be the most stressful, after the fact. An uncaring, impersonal shop can be a bride's worst nightmare.

Most stores carry either low priced, moderately priced, or expensively priced manufacturers. Some carry a mix of different gowns in varying price ranges. Your first priority: Find the shop that offers the best, most caring service. Your second priority: price. When it comes to your bridal gown, TLC and good service come first (for your own peace of mind). Price is secondary, but it shouldn't take a back seat. (For more information, see chapter 16, "Wedding Gowns and Bridesmaids' Dresses.")

• *Tuxedos and Formal Wear.* Shop price and service. Deal only with vendors who have been in business for a respectable length of time. (For more information, see chapter 19, "Formal Wear.")

• *Invitations.* Discounted invitations abound, or you may decide to make your own. The secret is to know proper etiquette, or if buying invitations, to find a vendor who is knowledgeable and who can advise you. There's nothing worse than an improperly worded wedding invitation. (For more information, see chapter 15, "Invitations.")

Shopping for the Nontangibles

I call the second type of wedding components the nontangibles. They include entertainment, flowers, photography, videography, and wedding cake. These components require a vendor's talent and artistry. *These two intangible factors can make or break a wedding and a reception and can make shopping difficult.* How do you find exceptional talent and artistry? And how do you put a price on it?

These components are so critical that you must educate yourself to the point where you can look at a photo or a video or a fresh-flower bouquet and say with confidence, "That's good . . ." or "That's not . . ." and know the reason(s) why. *Education* is your key to success.

These components may also require that you spend more dollars than planned. For that reason, I call them *bite-the-bullet components.* To guarantee an elegant, successful wedding, it's best (for these components) to get the best vendors possible.

• *Entertainment*. Nothing makes a party hop like good, nonabrasive entertainment. Guests who are listening to good music, dancing, and having fun will be hard-pressed to leave a reception early. But play obnoxious or loud or unfamiliar music and look out! An avalanche of guests in an early exit from a reception will cut the party short and turn a bride and groom's celebration into a wedding day disaster. (For more information, see chapter 10, "Entertainment.")

• *Photography and Videography*. These are the tools that capture your memories. The best photos and video will be produced by the vendors with the best skills and the ones who exhibit the finest artistry, talent, and expertise. They will also utilize the best equipment and employ the latest, most up-to-date technology. This blend of talent, artistry, equipment, and technology, and their adeptness with it, will produce your tangible memories. For that reason, *you must get the best vendors that good sense, knowledge, and your budget dictate*. (For more information, see chapter 11, "Photography" and chapter 12, "Videography.")

• *Flowers*. Fresh, expertly designed flowers make for a beautiful bride, bridal party and wedding photos. Flowers require a talented, skilled artist to release their full potential and their beauty. They, too, are a part of your memories. They make weddings (and pictures) unforgettable. (For more information, see chapter 13, "Flowers and Decorations.")

• *Wedding Cake*. Disregard the advice of a caterer who says, "Wedding cakes are to be seen but not eaten," like little children who once upon a time were to be seen but not heard. People *will* eat your wedding cake, if you shop diligently for a great baker (or you make your own), and if you *don't* serve an opulent dessert with dinner.

Unfortunately, wedding cakes have become a symbol—to be admired but not devoured. This is nonsense! The wedding cake is dessert, and it's expensive, even if you buy it at the local supermarket. It's time to put the cake back in perspective. Make it edible and admirable (and put your money [and your cake] where your mouth is!)

In Conclusion: Your Top Four Priorities

It's now time to make an analysis. Which components are the most important? And where should you spend the majority of your time, effort, and dollars?

Here are your *top four* priorities:

• An unforgettable, meaningful ceremony
• A reception with plenty of good food and drink
• Fantastic entertainment to keep the party hopping
• Outstanding photography and videography (to safeguard your memories)

Part III: Finances

MAKING YOUR BUDGET WORK

PREPARE YOURSELF

Now that you understand a little about the value of each component, let's get a grip on your finances. Sit down with your fiancé and decide the total budget for your wedding. Don't plan on your families' contributions until *their* money is in *your* bank. Once you agree on the budget, stick to the bottom line, but learn how to juggle it for success. (I'll show you how later in this chapter.)

Recently, I received an E-mail from a distraught groom who told me that his fiancée's family had promised to pay for the wedding. They gave the couple the deposit monies, but then backed out. The couple didn't have the money to pay the balances and he asked if I knew of any wedding charity that could help. Alas, no.

Don't let yourself in for this kind of stress and unhappiness. It will make you miserable. Have most of the money in the bank before you begin (and budget wisely for the rest). And whatever you do, *don't go into debt*. That's no way to start a marriage. Don't ever be one of those brides who says, "Gee, I hope we make a lot of money at this reception or we're in big trouble!" This is a disaster in the making. And it's so easily avoidable with proper planning.

WHO PAYS FOR WHAT?

The days of the bride's parents paying for the entire wedding celebration are long over. Weddings today are just too expensive. If your fiancé's parents are from the old school, he'd best sit down with them and explain the facts of wedding life. Nothing can cause more hurt feelings, on the bride's side, than uncom-

promising, uncaring, noncontributing future in-laws.

Today, it's best that everyone contribute emotionally, physically, and financially (if all are able). If not, everyone must contribute what they can afford. *The key is to work with what you have and to compromise!* Plan your wedding around a realistic, well-charted budget and stick with it.

Tip: Are you a parent who's footing the bill? If you are, here's some advice. Give the couple the money for the wedding up front or in installments (depending on your finances). *Let them decide on how they want the money spent* (with your input) *and let them write the checks.* They'll soon see that budgeting for a wedding is not easy. This is a terrific learning experience, and one that will teach them the value of shopping, researching, and finding the best value for their dollar. If they go over budget, it's up to them to make up the difference.

DEPOSITS AND RECEIPTS

A place or vendor is not booked unless you leave a deposit and get a receipt. A receipt should contain all pertinent information about the purchase (including dates and times). It must list the amount that's been paid. All receipts must be signed and dated by the vendor.

It's critical that all deposits are refundable if you change your mind within forty-eight hours. (This does not apply, however, to custom orders—wedding gowns or invitations). You must also add this clause to your receipt: *Deposits are refundable if the contract is not mutually agreed upon.* It's also essential that *the deposits are transferable if you change the date* (provided that you book another affair with the facility or vendor within a year of the date of the affair). *Do not sign a contract when you get your receipt. Negotiate one later* (more about contracts later in this chapter).

A catering facility's receipt, for example, should contain the wedding date, the room(s), and the time-period(s) that's reserved, for example:

The Wedding of Carolyn Jones and John Smith, Saturday, March 10, 2010. Cocktails, The Empire Room, 4 P.M. to 5 P.M. Dinner and Dancing, The Starlight Ballroom, 5 P.M. to 9 P.M.

It should list the deposit amount that's been paid. This receipt must state that the deposit is refundable if you change your mind within forty-eight hours, and that the deposit is *transferable* if the date should change. And that it's completely refundable if the contract is not mutually agreed upon.

PROTECT YOUR INVESTMENT

Always put your deposits (and the balances due, if possible) on a credit card. Should the business go under or if it's hit by a hurricane, you'll be protected. If the vendor or place will not take a credit card, give them a check made out to their place of business. *Never give cash, a check made out to cash, or a check made out to an individual.* Cash is not traceable, and a check made out to cash or to an individual could easily be disputed in court.

Part IV: Budgeting for—and Booking—Your Wedding Components

Now it's time to budget for and reserve those wedding components, but what do you do first?

The following Priority Schedule lists your priorities in order of importance, 1–20:

PRIORITY SCHEDULE—RESERVING WEDDING COMPONENTS:

In Order of Importance

Engagement ring (can be purchased at any time)
Wedding consultant (optional)

1. Ceremony (site, officiant, musicians, etc.)

2. Reception site

3. Entertainment

4. Photography/videography

5. Flowers

6. Honeymoon reservations (traditionally the groom's job)

7. Invitations, place cards, brochures, programs (start early)

8. Wedding gown, headpiece and veil, accessories

9. Bridesmaids' dresses

10. Wedding cake

11. Groom and bridal party wear (if near prom time)

12. Rented transportation (if near prom time)

13. Rehearsal dinner

14. Wedding rings

15. Hair and makeup

16. Marriage license, including blood test (if applicable)

17. Testing for genetically transmitted diseases (if applicable)

18. Testing for STDs (sexually transmitted diseases)

19. Factors to consider:
    a. wedding cancellation insurance
    b. premarital agreement
    c. premarital religious and/or nonreligious counseling

20. Gift expenses for the:
    a. bridal party
    b. host(s) of wedding and parties
    c. each other (if deemed necessary)

PUT IT ALL TOGETHER WITH A DAILY PLANNER

Go to an office supply store and buy a daily planner that divides your time into months, days, and hours. After you read the information in this chapter, pencil in, for example, the month (and the days within that month) that you plan on researching reception sites, bands, wedding gowns, etc. Pencil in your plans for making that practice cake or those invitations.

Schedule all of your time, from the day you get engaged until your wedding date. Customize your planner to meet your needs. Let's say that you decide to buy wedding invitations rather than make them. You must schedule shopping time, time to place the order, the approximate delivery date, and the time to address them. You must schedule in the dates you'll send them to out-of-town guests and to local ones. And you must make a note of the *respond date* (the date when replies should be in). Make your planner your Time Bible. Schedule well and efficiently and stick with it! Make a copy of the Priority Schedule and tape it onto the first page of your planner. After you plan for each item, put a check beside it.

USE THE PRIORITY SCHEDULE TO BUDGET SUCCESSFULLY

After you've researched and shopped, you'll know the estimated cost of each wedding component. Make a sheet entitled Finances (for each component listed on the Priority Schedule) and put it under the appropriate heading in your notebook. On each sheet, list the amount you're budgeting for each component and how you plan to pay for it. Let's assume you find a terrific videographer who's expensive (and over budget). No problem. *If you go over budget on one component, just juggle another to make up the difference.* The result: *The bottom line always remains the same.* Don't let it waver!

HERE'S HOW TO JUGGLE

Let's say that you've reserved Club A for your reception at a discounted rate. (You've just saved a bundle and are under budget for this component!) But you also elect to spend a bundle on a very special videographer—about 50 percent more than you planned. How do you come up with the extra money? You juggle!

But how? Put the money you saved on the reception toward the videographer. If that doesn't cover it, you may decide to knock a couple of people off the guest list to make up the difference. Or you may buy less expensive invitations or make them. Or you may decide to make your own wedding cake or headpiece and veil. You may also determine that a great DJ is just as good as a band. And you may even forego a limo. It's all in the quid pro quo. The secret: Juggle now! Get it all on paper and stick with it! And now on to . . .

Your Top Four Priorities

If your cherished cathedral is booked in June, you'll have to marry elsewhere or in a different month. If your father's country club (the site you've dreamed about for your reception) is taken on your wedding day, you'll have to find another place. If that top photographer, videographer, or entertainment is reserved, you're stuck with second best. *These places and these vendors are your top priority.* They must be reserved as expediently as possible because of their *limited availability.*

First, reserve (in this order) the:

1. Ceremony site
2. Reception site
3. Entertainment
4. Photography/videography

Your first month(s) of wedding planning (depending upon your time frame) must be spent shopping, researching, and ultimately reserving these components. These four must be booked immediately. Take your list of referred places and vendors and call to arrange for appointments (make sure your date is available). Get all the information you can gather—especially brochures and price lists. Talk casually with the person(s) in charge and take plenty of notes. Take a tour and get a feel for the places and vendors and measure your comfort level. If you don't feel good about the place or person, don't go back. Take your brochures and price lists home to study. Put them in your notebook.

Review Your Top Priorities — Include Price and Value

Take a look at the brochures and price lists you've gathered (ceremony and reception sites, entertainment, photography, and videography). After you evaluate each component for quality, ambiance, facilities, services, etc., it's time to analyze their cost.

1. The Ceremony

Calculate ceremony expenses, including:

- Church fees or ceremony site fees
- Clergy or officiant's fee and/or donation
- Church musicians, organist, vocalists, etc.
- Church consultant (if applicable)
- Vendor fees (if applicable)

If the ceremony is to be conducted at your house of worship, you will be restricted by their rules. Many places, for example, require you to pay for the services of a consultant that they provide. Others that have reception facilities may require, for example, that you only use one of their florists or bands or caterers. These vendors pay big bucks to be on their preferred vendor list and charge you big bucks for their services.

If your church or synagogue charges excessively or forces unnecessary services upon you, resulting in unnecessary expenditures, you must decide if it would be more advantageous, economically, to move your ceremony elsewhere— as much as it may hurt you to do so.

If you desire a combination ceremony and reception (at the same location), calculate all fees, set-up charges, taxes, and gratuities. Pick the place that has the best ambiance, facilities, and price.

Don't Forget the Officiant, Vocalists, Musicians

If you need an officiant, start looking now. Ask your caterer or catering director for a list of names. Most keep preferred lists of officiants (and vendors). Don't forget to ask recently married friends, relatives, and business associates.

A wedding in a sanctuary will require an organist and maybe some vocalists and musicians. Meet with clergy to review all options and cost. If the wedding is held in a place other than a sanctuary, meet with your entertainment director, who will help you plan and implement the music for your ceremony.

2. THE RECEPTION

- Caterers fees
- Rental fees
- Food and liquor costs
- Extras, such as valet parking
- Overtime fees (should you extend the reception)
- Applicable sales tax and gratuities (usually found at the bottom of most price lists)

This last point is a *major* expense! Be prepared. It can be as high as 26 percent of the total cost!

Once you compare costs and make a tentative decision, meet again with the catering director or caterer. Start negotiating to get the best price and the most value possible.

3. ENTERTAINMENT

- Cost
- Extra fees (setup and music for the ceremony)
- Overtime fees (should you extend the reception)
- Taxes and gratuities

4. PHOTOGRAPHY/VIDEOGRAPHY

- Costs
- Extra fees (portable studio)
- Overtime fees (should you extend the reception)
- Taxes

MAKE THE ANALYSIS

You've compared vendors and places and evaluated their cost. It's time to make a decision.

Once you do, leave a deposit and get a receipt. Negotiate a contract at a later date.

Part V: The Other Components

Visit at least three vendors per wedding component. Once your shopping and researching is complete, make a cost analysis (like the one above). Ask yourself The Five Questions. Consider all factors. Then make a decision.

Book these components next (in order of priority):

5. *Flowers.* Most shops can handle more than one wedding on a given day, but it's best to schedule and reserve as soon as you make a decision.

6. *Honeymoon Reservations* (traditionally the groom's job). It takes time to research the right spot for a honeymoon. Give this responsibility to the groom and start early,

especially if you plan to use those frequent-flyer miles. (See chapter 14, "The Honeymoon" for more information).

7. *Invitations, place cards, brochures, programs*. It's my advice to order your invitations, etc. when your stress levels are low. Once your ceremony and reception sites are booked and your guest list completed, you can proceed.

   If you make your own invitations, brochures, or programs, be sure to schedule plenty of time. (For more information, see chapter 15, "Invitations.")

8. *Wedding gown, headpiece and veil, accessories*. Begin shopping early. If ordering a dress, *do it six months in advance* if possible. Wedding dresses are normally delivered within three months, although some take longer. Don't let yourself in for unnecessary stress. It's my advice to make your own headpiece and veil (it will take a couple of days). If, however, you choose to buy a headpiece and veil, select it *only* when trying on your dress, the same with your jewelry. To be a picture perfect bride, everything must be in harmony (including your hairstyle, see #15). Accessories, like shoes and the right bra, must be bought in advance and taken to the first fitting (unless purchased from the bridal salon). This is a must.

9. *Bridesmaids' dresses*. First decide on your gown, then select your maids' dresses (they must complement your gown). If ordering dresses, do it a week or two after placing the order for your wedding gown—no later (about six months in advance if possible). Bridesmaids' dresses are normally delivered within three months, although some take longer.

10. *Wedding cake*. Want to try your hand at making your own? Schedule a weekend or two to make the practice cake. If it works out, schedule the actual cake into your

daily planner. (See chapter 18, "The Wedding Cake.")

   If purchasing a cake, give yourself time to visit vendors and have a tasting! Most custom bakers are limited by the number of cakes they can bake per weekend. If you go this route, be sure to book at least four months ahead of the wedding date.

11. *Groom and bridal party wear*. Most times, formal wear can be booked about one month before the date. The exception: prom time. If your wedding is in May or June, book your formal wear at least four months in advance.

12. *Rented transportation*. Most times, rented transportation can be reserved a month in advance. The exception again is prom time. If your wedding is in May or June, book at least four months in advance.

13. *Rehearsal dinner*. (Put it in your daily planner and budget for it if you're the host.) Make plans three months ahead of time.

14. *Wedding rings*. These may be purchased or ordered at any time. If they're being custom made, give yourself additional time. Also, purchase or order these when your stress levels are low. Don't wait until the last minute.

15. *Hair and makeup*. Don't wait until the last weeks to determine how you'll wear your hair on the most important day of your life. After you purchase your dress or after it's delivered, start experimenting with hairstyles. *Decide on your hairstyle first, then pick your headpiece*. Your headpiece should complement your hair and your gown; it comes second.

   Many brides employ makeup artists. If you want one, experiment with him or her before the fact; don't wait until the last week to make your choice. If you want to do your own makeup, go to the library and research the best way to do it *for the camera*, to produce the best photos. Educate yourself!

Money-Saving Tip: Many brides schedule an appointment with a makeup consultant at their local department store the morning of the wedding and get their makeup done *free*! If you want to try it, schedule a trial run first with the consultant. Make sure you like their work. (Also, buy a few of their products in appreciation! Or, tip them.)

16. *Marriage license. Know the law.* Many states, for example, require blood tests that take time to process. You must also know when and how to apply for a license, when it goes into effect, when it expires, and the documents that are required (for example, birth certificate, divorce decree, etc.).

17. *Testing for genetically transmitted diseases* (if applicable). For Jews, for example, testing for Tay-Sachs disease is a must. (For more information, see appendix I.)

18. *Testing for STDs* (sexually transmitted diseases). It's essential.

19. *Factors to Consider* (I suggest them highly!):
    • Wedding cancellation insurance. (See this chapter and appendix I.)
    • Premarital agreement. Every woman should have one. It protects her rights and assets and guarantees a proper settlement should divorce occur. It can also minimize the misery of divorce and guard against excessive legal fees. (For more information, see appendix I.)
    • Premarital (non)religious counseling has been proven to slash the divorce rate among participants. Two programs have been particularly successful. One is PAIRS (Practical Application of Intimate Relationship Skills), the other PREPARE. (For more information, see appendix I.)

20. *Gift Expenses* (pencil in shopping time):
    • Gifts for the bridal party
    • Gifts for the hosts of the wedding and the prewedding parties (for example, engagement parties and showers)
    • Gifts that the bride and groom give each other (not necessary)

Make the Analysis

After each component is evaluated for value, service, and price, it's time to make a decision. Leave a deposit and get a receipt. Negotiate a contract later. *Make sure all of the above components are scheduled into your daily planner.* Make sure each item is budgeted. When they're reserved or finalized, cross them off the schedule.

Part VI: The Contract

Your places and vendors are now reserved. You've left a deposit and retained a receipt that contains all vital information. *It's time to think about a contract.*

Most vendors will ask that you sign their contract. Ask for one and take it home to read it and study it. *Make sure that all the terms you* discussed *(before you booked them) are included in your contract.* Get out your notes and add all the items they promised you (if not listed). The hotel, for example, may have offered you a free room for the bride and groom's wedding night or a special rate if you booked a block of rooms for guests. The videographer might have offered you a superpackage for the same price as his regular one. The photographer may have offered you a free portrait or parents' album. Take nothing for granted! *Make sure every item appears in the contract, and be sure to have both parties initial the changes.*

The contract must contain a cancellation clause. This clause must be worded so that you don't lose the deposit(s). (See "Deposits and Receipts," this chapter.) And the ultimate, consumer-protecting clincher? Add this clause: *This contract is subject to approval by my attorney.*

List the vendors' (or professionals') names who will be present at the wedding. This will help ensure that the same people you think you booked will show. (This is critical when booking bands, DJs, photographers, and videographers.)

Leave nothing to chance. If you want to put the color of the linens the caterer promised you into the contract do it. Your contract is your only legal recourse should something go amiss. Read it. Study it. Amend it to meet your needs. Don't take it lightly.

IN CONCLUSION . . .

Plan your time and your financial budgets with good old common sense and forethought. You know what's important to you and *keep those top priorities in mind*—the ones that will have your guests talking about your amazing, elegant wedding!

Chapter Six

THE ENGAGEMENT

Nos deux coeurs sont unis. (Our two hearts are united.)

—From an eighteenth-century ring inscription

THE ENGAGEMENT ANNOUNCEMENT

Announcing an engagement in a newspaper is, most times, expensive. Newspapers charge for the honor (and big, prestigious newspapers charge *big* bucks). Many brides also like to feature a photo of themselves alone or together with their fiancé. This means employing a photographer. It's money that can be better spent.

Many experts warn against newspaper announcements. Many a bride and her family have been ripped off by burglars while attending the wedding. As a solution, they suggest not mentioning the wedding date, the host's address, or even the town where the wedding will take place. For example: Mr. and Mrs. Paul Smith announce the engagement of their daughter, Alice Marie to Walter Preston Jones, son of Mr. and Mrs. Donald James Jones. Miss Smith is a teacher with the Fulton County Schools. Mr. Jones is an attorney with the firm, Springman & Springman. A summer wedding is planned.

If you are dead set about announcing the engagement, do so in a small, local paper. They are much less expensive (and many don't charge). If you must feature a photo, use a recent one taken by friends or family. A good quality glossy black-and-white print, either eight-by-ten inch or five-by-seven inch will do. It's not necessary to employ a photographer for an engagement photo.

PRINTED ENGAGEMENT ANNOUNCEMENTS

It's in poor taste to send printed engagement announcements, the implication being, "Send a gift!" Let friends and family know through the grapevine that you're engaged or drop personal notes to your close relatives and friends. If they choose to send a gift, they will. Always respond with a thank you note within three weeks of receiving the gift.

ENGAGEMENT PARTIES—AN EXTRANEOUS EXTRA

If your relatives want to host an engagement party, why not? As long as it doesn't interfere with the wedding budget. For example, the groom's family might choose to host one (but might also decide that's all they're going to do). If that's the case, it's best that your fiancé discuss your priorities with his parents. For example: "Sue and I are very grateful, but we'd rather have the money put toward our photographer (or band or flowers, etc.). Our wedding is more important to us than an engagement party."

In the beginning (no matter who is hosting the wedding), it's best to sit down with both sets of parents to discuss your wedding plans and your priorities and theirs. It's the respectful thing to do. It will also give everyone direction, a sense of involvement, and put them on the same wavelength.

If your family decides to host a party, it may be as formal or informal as you'd like. Formal parties require formal invitations and all the added extras that go with them: food, drink, entertainment, flowers. They are expensive.

You may, however, have a formal wedding and an informal engagement party—a barbecue or a pool party, for example. You and your family may do your own cooking, buy your own liquor, and make your own decorations. It's up to you. But once again, if it infringes upon your wedding dollars—*don't do it!*

ENGAGEMENT PARTIES AND GIFTS

Contrary to popular belief, guests are not expected to bring gifts to an engagement party. They may, but it's not a requirement. Today, attending a wedding means spending money and lots of it. Many guests may travel long distances to attend and must pay for the trip and their lodging. They are also expected to dress appropriately and to bring a gift. And they may also be invited to a shower or two. To expect them to bring a gift to an engagement party (or to send one) is asking too much.

Be careful about whom you invite. Knowingly inviting out-of-town friends or distant relatives (those who can't possibly attend) is, once again, screaming for a gift. Be diplomatic and leave them off the guest list. This doesn't apply to close friends or relatives who would be insulted if they weren't invited. It's up to you to make tactful choices.

Be aware that all those who are invited to prewedding festivities must also be invited to the wedding. It's in the worst of taste to invite people to an engagement party or a shower and not invite them to the wedding.

IF THE ENGAGEMENT IS BROKEN

Recently a woman E-mailed me for advice. A friend of hers had called off the wedding, but had not returned the gift. A couple of months had gone by and the woman wanted her gift back. She asked me if she could write and ask for it, or if it would be considered rude.

My answer: The only rude person in this scenario is this woman's so-called friend. Since she chose not to return the gift, it's perfectly appropriate to ask. Hopefully, she'll be embarrassed enough to return it with a letter of apology.

WHO KEEPS THE RING? A WARNING!

Once, a client of mine, a flight attendant who lived in Florida, decided to make a surprise visit to her fiancé, who lived in New Orleans.

When she took out her key and opened his door, she found him in bed with another woman. His response: "I have something to tell you . . ." My client was so incensed that she threw her engagement ring at him (three carats!) and walked out. The bride's mother was so angry that she called the man and asked that he reimburse her for all the expended deposit money—about $30,000. He said she was out of luck. The woman called her attorney, who said that her only recourse was the ring. It belonged to the bride, and if she would have kept it, she could have sold it to recoup the losses.

Moral of the Story: Count to ten and keep that ring on your finger no matter what happens! Throw the nearest lamp.

Chapter Seven

THE ENGAGEMENT RING

A contract of eternal bond of love
Confirm'd by mutual joinder of your hands
Attested by the holy close of lips
Strengthened by interchangement of your rings:
—Shakespeare, *Twelfth Night*

A HISTORY

It was the pharaohs of ancient Egypt who first perceived the circle as a symbol of eternity, having no beginning and no end. A plain round ring, they deduced, should therefore symbolize love.

In ancient Rome, when a woman's family pledged her in marriage, the prospective bridegroom sealed the pledge with a ring. Even in the early Christian era, the wedding ring was integral to the marriage ceremony. In the seventh century, Isidore of Seville stated that the ring was "... given by the spouser to the spoused ... to join their hearts by this pledge and that therefore the ring is placed on the fourth finger because a certain vein is said to flow from thence to the heart."[1]

Ancient Jewish law required couples to perform three basic acts before they were legally married. The bridegroom had to give to the bride a gift of value (since the seventh century, a ring), while he recited the legal formula of acquisition and consecration, "Be thou consecrated to me with this ring in accordance with the laws of Moses and Israel." The ketubah (marriage contract) was signed and given to the woman. And the final act was consummation. Jewish couples basically follow these rituals today (although not necessarily in this order).

In the mid-seventeenth century, the Puritans tried to ban the wedding ring, describing it as "a relique of popery and a diabolical circle for the devil to dance in."[2] The public outcry was so overwhelming, however, they decided against it. Jeremy Taylor, a clergyman at the time, said this: "The Marriage ring ties two hearts by an eternal band; it is like the Cherubim's flaming sword, set for the guard of Paradise."[3]

When Prince Albert became engaged to Queen Victoria in 1839, he presented her with a coiled ring in the shape of an emerald-studded snake. At the time, snakes were popular for romantic jewelry. The snake symbolized eternity, the emerald faith. Throughout the ages, betrothal rings and wedding rings have changed in design but never in significance. In the twentieth century, there's probably no greater tale of the wedding ring and the love it bears than this one. It's a story marred by great tragedy, never to be forgotten by history.

In November 1963, as her husband, John Fitzgerald Kennedy, lay dead on a trauma table in the emergency room at Dallas's Parkland Hospital, Jacqueline, his wife, racked her mind for something of significance to give him. She chose her wedding ring, a plain gold band. She slipped it on his finger.

A day later, Mrs. Kennedy asked Senate Majority Leader Mike Mansfield to eulogize her husband in a memorial service to be held in the Capitol rotunda. Mansfield thought and thought but could not shake the image of Jacqueline and her ring. His eulogy was so poignant and raw that it will never be forgotten. As it progressed, he stopped periodically and repeated this refrain: "There was a father with a little boy and a little girl and the joy of each in the other, and, in a moment, it was no more. And so, she took a ring from her finger and placed it in his hands . . ."[4]

Choose your engagement and wedding rings carefully. You will wear them forever, never knowing what the fates may bring. Hold dear their ancient significance and wear them in love and joy for each other.

Who Needs a Ring?

If a man asks you to be his wife and you accept (or if you ask a man and he accepts!), you are engaged. A ring is but a luxurious formality and one that also becomes a treasured keepsake. It's tradition. It's also a great expenditure (the second largest wedding expense), and one that can take you to the cleaners but good, if you don't take precautions.

You need to educate yourself about diamonds before you purchase. And I don't mean the 4 Cs; that's kid stuff! In this book, I give you the technical information you need to shop wisely and well. Study it. I also offer an unusual shopping alternative. It's one that will save you hundreds, if not thousands of dollars, but it's also one that's going to take time to implement with success.

How This Chapter Can Save You Hundreds of Dollars — or More

Rings are the second largest expense of a wedding. They don't have to be. If you're a savvy shopper you can buy your rings for a fraction of the cost that you'd pay in a traditional jewelry store or a wholesale outlet. All it takes is a little self-education, a sense of adventure, and a willingness to shop. *This chapter is one of the most important ones in this book.* Not only will it save you money; it will open a whole new world to you. You will probably never shop at your local jewelers again.

A Secret Divulged

Hidden treasure lies in every major city and in every small town in America and it's buried in stores called *pawnshops*. These shops originated in China thousands of years ago, and their concept—an easy, fast way to get money with little aggravation—spread like wildfire throughout the civilized world. It's even said that Queen Isabella of Spain pawned the crown jewels to finance Christopher Columbus's expedition to the New World.

Pawnshops have come a long way since then. Over fourteen thousand exist in the United States today. If you're a savvy shopper, you can buy jewelry, crystal, guitars, computers, and even golf clubs in pawnshops—*at great savings*. Most people are apprehensive about buying in pawnshops, but there's no reason to be. You don't have to drive to the seedy part of town to find a pawnshop. Just open your eyes. Look closely at those little shopping centers you never noticed before as you make your way to work. Chances are, you'll find a pawnshop. They even exist in such places as Beverly Hills.

The Retailer and the Pawnbroker

We assume (and hope) that the retail jeweler we do business with is ethical. But *Primetime Live*, in a program entitled *"Everyone's Best Friend,"* proved that ethics was the least of the problem.

Primetime bought diamond rings from jewelers on Forty-seventh Street (The Diamond District) in New York City, two different Macy's department stores, and the Home Shopping Network. Here's what they found: The jewelers grossly misrepresented the color of the diamonds they sold them. Macy's misrepresented the color, and in one instance, the clarity (or flaws). The Home Shopping Network sold diamonds so poor in quality they should have been ground up and used for industrial purposes. The result: *Primetime Live* was taken!

Apparently there was no legal aftermath. The reporters did not say they were going to relate their findings to the police and there was no mention of a pending investigation. The moral of their story: *Buyer beware!*

It's been my experience that most pawnbrokers will *not* offer a consumer *their* evaluation of a diamond (unless they're a gemologist).

They will show you a grading report or appraisal if available. They may even say, for example, that the diamond has good color or is fairly free from flaws. Therefore, in most cases, it's left up to you to make the final determination. And as *Primetime* proved, *you had better know how to evaluate a diamond—no matter where you shop!*

Pawnbrokers must run honest businesses. They are required to report to police any items brought to them for pawn that they think may be stolen. And they are thoroughly investigated by police or other state agencies before they can open their doors. Police also regularly monitor pawnshops for stolen items.

The National Pawnbrokers Association

The National Pawnbrokers Association is an organization of approximately 3,200 pawnbrokers. The organization promotes honesty and integrity among its members and is dedicated to improving the industry's public and political image.

The organization also works closely with

the Gemological Institute of America (GIA), the most prestigious gemological society in the world. Many of its members are also very active with a distinguished professional online service called Polygon Networking, which allows them access to information and advice about diamonds and colored gemstones. The association also has its own web site. (For contact information, see appendix I.) When shopping, it might be wise to ask your pawnbroker if he is a member of this highly informative, upstanding organization.

According to Tom Horn, the association's executive director, pawnshops fall under the Federal Truth and Lending Act, whose regulations were written by the Federal Reserve Board. Compliance is overseen by the Federal Trade Commission, and pawnshops must abide by those regulations.

Mr. Horn also stated that about ten years ago, Dr. John Caskey, Swarthmore College, researched the pawnshop industry. At first he considered it to be a necessary evil. But after extensive study, he became impressed with the integrity of the industry and the service they offered the public.

HOW A PAWNSHOP WORKS

Let's say a man who paid $2,000 for a three-quarter-carat diamond ring needs a quick loan. He takes it to a pawnshop. He has a diamond grading report from a respected gem laboratory vouching for the authenticity of the stone. The pawnbroker makes a copy of the certificate but examines the diamond himself before deciding to loan the man $250. Every month the man returns to the pawnshop to make payments on the loan. If he misses payments, the ring becomes the property of the pawnshop.

The unclaimed ring is then taken *out of pawn* and put up for sale. In this case, the pawnbroker prices the ring at $900. A savvy shopper spots it, examines it (and the grading

report), negotiates an even better price, and walks away with a bargain. (In the meantime, the pawnbroker has made a hefty profit.)

I find pawnbrokers to be very honest. They are also very well versed, experienced with, and educated about diamonds. After all, their livelihood depends on how well they evaluate stones (and other goods they take in for pawn). Because of the regulations they fall under and because I respect their knowledge and the responsibility they bear, I feel very comfortable dealing with them. An act of dishonesty could be their downfall. I've never had a problem with a pawnbroker or walked away without a bargain. I am, however, an educated consumer.

I've found buried treasure in pawnshops. And I relish the experience. It appeals to my sense of adventure. It's not like looking for a needle in a haystack or panning for gold or digging for diamonds in the fields of Arkansas. I guarantee you: You will find treasure in every pawnshop you visit. I'm going to teach you how.

BEFORE YOU SHOP: RULES TO FOLLOW

Many pawnshops have gone into the retail jewelry business, therefore it's essential that you know whether the jewelry you're considering is out of pawn or new. *The bargains are found in jewelry that is released from pawn.* If you'd wanted to buy a new ring—and pay retail—you could have gone to a traditional jewelry store. *Ask the pawnbroker if the jewelry is new or out of pawn. Only consider jewelry that is out of pawn. And don't be afraid to negotiate.* Pawnbrokers expect it. I've never bought a piece of pawned jewelry for the asking price. Be a tough negotiator.

If the stone you're considering is expensive and doesn't come with a grading report from a respected gem lab, have the pawnbroker get a grading report for you. *This is a must even if you have to pay for it!* (See "The Diamond Grading Report" this chapter.)

THE BIG FISH THAT DIDN'T GET AWAY

I tell no fish tales when it comes to pawnshops; the ones I hooked didn't get away. Once, while in a pawnshop, a bright, shiny cocktail ring caught my eye. Branching out from the center diamond—like a bicycle wheel—were gold spokes. At the end of each one was a small diamond. I asked the pawnbroker the weight of the center diamond. He said about 0.80 points, or just over three-quarters of a carat. It was so clear and white and brilliant I couldn't keep my eyes off it! I asked him for his loupe (a jeweler's magnifying glass) and examined it. From what I could see, it was virtually flawless. I went outside and examined the color and inspected the gold stamp on the inside shank of the ring. It was marked 18K. (*My rule:* Better stones will normally be set in better settings. It's doubtful, for example, that a diamond would be set in 10K gold.) I bought it for $800 and rushed to my jeweler. He offered me $2,000 on the spot. No thanks! I asked him to remove the shank, add a bale (a gold loop), and make it into a pendant. I wear it to this day.

A couple, looking for an engagement ring, could have bought this ring and reset it into the ring of their dreams for less than half the cost (or a third of the cost) that they would have paid in a traditional jewelry store. (There's no telling what price my jeweler would have asked for the ring!)

BE CAREFUL . . . NOT ALL EMERALDS ARE GREEN

When it comes to colored gems (if you're thinking of one), even the experts can be fooled—so *beware!* Antoinette Matlins, a top gemologist and author of many books about jewelry, recounts the story of a woman who had what she thought to be a very fine emerald ring. She took it to a very knowledgeable jeweler, who happened to be a friend of Ms. Matlins's father (Antonio Bonanno, also a top gemologist and once curator of gems for the Smithsonian Institution). The jeweler looked at the ring and pronounced it an inexpensive tourmaline because it had no flaws. The woman, however, was unconvinced and later took it to Mr. Bonanno. It was one of the finest emeralds he'd ever seen.[5]

The jeweler made a mistake because he had never seen an emerald without flaws—a rarity. Flaws are characteristic of emeralds. In fact, some flaws in certain emeralds are like fingerprints; they can tell experts where they originated and will actually *increase* the price of the stone because they prove its authenticity. If I look at an emerald and see flaws, I can be pretty certain it's the real thing.

One day, while browsing in a pawnshop, a stunning green emerald caught my attention. After examining it with a loupe, I found it flawed, but minimally. I also noted that it was mounted in 18K gold. (This gave me another clue that the stone was a good one.) And the color was a translucent pea green. It weighed a little better than two carats. I bought the emerald for $600 and this time took it to a friend who is a wholesale jeweler. I wanted to sell it. He sent it to a client who owned a prestigious jewelry store in a historic hotel in Washington, D.C. After a few months we heard no news; I asked my friend to retrieve the ring. On the day he received it, he called me. "Meet me later. I have something to show you." When I met him, he told me to look at the ring. It still carried the price tag from the jewelry store. It was marked $5,000. My friend said, "No wonder they couldn't sell it." I said, "I'll keep the ring."

Many women prefer colored gemstones for engagement rings and this emerald would have made any bride-to-be proud. Imagine it reset in an engagement ring? *And all for $600 plus the cost of resetting!*

Warning: Many pawnbrokers and jewelers are at a loss when it comes to colored gemstones. Even the best, most experienced jeweler may be duped into thinking a colored gem is a natural one rather than a synthetic or a treated stone; it's that difficult to determine accurately. Therefore, when it comes to colored gems, I'm wary. I never spend more than I can afford to lose (just like when I go to Las Vegas).

Pawnbrokers are very honest in this regard. Whenever I've asked about a colored gem, I've always received the reply, "I really don't know what it is." That's because they don't. Colored gems and whether or not they're synthetic can't be determined by the human eye or a loupe (unless you find a gemologist who specializes in the field). And don't be fooled by an antique setting. Good synthetics have been produced in this country since the early 1900s, and there's been many a reputable, experienced jeweler who's been hoodwinked.

Be aware that many techniques are commonly used to alter the color of gemstones, from heat to radiation to dyeing. A colored gem may also be a *composite*, a stone that's made up of layers of different materials—including glass. A composite may even be difficult for the trained eye to spot.

Before the purchase of a fine colored gemstone, send it to the GIA or other respected gem lab to have it evaluated. It might cost a little more, but an ounce of prevention is worth a pound of cure. (For more information, see appendix I.)

A WORD ABOUT BIRTHSTONES

Birthstones make lovely engagement rings—especially for those who would *not* prefer a diamond. But once again (except for the months of April [diamond] and June [cultured pearl]), you're dealing with colored gems. Risk no more than you can afford to lose. Check the mounting and buy only those rings set in 14K or 18K gold or platinum.

The Month and the Birthstone:	The Zodiac and the Stone:
January: Garnet	*Aquarius:* Garnet
February: Amethyst	*Pisces:* Amethyst
March: Aquamarine/Bloodstone	*Aries:* Bloodstone
April: Diamond	*Taurus:* Sapphire
May: Emerald	*Gemini:* Agate
June: Cultured pearl/Moonstone/Alexandrite	*Cancer:* Emerald
July: Ruby	*Leo:* Onyx
August: Peridot/Sardonyx	*Virgo:* Carnelian
September: Sapphire	*Libra:* Peridot
October: Opal/Pink tourmaline	*Scorpio:* Beryl
November: Citrine quartz/Topaz	*Sagittarius:* Topaz
December: Turquoise/Zircon	*Capricorn:* Ruby

THE MEANING OF COLORED GEMSTONES

In the ancient world, it was believed that a gem could impart its attributes to its wearer. An amethyst, for example, was said to prevent drunkenness (so brides-to-be, get him a great big one before the bachelor party). If thinking of buying a colored gem, why not one whose meaning you'll hold dear?

The Meaning of Popular Colored Gems:

White pearls—love and purity
Blue sapphire—hope
Amethyst—perfection
Topaz—affection
Agate—strength
Peridot—friendship
Moonstone—good luck

Ruby—passion
Emerald—steadfast love
Opal—fidelity
Garnet—devotion
Aquamarine—vitality
Turquoise—love and success
Alexandrite—good omen

DIAMONDS

In the ancient world, diamonds were perceived to have magical powers and were said to bestow the wearer with great strength. Because of their hardness, they also signified undying love and fidelity. Today, close to 70 percent of American women receive diamond engagement rings. For that reason, I'm going to concentrate on diamonds and what you should look for before you purchase one.

THE DIAMOND GRADING REPORT

A grading report is an evaluation of a diamond based on standards developed by the G.I.A.

Many respected gem labs throughout the world, however (other than the G.I.A.), grade diamonds. For a list of top gem labs, see appendix I. (Grading reports are also available for colored gemstones.)

When you buy a diamond of a carat or more from a respected traditional jewelry shop, it should be accompanied by a *grading report* from a respected gemological lab. (Not to be confused with a *certificate* issued by the jeweler, which is *his* appraisal of the stone.) *Don't buy a diamond of a carat or more unless it's accompanied by a grading report from a respected gem lab.* Ask your pawnbroker or jeweler to obtain one for you (or do it yourself). He'll charge you for it, but it will be well worth the price.

Rings are the second largest expense of a wedding; they are an investment. It's important to understand what you're buying, inside and out. A grading report will tell you in no uncertain terms.

How to Use a Loupe

Before you begin diamond hunting, you must learn how to use a *loupe*. A loupe is a jeweler's magnifying glass and is 10x, an international standard. (*Look at diamonds or colored gemstones only with a 10x loupe.*) Loupes are inexpensive and can be purchased through a jewelers' supply house. Consult your Yellow Pages (or see appendix I).

Once you get a loupe, practice with it. Hold it between your thumb and index finger, about one inch from your eye. Borrow your mom's diamond engagement ring. Hold it with your other hand and move it back and forth in front of the loupe—one to two inches away until the diamond comes into focus. To steady the ring, make sure your palms touch one another. With practice, you should be able to see the diamond clearly, inside and out.

Many jewelers and pawnshops also have microscopes to inspect diamonds. The advantage is that they provide background light, which makes the diamond more clearly visible. But a word of caution: *Focus the microscope yourself.* There's less of a chance of missing *inclusions* (flaws within the diamond) than if the microscope is focused for you.

The Next Factor

Is the diamond clean? *Make sure the ring is cleaned before you inspect it.* This is a must. Dirt will mask the color of the stone and may even hide its flaws.

Unmounted Diamonds

A reputable jeweler will tell you that the only way to evaluate a diamond is to look at it *unmounted.* Unfortunately, most pawnbrokers are not the type of jewelers who remove stones from their settings, so we'll just have to shoot from the hip. There's nothing like educating yourself and using your common sense to help you arrive at the right decision. I'm going to give you tips on what to look for when evaluating a mounted diamond.

What Mounting?

Look only at a diamond that is set in prongs, preferably one where the prongs elevate the stone from the shank of the ring. An example of this type of mounting is the classic *Tiffany.* In this setting, the thin prongs that hold and suspend the diamond also allow the optimum amount of light to enter it and be refracted back to the eye. The degree to which a diamond properly refracts light determines its fire and life, or *brilliance.*

Beware: Diamonds are mounted to hide flaws and flaws may be hidden by prongs. Therefore, look closely at the diamond near the prongs.

Don't consider a diamond that's mounted in a *bezel*. A bezel encases the *girdle* (the fine rim that separates the top of the diamond from the bottom) in metal. This makes it impossible to examine the girdle for flaws or to determine if it's been cut too thin or too thick (essential in determining the diamond's fragility). Stick to elevated, prong-set diamonds. It's a necessary precaution.

If you wanted to be chancy, you could consider a *channel*-set diamond. A channel setting suspends the stone from opposite ends with no metal touching the sides. You should, however, be able to see the entire diamond (except the ends, where flaws may be hidden).

Rule: Make sure that you see the table (the top of the diamond), the facets above and below the girdle, the pavilion (the area below the girdle), the girdle, and the culet (the polished facet on the point of the pavilion) to make a proper evaluation.

THE MAKE

I'm forever frustrated by those who put too much emphasis on flaws. Unless you can see them with the naked eye, who's going to know they're there? Do friends pull a loupe out of their pocket when you show them your ring? No, of course not. They look at the diamond, how bright and sparkly it is, and the color. (People generally know that diamonds should not look yellow.)

Our goal is to buy a *beautiful* diamond, not an *investment-quality* diamond (one that's near flawless, close to colorless, and cut to excellent proportions). Even a very small diamond of this quality will cost thousands of dollars. We're not interested, but it is important to know the factors that constitute a beautiful diamond. The first, and most important factor, is its *make. The make is the cut, proportioning, and finish of a diamond.* If the make is bad, the stone will look lifeless and pasty, even if it's near flawless with great color.

In 1919, Marcel Tolkowsky mathematically calculated *ideal dimensions* for the cutting and proportioning of round (called *brilliant*) diamonds, which are followed to this day. Your goal is to find one cut as close to his standards as possible. Once you start to compare diamonds, you'll begin to notice the difference between good make and bad.

The importance of make cannot be exaggerated. Tiffany's, in its *How to Buy a Diamond* brochure, notes that *cut* is the most important factor in determining a stone's beauty and brilliance. But how does it affect its dollar value?

Jay Feder, author of *The Practical Guide to Buying Diamonds*, states, "It is not uncommon for a diamond merchant to push color and clarity and almost disregard the quality of the cut. This sometimes results in the purchase of a diamond that is really worth 20, 30, or 40 percent less than what the merchant is charging you, just because of the poor cut."[6] *Now that's something to think about!* (To contact Mr. Feder, see appendix I.)

FACET ARRANGEMENT OF A STANDARD ROUND BRILLIANT CUT

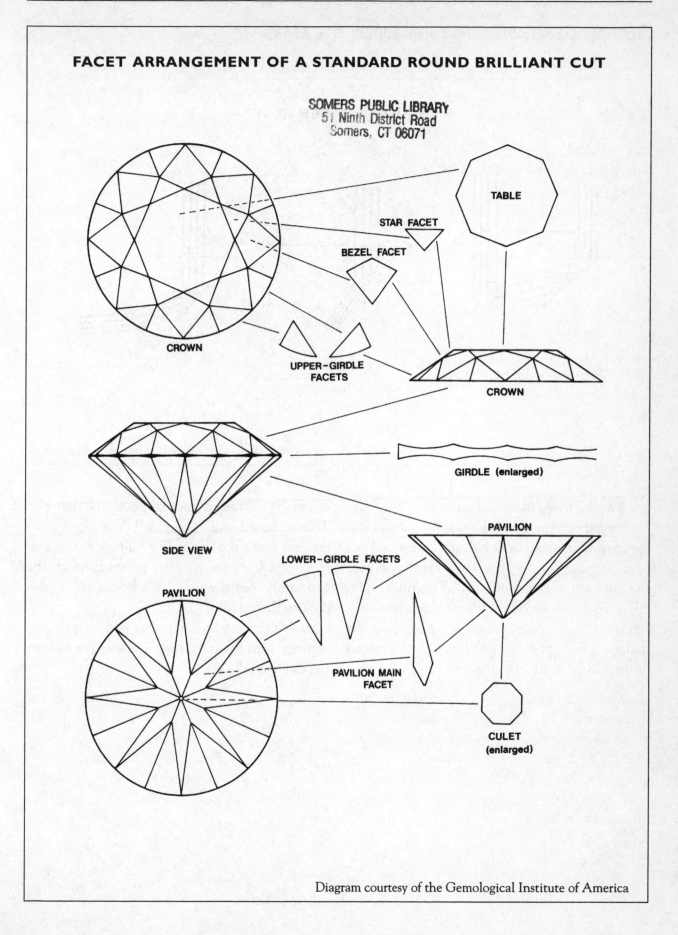

TABLE

STAR FACET

BEZEL FACET

CROWN

UPPER-GIRDLE
FACETS

CROWN

GIRDLE (enlarged)

SIDE VIEW

PAVILION

LOWER-GIRDLE FACETS

PAVILION

PAVILION MAIN
FACET

CULET
(enlarged)

Diagram courtesy of the Gemological Institute of America

HOW TO DETERMINE THE QUALITY OF THE MAKE

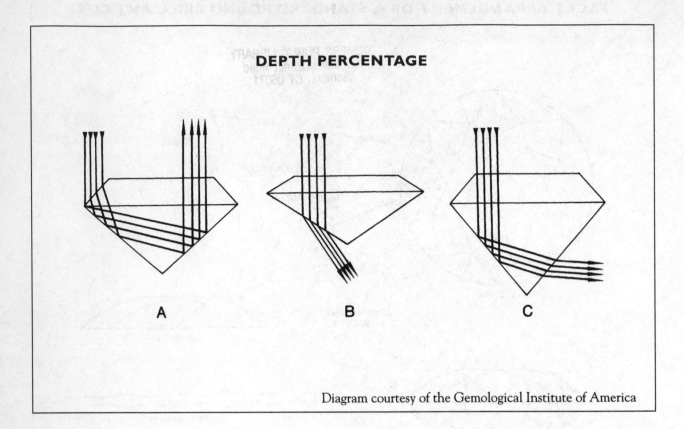

DEPTH PERCENTAGE

A   B   C

Diagram courtesy of the Gemological Institute of America

Look at the three diamonds above.

The diamond on the left has ideal *depth percentage* (the depth from table to culet, expressed as a percentage of the diamond's average diameter at the girdle in round diamonds). This diamond is cut so that the majority of light that enters it is refracted back to the eye. When this occurs, the diamond has optimum brilliance. *The diamond in the middle* is cut too shallow. The light that enters it is *not* refracted back to the eye. This diamond will appear dull. *The diamond on the right* is cut too deep. The light does not exit the stone from the top, but passes through the center and out the side. This stone will appear dark in the middle.

It's fairly easy to determine good depth percentage with the naked eye. Look at the following diagram.

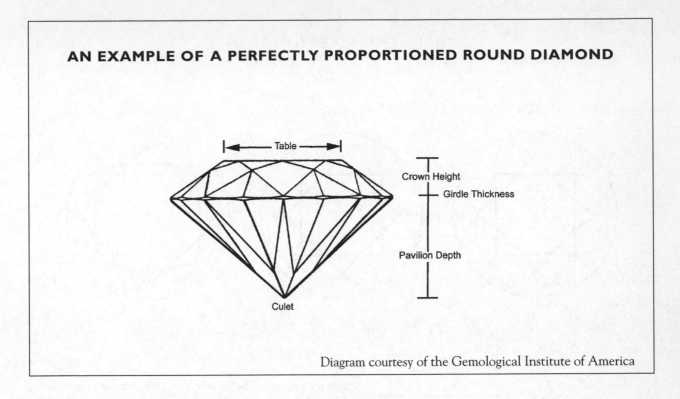

AN EXAMPLE OF A PERFECTLY PROPORTIONED ROUND DIAMOND

Table

Crown Height

Girdle Thickness

Pavilion Depth

Culet

Diagram courtesy of the Gemological Institute of America

You will notice that the pavilion is approximately 2½ times greater than the size of the crown. *To find a diamond with good depth percentage, make sure that it falls as close within this range as possible.* This is fairly easy to accomplish with the naked eye and a loupe.

THE TABLE PERCENTAGE

The next factor to analyze is the *table percentage* (the size of the table expressed as a percentage of the average girdle diameter in round diamonds). This is a critical factor to understand for a number of reasons. *Most diamonds are cut to increase the size of the table.* This makes a stone look larger, but it also decreases the size of the crown facets, diminishing the diamond's fire. A diamond cut this way is called *spread. The cutter has sacrificed the diamond's beauty and brilliance for size.* A spread diamond often looks lifeless. *Stay away from them.*

If you ever hear a pawnbroker or jeweler say, "It spreads just like a one-carat diamond," *run!*

What he's telling you is that the stone weighs less than a one-carat diamond but *looks* as big. *Beware: It's not and never will be a one-carat diamond. And: If it spreads like a one-carat diamond, it's been cut wrong.* Tiffany's, in its *How to Buy a Diamond* brochure, says that most diamonds are spread, "*. . . and the customer is unknowingly paying for this extra padding.*"[7] By educating yourself about diamonds, you should never fall into this trap. Why pay more for a poorly cut diamond when it's so easy to buy one that's cut for maximum brilliance? To ensure your diamond has good table percentage, look at the *Table Spread Estimation* chart. Notice the two squares formed by the facets that intersect each other. If the sides of the squares bow in, you're looking at a diamond with great table percentage. If the sides of the squares are straight, as in the middle example, the table percentage is passable. But if the sides bow out, as in the third example, you should do the same! This diamond has a spread table. Once again, this is easy to observe with the naked eye and a loupe.

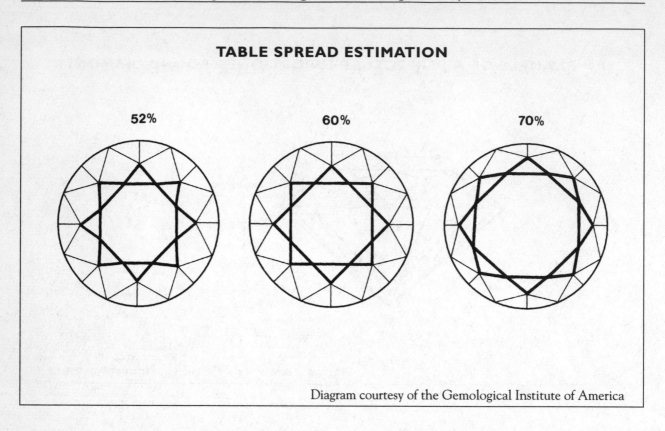

TABLE SPREAD ESTIMATION

52% 60% 70%

Diagram courtesy of the Gemological Institute of America

A Word About Make and Fancy Cuts

A fancy cut refers to any diamond that's not round. This would include pear-, marquise-, oval-, heart-, and emerald-shaped diamonds, and trilliant (triangle) and quadrillion (square) diamonds. Be aware that it's more difficult to assess proper make in fancy cuts and it takes practice. But the most common indicator, and the one that's the easiest to spot, is called the *bow-tie effect*. The bow-tie in a diamond looks exactly like its namesake; it's a dark area that resembles a bow-tie shape and stretches from one side of the diamond to the other. The bigger and darker the bow-tie, the worse the make.

Fancy cuts should fall close to industry standards. Look at the Length-to-Width Preferences chart. Try to stay as close to these proportions as possible. They're easy to judge with the naked eye. A fancy cut diamond that deviates too far from the standard, however, should cost much less. (Be aware that dimensions are also a matter of taste. Some women, for example, may prefer a thinner marquise and others a more rounded one.)

With practice, by comparing fancy cuts, you should be able to determine those with good make, ones that have the best brilliance and color. Make sure they're not cut too shallow or too deep, and keep an eye out for that bow-tie!

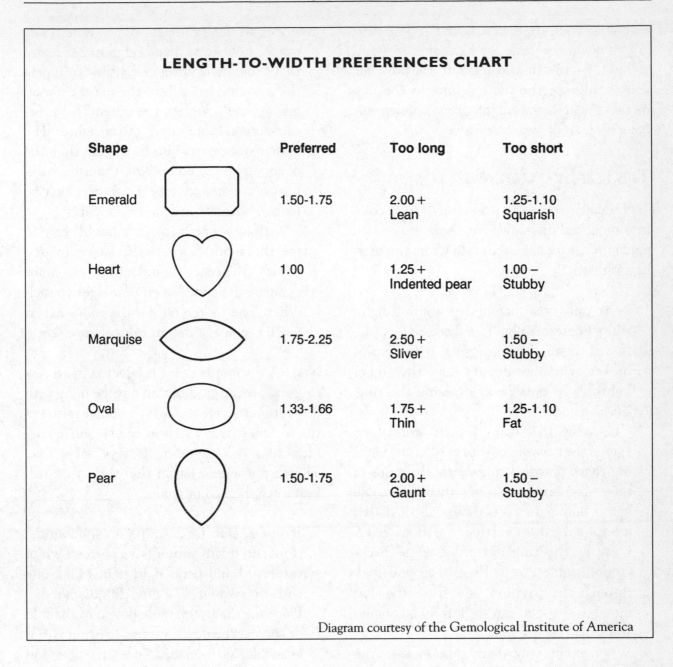

LENGTH-TO-WIDTH PREFERENCES CHART

Shape		Preferred	Too long	Too short
Emerald		1.50-1.75	2.00 + Lean	1.25-1.10 Squarish
Heart		1.00	1.25 + Indented pear	1.00 – Stubby
Marquise		1.75-2.25	2.50 + Sliver	1.50 – Stubby
Oval		1.33-1.66	1.75 + Thin	1.25-1.10 Fat
Pear		1.50-1.75	2.00 + Gaunt	1.50 – Stubby

Diagram courtesy of the Gemological Institute of America

COLOR

In the quest for a beautiful diamond, it's my opinion that color and make go hand in hand. If the make is bad, the color, no matter how good, will be dwarfed. On the flip side, if the color is faint yellow (undesirable) and the make is terrific, the stone will look brilliantly off-color, the last thing you want. *Our goal is to find a diamond with good make and good color.*

This is how the GIA grades color in dia-

monds. The optimum grade is D. A D-color diamond is *colorless* (not white or blue-white as some think). If you can envision looking into a brook of pure, clean, cold mountain-spring water you can imagine a D-color diamond.

From D, the scale progresses through the alphabet to Z (light yellow). The grades that demand the highest price are D, E, and F (considered colorless). The next grades (called near-colorless) are G, H, I, and J. The next grades down the scale are K, L, and M (faint yellow). By the time you get to M, however, you should see the faint yellow in the diamond. As a diamond progresses down the color scale, it decreases in value.

TIPS FOR EVALUATING COLOR

Technically, you can't accurately assess color in a mounted diamond, but there are certain precautions you can take and factors you must be aware of:

1. Look only at a diamond in natural light, white fluorescent light, or *diamond light* (designed to simulate daylight). If the pawnbroker or jeweler doesn't have the proper lighting, go outside to examine the ring. *This is a must!*

   Be aware that many jewelry stores (and even some pawnshops) use very strong lighting that's designed to *enhance* the color of their diamonds, meaning that you could spend hundreds, even thousands of dollars more, for the diamond than you should have.

2. Look at the ring against a white background, table down. Pick it up and look through the pavilion side. Turn the diamond so that you can see it from all angles. *You should see no yellow.*

3. When comparing diamonds, look at the color near the girdle with the diamond turned on its table. The girdle is the thinnest part of the stone with the least mass. The chances of color distortion are less from this angle.

4. Ask to compare the diamond to a set of *master stones*. Master stones are a set of cubic zirconia that meet the GIA's standards for color. This is how the GIA's experts grade diamonds (under very controlled conditions, but don't forget, they're experts!).

   Put the diamond next to the master stones to determine its color grade. (The master stones and diamond must be clean.) Make sure there's proper lighting. Compare the diamond to each of the master stones, first on one side then the other. This is because one side may appear to be lighter. The master stones may also be smaller than the diamond you're comparing them to, making your diamond appear darker. Don't be fooled, however, and downgrade it.

   With lots of practice, you should begin to see the subtle variation in color in diamonds. If master stones aren't available, compare diamonds of equal weight to each other. The more you do, the more expert you'll become at determining *white* color.

Note: A diamond's color is affected by its setting and precise grading can only be done with unset stones. Even the GIA can make mistakes (most times in borderline cases) and recognizes that color grading is very subjective. There's not a gem lab in the world that will guarantee their color grades.

5. If you're able to examine an unmounted stone, do it this way. Take a piece of white cardboard and bend it in half. (Take one with you when shopping for diamonds.) Place the diamond, table down, in the fold of the cardboard. If proper lighting is not available, go outside. Turn the diamond around and move the cardboard so that you can see the stone from all angles. The more yellow you see, the less the value of the diamond.

Note: If you see yellow in a diamond, don't consider it. There's a pawnshop on every corner.

A WORD ABOUT FLUORESCENCE

The GIA estimates that about 50 percent of the world's gem diamonds fluoresce. It's essential to know—in terms of color—whether yours does or doesn't. *Fluorescence* means that the diamond will glow when placed under direct light, especially violet and ultraviolet rays (sunlight). Because fluorescence may negatively affect a stone's color, it's analyzed by gem laboratories. The results are listed on the diamond grading report: whether the diamond fluoresces, the degree of fluorescence, and the color it fluoresces.

Diamonds usually fluoresce blue, although many fluoresce yellow. Let's say you're looking at a diamond under normal lighting conditions and it appears to be white. But when you go outside, the stone appears whiter and bluer. Are your eyes playing tricks? No, the diamond is fluorescing.

THE PROS AND CONS

The diamond that fluoresces blue will make it look whiter, a real plus if the diamond doesn't have terrific color. The advantage: Stones that fluoresce don't cost more than their nonfluorescing counterparts. The drawback, however, is twofold: If a diamond has terrific color but fluoresces, the fluorescence will mask it. This is undesirable. The other disadvantage: Too much fluorescence may make the diamond appear waxy, hazy, or dull, affecting its brilliance. This is unacceptable.

To know if a diamond fluoresces, look at it outside under a white fluorescent light, or if possible, under a *black* light. If you see a blue or yellow tint that wasn't visible before, the diamond fluoresces. If the diamond retains its brilliance, it's nothing to be concerned about. But if it looks hazy, milky, greasy, or dull, it's best to look for another diamond.

Note: The subtle differences in color grades can mean thousands of dollars to you. If buying an expensive diamond, have it graded first by a respected gem lab. Don't trust jewelers to make this determination, no matter how experienced they are.

A WORD ABOUT FANCIES

A *fancy* is a colored diamond. Diamonds occur naturally in almost every color: red, purple, green, yellow, and even black. These diamonds are very rare. The only way to be certain if a gem's color hasn't been artificially changed is to have it analyzed. Many diamonds are treated to alter their color and even an experienced jeweler may not recognize one that's been tampered with.

CARAT WEIGHT

The carat refers to the weight of the diamond, *not its size*. A metric carat equals .200 grams. To determine a diamond's weight, a jeweler throws it on a scale (designed for the purpose) and weighs it. According to the *GIA Jeweler's Manual* ". . . diamond weight is usually measured to a thousandth of a carat and rounded to the nearest hundredth (or point)."[8] A one-carat diamond is composed of 100 points. A

half-carat, for example, would be 0.50 points, a three-quarter carat, 0.75 points.

Pawnbrokers may not be able to tell you the exact weight of a diamond but I've found them to come very close. Weight, however, is important in terms of dollars. In the diamond world, the value increases with specific increments of weight, i.e., 0.25, 0.50, 0.75, and one carat. That's why diamonds slightly less than one carat are significantly less in price than a one-carat diamond of the same quality. *By buying a diamond slightly under the specified increments, you can save a bundle.*

CLARITY

The clarity of a diamond refers to its *clarity characteristics*—or how free it is from flaws, both external (called *blemishes*) and internal (called *inclusions*). Don't be concerned if a diamond has a flaw or two that can't be seen with the naked eye. It just means it's genuine. Most diamonds are flawed. The key is to find a diamond whose flaws don't mar its beauty.

EXAMINING THE DIAMOND: BLEMISHES

Diamonds with flaws that can be seen with the naked eye should be avoided. These include:

1. *Cracks*. A deep crack that cuts across the table, for example, will weaken a diamond. A small crack, on the other hand, near the girdle and not seen from the top, isn't considered detrimental.
2. *Dullness*. If the diamond appears cloudy, hazy, not bright, or milky in appearance, it's best to avoid it.
3. *Chips, nicks, pits, scratches*. They speak for themselves.
4. *Black or white spots or lines*. Black marks are considered worse than white ones in the world of clarity grading. Lines that are seen on the diamond's surface may be caused by poor polishing and should be avoided (although if barely seen from the pavilion should not lower the value).
5. A *natural* is a piece of the original diamond crystal left on the diamond by the cutter, usually at the girdle (it looks rough and scratchy). As long as it doesn't interfere with the diamond's roundness and you can't see it from the top, it's considered minor.

INCLUSIONS

Next, take your loupe and examine the diamond internally. Hold it table down and look through the pavilion. Examine it from one side, put it down, turn it, and look at it from another side. View it from all angles. Then examine the diamond through the table and the crown facets. Inspect for:

1. *Dark or white spots, bubbles, or crystals*. Make sure they don't affect the stone's brilliance; they shouldn't be seen through the table by the naked eye.
2. *Cracks*. The smaller the better.
3. *Growth or grain lines*. Seen in the diamond as fine parallel lines.
4. *Bearded girdle*. These are small lines that emanate from the girdle. Minimal bearding is not considered a major flaw.
5. *Cloudy areas, haze*. Make sure they don't affect the brilliance of the diamond or the color.

WHERE'S THE FLAW?

The position of flaws in a diamond is pivotal. Stay away from stones that have flaws under the table or the crown or star facets. They're easily visible and will decrease a diamond's value. The best place for a flaw to be is near the girdle and the optimum is one that's seen only from the pavilion side.

How the GIA Determines Clarity Grades

The GIA determines clarity in diamonds with the following classifications:

FL *(Flawless)*: No blemishes or inclusions visible under 10x magnification.

IF *(Internally flawless)*: No inclusions, but small blemishes visible under magnification.

VVS1 and **VVS2** *(Very, very slightly included)*: Very small inclusions that are difficult to see even if magnified.

VS1 and **VS2** *(Very slightly included)*: Very small inclusions that may range from difficult to fairly easy to see under magnification.

SI1 and **SI2** *(Slightly included)*: Inclusions that are fairly easily seen when magnified.

I1, I2, I3 *(Imperfect)*: Inclusions you can see with the naked eye. In **I3** diamonds, they may even affect durability. *Stay away from them.*

Note: The Rappaport Diamond Report is to diamonds what the Blue Book is to cars. It has recognized a new classification for diamonds, **SI3,** slightly above the imperfect (I) grades. If the make and color is good, these may be a good buy, especially for the budget conscious. Be aware that the GIA doesn't recognize this classification.

A Word About Lasers

Lasers are being used to treat diamonds and it's a legitimate practice. Thin, long holes are drilled into the diamond with a laser. Chemicals are then poured in to bleach out dark areas. The question is: Do I want a diamond that's been treated? If the stone is poor quality, there's no doubt that the treatment will improve its appearance. But a fine diamond shouldn't be treated; natural clarity is what you're paying for. Laser lines can be seen by using a loupe. Look at the diamond from the pavilion and tilt it slightly. Laser lines look like very fine white lines. Watch for them.

Symmetry Characteristics

It's important to look at the diamond to ensure it exhibits *proper symmetry*. This means that the facets of one side are in line with the facets on the other, and that they're the same size. Look at the chart, Symmetry Characteristics in Rounds. Inspect the diamond for these flaws:

1. *Off-center culet*. The culet should be small, not large, and should not be visible by looking into the stone. Examine the culet to see if it's chipped, broken, or off-center.
2. *Misshapen facets*. Easily seen by looking directly at the table with a loupe.
3. *A misshapen table*. The table should be an octagon (in a brilliant diamond).
4. *Extra facets*. Look at the diamond from the side. You should not see extra facets. Round-, oval-, marquise-, pear-, and heart-shaped diamonds have fifty-eight facets. Trilliants have forty-four facets. Quadrillions have forty-nine.
5. *Out-of-round*. This means that the stone is *not* round. Do not buy a diamond that's visibly out-of-round.
6. *Crown and pavilion misalignment*. The top facets, those above the girdle, have to meet and line up with the bottom facets, those below the girdle.
7. *Facets not properly pointed*. Facets should meet and end in neat points.
8. *Wavy girdle*. Undesirable.

Note: A girdle should appear to be a fine white line in diamonds of up to two carats.

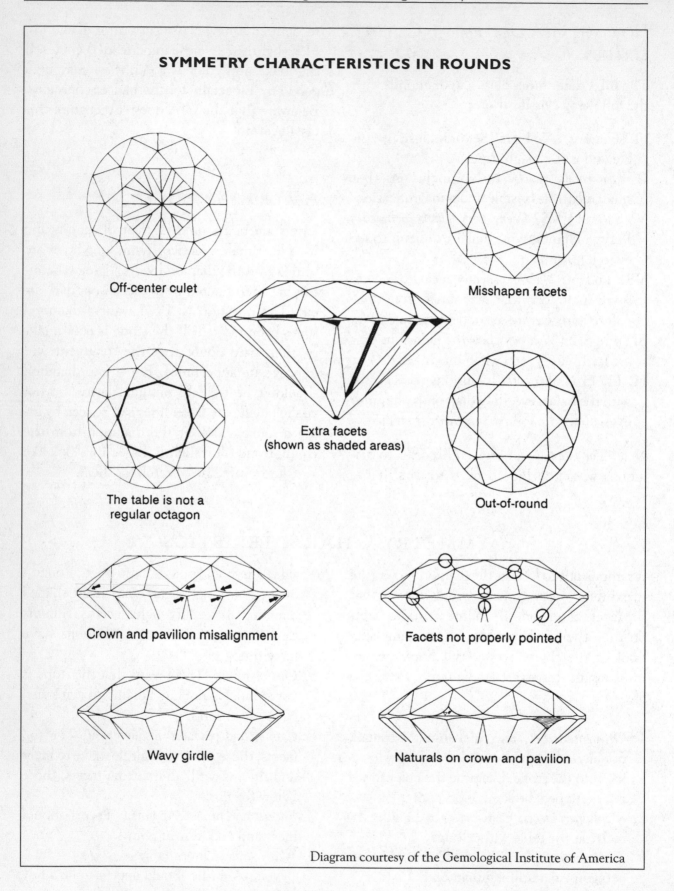

SYMMETRY CHARACTERISTICS IN ROUNDS

Off-center culet

Misshapen facets

Extra facets
(shown as shaded areas)

The table is not a
regular octagon

Out-of-round

Crown and pavilion misalignment

Facets not properly pointed

Wavy girdle

Naturals on crown and pavilion

Diagram courtesy of the Gemological Institute of America

Some are even scalloped or faceted. The girdle's thickness determines the fragility of a diamond. One that's too thin may break or chip. One that's too thick will make a stone look smaller and detract from its beauty.

9. *Naturals* (*on crown and pavilion*).

Symmetry and Polish Equal Finish

Finish is very important to a diamond's value and is a factor solely determined by the skill of the diamond cutter. To determine the quality of the finish, it's crucial to analyze the symmetry characteristics of the diamond (see the chart in this chapter). Its quality is easy to determine with your eye and a loupe.

Buying Diamonds from Retail and Wholesale Jewelers

Colorless diamonds, just like FL diamonds, are rare and are rarely carried, even by the finest jewelry stores. Near-colorless stones and IF grades are hard to find even in an above average shop. VVS1 and VVS2 stones are also seldom stocked, especially in larger diamonds, although some fine jewelers will carry diamonds with near-colorless grades. Discount stores, however, will rarely have this quality in their jewelry. It's too expensive. *Faint yellow color and lesser quality clarity grades are what's commonly found.*

Note: This gives the pawnshop a terrific advantage over retailers and wholesale jewelers! You will have the opportunity to see *all* kinds of diamonds (from the very fine to the dregs) in pawnshops. It's your job to be able to tell the difference.

Protecting Your Investment

There are several ways to protect your investment. The GIA, when grading a diamond, will inscribe the certificate number along a diamond's girdle (if you pay an additional fee). This is a must. If the stone is missing or stolen, the police will have a means of positive identification. Tell your insurance company. Give them the certificate number and list it on your policy.

Tip: when shopping for diamonds, look for an inscription along the girdle. Write down the numbers and then go home and call the GIA. You never know what you may find.

Another terrific system for identification is called *Gemprint*. For a nominal fee, Gemprint records the unique reflections that a diamond (or a clear colored gemstone) creates when hit with a laser (no two are alike). One Gemprint is given to the customer and one is kept on file with the company. (Once again, notify your insurance company. Many offer discounts to those who have their jewelry Gemprinted.)

Gemprint is an invaluable tool, especially if you think your diamond or gemstone (that you left to be repaired, for example) has been switched by an unscrupulous jeweler. (To contact them, see appendix I.)

Your last means of protection is insuring your investment, but insurance companies will require an estimate and a special rider. Coverage through homeowner's insurance is minimal, but there is a company that can help. (For contact information, see appendix I.)

THE SETTING

After you buy a ring from a pawnbroker, you may want to have it reset. If you're active, set the diamond in a mounting that will protect it. A bezel will minimize chipping. A channel setting is also a good choice for an on-the-go individual. The classic Tiffany setting is *the one* that displays a diamond to its best advantage. Make sure it has six prongs. If one lets loose, it's doubtful you'll lose the diamond.

Set white stones in white gold or platinum prongs, bezel, or channel. Set diamonds with faint yellow color in yellow prongs, bezel, or channel. The yellow metal will blend with the yellow color of the diamond. A white setting, on the other hand, will emphasize it.

A WORD ABOUT GOLD AND PLATINUM

Pure gold, 24K, is considered too soft for jewelry. 18K (75 percent gold) is acceptable although it marks easily with wear. 14K (58.5 percent gold) is perfect for an active lifestyle (and what you'll find in most jewelry stores in the United States). The ring will be stamped (unless very old) 14K or 18K (or 585 and 750, respectively, if the ring is European). If the ring is not stamped, have the pawnbroker or jeweler test for gold content.

White gold is more brittle than yellow so check the setting regularly. And platinum, the most expensive of all, is strong, durable, and white. A platinum ring will be stamped "plat" or "PT." If it's European, the stamp will read "PT 950."

HOW TO BUY THAT PLAIN GOLD WEDDING BAND

You may buy wedding bands in pawnshops and you should find some terrific bargains! Pawnshops charge much less per *pennyweight* (or *gram*) than their jewelry-store counterparts. (Gold is weighed in pennyweights or grams. There's 1.555 grams to one pennyweight.)

CHARACTERISTICS OF GOLD WEDDING BANDS

1. Gold wedding bands are flat, half-round (curved), with a milgrained edge (like a saw-tooth blade) or without.
2. They may be *comfort-fit*. (Gold is added to the inside of the ring, which rounds it and makes it more comfortable. It also makes the ring heavier and more expensive.)

3. In the United States, bands are usually 14K or 18K, yellow or white.
4. They are priced by their weight, the size (the bigger, the more gold required), and the karat—18K being more expensive than 14K. A milgrained edge is also more expensive.

TIPS TO ENSURE THE BEST PRICE

Decide what kind of ring you want, then shop price. Compare apples to apples. For example, "I want a 14K yellow gold, size 6, half-round with milgrained edge." Next, have the jeweler or pawnbroker weigh the ring. Let's say it's three pennyweight. Go from store to store and shop price.

HOW ABOUT A LITTLE ROMANCE TO END THIS CHAPTER?

THE POSY RING

In the fourteenth century, rings that denoted love or courtship were inscribed with posies—or poetry—often written in French, Latin, or Italian, and later English. The custom remained for centuries and was so important to the ring's intrinsic value that a suitor would *never* give a ring to his intended without an inscription. He would even measure her finger to ensure that the ring was made large enough to encase it. And indeed, history has recorded some profound posies, as relevant today as they were five hundred years ago:

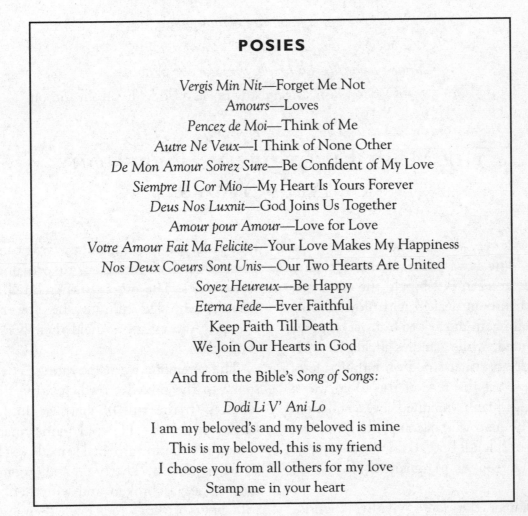

POSIES

Vergis Min Nit—Forget Me Not

Amours—Loves

Pencez de Moi—Think of Me

Autre Ne Veux—I Think of None Other

De Mon Amour Soirez Sure—Be Confident of My Love

Siempre II Cor Mio—My Heart Is Yours Forever

Deus Nos Luxnit—God Joins Us Together

Amour pour Amour—Love for Love

Votre Amour Fait Ma Felicite—Your Love Makes My Happiness

Nos Deux Coeurs Sont Unis—Our Two Hearts Are United

Soyez Heureux—Be Happy

Eterna Fede—Ever Faithful

Keep Faith Till Death

We Join Our Hearts in God

And from the Bible's *Song of Songs:*

Dodi Li V' Ani Lo

I am my beloved's and my beloved is mine

This is my beloved, this is my friend

I choose you from all others for my love

Stamp me in your heart

Early Jewish wedding rings were often inscribed with the words *Mazaall Tov* (good luck). Later, beautiful verses were engraved in rings, many from the Bible's *Song of Songs.*

I often see posts in the wedding newsgroups (on the Internet) that ask this question: "What can we inscribe in our wedding rings? We want to make them special." And special they can be. Dedicate a posy to your beloved that will be worn until the end of time.

Chapter Eight

THE CEREMONY

The organ booms, the procession begins,
The rejected suitors square their chins,
And angels swell the harmonious tide
Of blessings upon the bonnie bride.
But blessing also on him without whom
There would be no bride. I mean the groom.
—Ogden Nash, "Everybody Loves a Bride, Even the Groom"

THE MOST ELECTRIFYING CEREMONY OF ALL—YOURS

When I was very young, I attended my first Jewish wedding. It was unforgettable. Held in a prestigious hotel in Pittsburgh, the ceremony was in a ballroom decked with flowers from floor to ceiling, from back to front. The lights were dimmed, while candles flickered softly from candelabra that stood on either side of the chuppa. At the rear of the room was a baby grand piano, manned by a talented pianist. The man who accompanied him had a voice so splendid it could have jumped from the screen of a romantic Hollywood musical.

I remember the songs vividly: "Sunrise Sunset" from *Fiddler on the Roof*; "The Love Theme from *Romeo and Juliet*"; and *Camelot's* "If Ever I Would Leave You." Before the ceremony started, there wasn't a dry eye in the room. It was moving, relevant, and exciting.

The processional, led by the cantor in full voice and the rabbi in magnificent garb, were followed by the grandparents. Next came the groomsmen in elegant black tuxedos and crisp white shirts. The groom was escorted by his parents, who led him to the flower-laden chuppa. And everyone held their breath for the bride.

The ceremony was captivating. The rabbi spoke to the mixed crowd, relating the differences in the rite of marriage in Judaic-Christian culture. He told funny anecdotes about the bride and groom. He made you laugh, he made you cry. The bride and groom were united, the glass broken, and, with their guests' wild shouts of *Mazel-Tov!*, made their way happily, laughing, arm-in-arm down the aisle.

The ceremony lasted about forty minutes and I shall never forget it. I've attended hundreds of weddings over the years, but it's the one that stands out in my mind. To this day, it brings tears to my eyes. It's the way every ceremony should be.

WHATEVER YOU DO—
NO SLAM-BAM OR WAR AND PEACE

The wedding ceremony is the most important one of your life. When your guests leave your ceremony, they must think so too! Don't do a ten-minute slam-bam special, or make it longer than *War and Peace*. The former is insignificant and cheapens the ceremony. The latter is boring.

CHOOSING THE CEREMONY SITE

Recently, I attended a large formal wedding at a huge cathedral. The place was so immense that the two-hundred-plus guests didn't make a dent in its seating capacity. Everyone was positioned in the front third of the church. When the processional started, the guests turned their heads and looked to the back of the cathedral. What they saw was an interminable aisle—longer than a football field—and row after row of empty wooden pews. The bridal party looked as if they were at the end of a tunnel.

But the worst was yet to come. The cathedral was so old and so big and the acoustics so bad that you couldn't understand one word of the ceremony. The music, which cost a fortune, was loud and muffled, the voices of the vocalists incomprehensible. This bride and groom may have selected a historic cathedral for their marriage, but the charm ended there. The place was massive, cold, and impersonal, and expensive to boot!

Use your common sense—not only to save money—*but to achieve elegance and beauty.* Besides, what's the point of having a marriage ceremony in a place that's so large it imparts a feeling of indifference, or a place where no one understands your words or hears your vows?

RULES FOR CHOOSING A CEREMONY SITE

1. Make sure it's the right size to accommodate the size of your wedding.
2. Check the acoustics.
3. How's the ambiance? Is it warm or can it be easily decorated to achieve the desired effect?

Brides are often married in their place of worship, or at a place other than a sanctuary, which may not be aesthetically beautiful. A few inexpensive rental trees placed around the room may spice things up and create a warm atmosphere, as will a few rented candelabra and some pew- or chair bows. (For more information, see chapter 13, "Flowers and Decorations.")

SITE ALTERNATIVES (TO SAVE MONEY)

If your home or your family's is a hostess's dream and can accommodate a wedding and reception, do it. You'll save a ton of money. But do it right. The bride and groom should not worry about cooking or decorating or wondering if the tent has arrived. If your families and friends are willing to relieve you of these burdens, consider it. You may decide to hire a caterer to handle all details (if it's less money than a hotel or a catering facility). Thoroughly evaluate the pros and cons before making a decision.

Many brides like to be married in a public park or on the beach, and it can save money, provided there's a contingency plan if the weather turns bad. It might be more economical, however, to employ a full-service facility.

A wedding and reception, held at the same location, may also save you money. Once again, weigh the pros and cons and determine what's best for you. And don't forget organizations like the Elks, American Legion, and women's clubs. Sometimes they offer charming facilities for weddings. Not only do they provide a place for the ceremony and reception, they often provide catering and allow you to buy your own liquor. This means *big* savings!

AVAILABILITY AND MORE

Call and ask if your date is available. If not, you're going to have to move the location or change the date. Don't wait to make this decision or you might find yourself out of luck. (Places book fast!) Consider Friday or Sunday (if Saturday is reserved).

When first meeting with an officiant, ask for any pertinent information and brochures they may have. Put them in your notebook. If your date is available, ask the officiant (or the person in charge) to pencil it into their calendar. Get a written receipt that notes the date and time. Wait a week, then call to confirm that your date and time are on their schedule.

If hosting a wedding at a hotel, a catering facility, or a public location, it will be necessary to leave a deposit to reserve the date. Get a receipt containing all pertinent information.

DON'T DISCOUNT YOUR CEREMONY

Whether you're married by clergy or by a paid officiant, it's important to plot your ceremony every step of the way. Unfortunately, many times, clergy are not warm personages or good speakers. These factors can kill a wedding ceremony. It's important, therefore, to find someone who can address and involve your guests in a sensitive, feeling, caring way (while making you feel *oh so special*). This is the crux of a successful ceremony.

If your clergy's orating skills scare you, ask for another member of their staff. Or, ask if clergy from a different church (same denomination) or temple would be able to perform this solemn but uplifting ceremony. Ask recently married friends, relatives, and business associates for their recommendations.

Many times, brides prefer relatives or friends who are clergy to perform the ceremony. This requires clearance from the church or synagogue. (Be aware that out-of-state officiants may not legally be able to perform the ceremony. Check with local state authorities beforehand.)

Always observe your officiant performing a ceremony. Take notes about what you like and don't like and discuss it afterward with him. Plan your ceremony start to finish. Get involved every step of the way.

THE RELIGIOUS CEREMONY

Don't wear your blinders when you meet with clergy. Be aware that cohabitation is frowned upon and may even be a reason for the Catholic Church to deny your marriage. Many religions also require premarital counseling that may take months to complete. And don't count on an annulment (if you're waiting for one), until it's in your hot little hands.

If you have potential problems (annulment, for example), meet with clergy before setting a wedding date. Put the stipulations on the table. Schedule the time to complete them and work with clergy to establish a viable date.

COORDINATORS

Many churches and temples offer coordinators who help with wedding day setup. These people often volunteer their services (although some institutions may charge you for their help). I think they're a must (provided you're not charged excessively). On the wedding day, the coordinator arrives early; turns on the air-conditioning or heat; makes sure the place is clean; shows the photographer, videographer, and florist where to go; and attends to the bride and groom and their bridal party. Ergo, they're invaluable! If your place of worship doesn't offer a coordinator, ask if they could suggest someone who could help (for a small fee).

Sally Jessy Raphael has featured many shows about wedding disasters. Once, as her bridal expert, it was my job to tell the members of the panel (brides and grooms who had experienced wedding day trauma) what they could have done to avoid problems.

One groom fainted at the altar because some cold guest turned the church thermostat to over eighty degrees. Everyone was sweltering—not to mention the poor groom, who was flat on the floor. The bride was hysterical and thought he had died. Had she had a church coordinator, this scene (captured forever on video) could have been avoided.

IF A RELIGIOUS CEREMONY (IN A SANCTUARY) IS TOO EXPENSIVE

Unfortunately, the disease of making money via weddings has infected some religious institutions. If yours is charging you excessive fees or is thrusting unnecessary services upon you, you may decide to move the ceremony to another more reasonable place. Don't wait to make the decision. It will take time to find the right place at the right price. Sometimes it's better to conduct the marriage ceremony at the reception site. It may be more cost effective. (See chapter 9, "The Reception" and chapter 13, "Flowers and Decorations.")

A WORD ABOUT INTERFAITH MARRIAGE

A Jew marrying a Christian may have trouble finding an officiant to perform their ceremony or know where to go to obtain counseling. If you need assistance, call or write The Rabbinic Center For Research and Counseling (see appendix I).

NONRELIGIOUS, PREMARITAL COUNSELING

This wonderful, educational counseling is a must for all engaged couples. These programs have been known to cut the divorce rate among participants and in my opinion are essential! I recommend the programs PAIRS or PREPARE. Each provides a unique opportunity for you to learn more about each other and to discover and correct weak spots in your relationship before problems occur. (For contact information, see appendix I.)

CEREMONY MUSIC

There's nothing like the *right* music to set the mood and create the *right* ambiance for your ceremony. Many churches and temples, however, restrict certain music. Ask about regulations when you first meet with clergy. (For information about music for ceremonies, see appendix I.)

Music may also be expensive. You will have to pay for the organist and vocalists provided by the temple or church. If this proves costly, ask recently married people for referrals and shop diligently to find the musicians and vocalists who will fit the bill. Most times, religious institutions will permit you to use your own musicians, but ask clergy before proceeding.

A band, orchestra, or DJ may provide ceremony music if the reception and ceremony are at the same location. This will save you money; you're killing two birds with one stone. They should also give you a break on the price.

No matter who you employ, *audition them at the ceremony site.* That's the only way to know if they're acceptable and how the acoustics affect their sound. If there's a problem, they'll have time to correct it. *Audition everyone—* and that goes for those referred by your religious institution.

To Save Money

Call your local college or university school of music. Ask if they have musicians or vocalists (or both) who would like to participate in your ceremony for a small fee. They should be most agreeable. (It always helps to make a little extra when you're going through school.)

Decorations

Avoid excessive decorations. They are unnecessary. All you'll need are a couple of altar bouquets (flower arrangements that are placed on either side of the altar or the chuppa), pew or chair bows (that you can make yourself), an aisle runner (if the carpet doesn't suit you), and perhaps a unity candle.

Fees

Get an estimate of the total fees in writing, no matter where the wedding takes place. These may include janitor's fees, clean-up fees, set-up and rip-down fees, coordinator's fees, fees for musicians and vocalists, fee for rental of the site, and church or temple fees. Ask if there are taxes or service charges.

Donations

To Clergy and Others

In the not-so-long-ago good old days, people were married in their place of worship and gave a donation to clergy for the privilege. (That's the way it should be!) If your religious institution, however, charges excessively, skip the donation; they've made enough money. (Don't ever give a donation to paid clergy or a paid consultant.) Catholics, by the way, are expected to give gifts to the altar boys and girls who serve at their wedding.

If you're lucky enough to find (or have) a religious institution that's reasonable, then clergy should receive a donation, but only what you can afford. Don't go overboard. You might give cash or a gift certificate to their favorite bookstore or restaurant. And don't forget, they are always invited (with spouse, if applicable) to the reception. (They also receive a wedding invitation.)

The Paid Officiant

If a church or temple wedding is not in your plans, you'll have to hire an officiant. These people often charge hundreds of dollars for their services. Start your search early. Once again, ask for referrals and shop hard. (You'll find that officiants come in many different price ranges. Shop for one who is both compassionate and cost effective.)

Get videotapes of their performances or see them live if possible. Structure your ceremony with their input and be explicit about your requirements and expectations. Meet with them more than once. (I often tell the story of the officiant who had never met the groom and mistook him for the man who walked the bride up the aisle. It made for a funny video, but not one a bride would treasure. Don't let this happen to you.)

Rehearsals and Rehearsal Dinners

A rehearsal before a wedding is a trial run. It ensures that the bridal party is coordinated with the officiant and musicians and that they know their place and the order of events. A rehearsal should not last long (about forty-five minutes). And whatever you do, be punctual. Nothing gets an officiant's ire up like a tardy bride. (Be aware that rabbis don't conduct rehearsals.)

Rehearsal dinners, however, have gotten out of hand. They're not meant to be formal, elegant affairs (unless you plan it that way and have unlimited funds). They're not miniature weddings. They are a venue for the bride, groom, bridal party, and immediate families to relax and have a bite to eat after the rehearsal.

The dinner may be held at a restaurant, a club, your home, or the home of family or friends. It may be a barbecue, a picnic, or a sit-down dinner. It may be hosted by the groom's family, the bride's family, the bride and groom themselves, or a combination of the above. It may be potluck, where everyone brings a different dish. There are no set rules.

I once attended a very pleasant affair, hosted by the bride and groom. Their parents were throwing the wedding, so they decided to host the rehearsal dinner. They contacted a local gourmet grocery store, who delivered platters of hot and cold hors d'oeuvres, cold cuts, bread, salads, cheese, crackers, and fruit and pastries for dessert. There was plenty of soda, beer, and wine. And the best part, they hired a maid (through the store), who heated and served the food and cleaned up. It was relaxing, fun, and thoroughly enjoyable.

Who's Invited?

The people who are invited are the participants: clergy, musicians, the bridal party (including parents of the ring bearer and flower girl(s), parents and grandparents). Paid officiants and musicians—people you don't know—are not invited.

While some feel it's proper and essential to invite the dates and/or spouses of the bridal party, and all out-of-town family and close friends, that's not the rule, especially if money is tight. If relatives insist, however, it may be wise to throw the kind of rehearsal dinner that's affordable, a picnic or a barbecue, perhaps, that includes everyone (especially if your bridal party is primarily composed of out-of-towners, whose dates or spouses are sitting in a hotel room). It's the kind and wise thing to do.

Gifts and the Rehearsal Dinner

In appreciation for their help, the conscientious bride and groom extend gifts to their bridal party, most times, at the rehearsal dinner. Pretty earrings for bridesmaids are always a good choice (they should all wear the same jewelry for the wedding), but I dislike items like engraved beer mugs for groomsmen. Gift certificates are a terrific idea! Perhaps one of your maids or groomsmen likes the movies, another books, or perhaps one enjoys good wine. These personalized gifts will be used and treasured, and won't end up sitting on a shelf or in the garbage.

It's also customary for the bride and groom to give gifts to each other. But if you think the money would be better spent on your honeymoon—do it! Gifts are unnecessary.

AND A FINAL NOTE: BE PUNCTUAL

Don't be late to your wedding. It makes an officiant uneasy and miserable and guests irritated. It is not the way to be an elegant, caring hostess, or to get things off on the right foot.

I once handled a very upscale Jewish wedding at a hotel in Boca Raton, Florida. The entire day was spent decorating the ballroom for the ceremony (the bride paid a fortune for our services). The rabbi arrived in plenty of time, but the bride, who was upstairs getting dressed, was over half an hour late. The rabbi was angry. When the bride finally arrived and started up the aisle, I exited. No more than ten minutes had passed, when the door slammed open and out walked the rabbi, followed by the bride and groom. The ceremony was over! The rabbi didn't say one word to the couple and left in a huff.

We spent all day changing a mundane ballroom into a wedding wonderland for what should have been a very meaningful ceremony. All our work was down the drain, and the bride's money along with it. And just imagine how she and the groom felt! Don't let yourself in for this kind of heartache and aggravation, or you might learn a lesson about why it's polite to be on time.

Chapter Nine

THE RECEPTION

The Guests are met, the feast is set:
May'st hear the merry din.

—Samuel Coleridge,
The Rime of the Ancient Mariner

HOW HISTORY'S CHANGED

It seems that since the beginning of time, weddings have been occasions of celebration, feasting, and dancing. In Biblical times, the wedding celebration lasted seven days. Throughout the ancient world and for centuries beyond, wedding festivities were designed to impart feelings of happiness and plenty, good fortune, love, and fertility to *all* who attended, *not* just to the bride and groom.

Somehow along the way, the word "camaraderie" has been displaced by the word "elegance." The happy couple, prince and princess for a day, plan their wedding not around their families and friends but around each other. Having an *elegant* affair is an obsession. They'll go into debt for it; they'll even sacrifice the happiness and comfort of their guests for it. This is why *cash bars* (guests pay for their own drinks) and *dessert receptions* (bon-

bons and wedding cake are the only items on the menu) have evolved. I say: Let's go back to the good old days! Let's eat, drink, be merry—and married—*debt free!* But how do you do it on a budget?

Note: The reception is the largest expense of your wedding. Here's where you will budget the majority of your wedding dollars and *where you need to save the most money! If you do not keep within a rigid, self-imposed discipline, your reception will get out of control and you will experience financial hardship.* I can't tell you how often I've heard, "I hope we make a lot of money at this reception or we're in big trouble." A little common sense and practical planning will prevent you from falling into this trap. Don't begin married life heartbroken—and *broke*.

HOSTING A WEDDING

Your wedding reception is the first party you will host as husband and wife. It's your primary responsibility to see that your guests are as happy and as comfortable as you are. *They do not pay for their own beverages and they are given plenty to eat and drink—at your expense.* You invited them to a celebration, a party. It's no different than if you invite family and friends to your home for dinner or for a barbecue; it's on you! As the hosts of your wedding, your goals are to ensure:

- There's plenty of food and drink
- Your guests are comfortable
- Your guests are entertained
- *You don't go into debt*

IN PURSUIT OF ELEGANCE

Elegance, in terms of weddings, is not solely defined by sit-down dinners held on moonlit Saturday evenings. There are many ways to achieve elegance. Imagine an afternoon picnic, served under ancient oak trees, tables covered with eyelet cloths graced by bowls of fresh-fruit centerpieces that glisten, and a trio playing romantic songs. Envision an afternoon brunch by the pool of a family member or friend, made happy by the music of a one-man band. Picture a cocktail party at a restaurant or club, peppered by dancing to the *golden oldies* played by a discerning DJ. Visualize a late evening breakfast, preceded by a ton of hot and cold hors d'oeuvres, eaten to the pulsating beat of a fiery Latino band. Even an elopement can be elegant! Let your mind soar. Open your imagination to new ideas and thoughts. *Define elegance in your own terms (within your budget).*

THE KEY TO SUCCESS

Your guest list and how you control it is the key to the success of your forever-fantasized about, long-anticipated reception. There's nothing wrong with longing for succulent, icy cold pink shrimp and lobster appetizers followed by an entree of Chateaubriand and Lyonaise potatoes, while champagne flows from cherubim fountains! *You can have your dream.* But instead of inviting three hundred, you may have to invite thirty. *To attain your goal, control your guest list.* It's that simple.

If you desire, for example, a Saturday night sit-down dinner at a full-service catering facility, determine the number of guests you can afford based on a per-person food and beverage cost. Next, multiply the price by the number of guests. Don't forget to add applicable taxes, service charges, and gratuities. If you're over budget, take out your scalpel and cut your guest list. Or, *call the catering director and ask if there would be a significant price break if the reception were held on a Friday night or a Sunday night.* You may not have to cut as many people as you think. (More about this later.)

ELEGANCE AND NUMBERS

There's nothing wrong with a small, intimate, outrageously extravagant wedding, if elegance is your byword. It's better than having a humdrum, mediocre wedding for one hundred fifty people, many of whom you don't know well and may never see again. Imagine viewing your video twenty years later while asking yourself, "Who in the world is that?"

The biggest mistake that brides and grooms make when trying to achieve elegance is by overextending themselves. This results in the *Humdrum Wedding Syndrome*. The first indicator of HWS is an out-of-control guest list. The second is you begin to think of sacrifice: the lobster entree, the orchid centerpieces, the open bar, the band . . . all go by the wayside. The result: a mediocre wedding that you will both regret.

If you see yourself falling into this trap: Step back, take a deep breath, and regroup. Have the type of wedding you want. Cut your guest list, get your budget back in line, and don't make sacrifices!

THINK SMALL—IF ELEGANCE IS YOUR GOAL

You can't have a large, elegant wedding on a limited budget. It's impossible. But you can have a small one! A small, intimate wedding definitely has its advantages. Chances are, most who are invited will know one another. They'll mingle easily and be more comfortable. The atmosphere will be one of affable intimacy. You'll serve tenderloin of beef instead of stuffed chicken breast. Bowls of dew-laden roses in full bloom will sit on your tables. Champagne will flow and there will be an open bar. And most important, you'll be able to intimately enjoy your friends and families, and they in turn, will enjoy you. Isn't that what weddings are all about?

Part I: The Rules

Whether it's a picnic held on the grounds of an old-world hotel or a sit-down dinner at Luigi's Trattoria or a barbecue in your aunt's backyard, there are reception rules you must observe to keep your pocketbook in check and your stress levels low.

It's important to follow these rules. Keep them in mind before you begin to shop—and when you shop—for a reception site. *These rules are the blueprint for a successful, well-planned, economical reception*. Follow them to make your reception, for the money you have to spend, the best one possible.

REFERRALS A MUST

Get referrals from recently married friends, family, and business associates. Do not shop at any catering facility or interview any vendor that has not been referred to you. Trust your friends and family, not the Yellow Pages. Also, *get referrals from the caterer or catering facility*. Ask perspective caterers and catering facilities for the names and phone numbers of their five most recent bridal clients. Call these people and question them in depth. (Don't do business with any facilities or vendors who will not allow you to question their clients. Go elsewhere.)

I can't tell you the number of brides who say to me, "I've never heard of the country club (or catering facility) you mentioned. Do they do a good job?" If they had done their homework, they would have known about it.

Take the time to visit all the perspective vendors and catering facilities friends, relatives, and business associates suggest. Get all pertinent information and price brochures. Walk around the facilities to get a feel for their ambiance. Go home and analyze what they have to offer.

RECEPTIONS TAKE TIME

Caterers want to book as many receptions as possible. This is why you may hear, "We have a reception from eleven A.M. to four P.M. But we can be ready for you by five." Don't be so sure. In these situations, there's always a hectic, go-like-hell hour as waiters and the captain or maître d' try to prepare for the next reception.

And what about the poor bride and groom and their families (at the early reception) who don't want their day to end? They're left lingering, sadly watching as their room is torn down. This predicament is especially unfair, not only because they're pushed out, but because they couldn't extend the reception even if they wanted to.

Vendors in these situations are also put in a precarious position. Many times they have less than forty-five minutes to decorate a room or to assemble a wedding cake in time for their client's arrival. A wedding, and its preparation, should not be rushed. For these reasons, ask about time restrictions. If you have to be out by a certain time, it might be best to find another location.

HOW LONG SHOULD THE RECEPTION LAST?

A sit-down dinner reception for 150, with dancing, will take five hours. One hour for cocktails, four hours for dinner, dancing, and all the traditional wedding things in between—garter and bouquet toss, cake cutting, etc. A reception for one hundred or less guests may last four hours. (It will also save you money.)

Part II: General Information

THE CATERING DIRECTOR—OR CATERER—SHOULD BE THERE

The person who helped plan your reception (whether it be a caterer or a catering director) should be there for the event. This doesn't mean that he or she will be there for the entire affair, but he should stop in from time to time to see that everything is progressing satisfactorily. (This person is not to be confused with the captain or maître d', who will supervise the affair and who will be there from start to finish.)

Say No to Cash Bars

Your guests are your responsibility. You pay for their food *and drink*. I'll teach you how to buy liquor the right way—economically—and how to stay within your budget.

Dessert Receptions—Don't Do It

When you were a kid, you ate sweets until you got sick. Hopefully, you've outgrown the urge. So how can you expect your adult guests to eat nothing but bonbons, pastries, and cookies, topped off by wedding cake? You don't want to end up like Marie Antoinette, who said, "Let them eat cake!" Look what happened to her!

We live in a low-fat, low-cholesterol, low-calorie society. Don't invite your guests to a reception that will increase their chances of heart disease or one that will force them to leave early to get a tuna salad platter. *Have solid food at a reception and save the wedding cake for dessert.*

Make Sure There's a Room for the Cocktail Hour

Many facilities do not have an extra room for the cocktail hour and suggest instead having cocktails and hors d'oeuvres by the pool or outside. What happens if it rains—or worse?!

A facility must provide a back-up room in case of inclement weather. If they don't have one, look elsewhere.

Place Cards Are a Must

Use place cards to arrange seating for seventy-five guests or more. Guests milling about trying to decide where they want to sit makes the wedding look haphazard and unstructured. It also wastes valuable time.

Note: Always have reserved seating for the bride and groom, families, bridal party, clergy or officiant, and elderly guests.

Tipping

The only people you tip at the reception are the catering director and the maître d' or captain, if they do a superior job. (I do advise my clients, however, to tip them ahead of time if they want exemplary service.) *Tip only what you can afford.* You do not tip bartenders or waiters or anyone else employed by the caterer or property. That's why you pay service and gratuity fees.

Part III: Precautionary Measures

AVOID WEDDING MILLS

A wedding mill is any catering facility that can accommodate many weddings at once, robbing a bride and groom of exclusivity. Once, when attending a "mill" wedding, I walked into the ladies' room, only to find four brides standing in front of the mirror applying makeup. I thought it was Halloween.

I have seen brides, grooms, and guests hustled off the dance floor to make way for the next reception (whose guests wait patiently in the foyer for their turn). I've seen newly married couples hurried from "gardens" or "waterfalls" (pretty, man-made settings offered by mills for photo opportunities) so that the next couple may have their pictures taken.

It was my misconception that mill weddings were *dirt* cheap. Wrong! I later discovered that many of these properties charge as much as private clubs or hotels. I was dumbfounded. Reception opportunities abound. Do your homework and find a site that will make you proud, and one that genuinely cares about you and making your day memorable. Stay away from wedding mills.

AVOID WINTER WEDDINGS

If you live in Aspen or Albany (snow country), you should not chance a winter wedding. Or take the chance that guests (who have to travel from or through snow country) won't attempt the trip (at the last minute), due to warnings of inclement weather. Weddings are too much work and too expensive to take an unnecessary chance on Mother Nature. Book your wedding for spring or fall.

TENTS ARE A DOUBLE-EDGED SWORD

The tent featured in the remake of the movie *Father of the Bride* was stunning, no doubt about it. So was the one you saw in the movie *Betsy's Wedding*, until the rain hit. Every wedding-disaster talk show I've ever seen features a tent calamity.

Oprah, on one of her shows, highlighted an expensive tented reception. The heavens opened up and spewed so much water on the massive tent that its roof filled like a giant overinflated balloon and split. The ensuing flood made Niagra Falls look like a babbling brook. The bride, two years later, was still suffering emotional trauma. Her dream went down the drain—literally.

Note: Tents are great for a drizzle but not for a deluge.

Cleanliness Is Next to Godliness

Examine all properties for dirty walls and floors, torn and worn carpets, holes in upholstery, and unclean restrooms. Go in the kitchen and inspect it. An unkempt place or one in poor repair can only mean one thing: financial problems.

Are They Licensed and Insured?

Do not do business with any facility or vendor who's not licensed and insured. Check their licenses and insurance cards to see that they're up-to-date.

Don't Forget Taxes, Service Charges, Gratuities, etc.

Taxes, service charges, and gratuities may add up to 20 percent or more of the total cost. Inquire what the charges are and always include them in your budget. (It may even be necessary to knock a few people from the guest list or to juggle the budget to compensate for these charges.)

Warning Words: Relax and Enjoy Your Day

The road to economy should not be paved with the bride's and groom's blood. If you host an at-home wedding and hire a caterer, hire one who will handle all details, including all party rentals and all wedding related services. Leave everything up to them and enjoy your day.

A bride and groom on their wedding day should not be bothered about the physical details of their wedding ceremony or reception. In other words, you should not be doing the cooking or decorating the arch or chuppa or handling party rentals. This is not the way to have a stress-free wedding or to enjoy the most important day of your life. Even if your budget is tight, hand the details over to a caterer who will do the cooking and handle the party rentals for a small percentage over cost. Entrust the decorating to close family members or friends. Relax and savor your day.

Part IV: Saving Money

Ceremonies and Receptions — All in One

With the cost of a church ceremony these days, it might not be a bad idea to have the ceremony at the reception site. In our town, for example, many churches charge hundreds of dollars for the use of the sanctuary (even for members). It's hard to believe that some religious institutions have climbed on the marry-go-round, but they have. A club or hotel, on the other hand, may provide you with a ceremony room *free of charge or for minimal charge* because you're spending lots of money at their property. If you can, take advantage of the offer.

Many clergy will marry couples outside the confines of the church. You may also find it less expensive to pay an officiant than to rent the church and pay their fees. For the devout, however, this may not be an option. Catholics, for example, may find it difficult to get a *dispensation from form* and a *dispensation from place* to be married outside the Church.

The Four-Hour Reception and the Thirty-Minute Cocktail Hour

For the budget conscious, Christine Misiano, catering manager of the prestigious Four Seasons Resort in Palm Beach, Florida, says that a four-hour reception for one hundred or less is adequate and will keep your cost down. She also suggests robbing thirty minutes from your cocktail hour (it will last one-half hour) and adding thirty minutes onto your dinner! What a great suggestion!

Skip the Cocktail Hour (at a cocktail hors d'oeuvre reception)

It's unnecessary. Open the room, bring on the food, start the music and let the festivities begin! Christine Misiano suggests, however, that if the wedding is off-property, that you maintain a cocktail hour, which gives the guests time to arrive before the actual reception begins.

Skip Buffet or Station Receptions

Most people are under the misconception that buffet or station receptions are less expensive than sit-down dinners or luncheons. Not so. Buffets and stations are not manageable (from a catering perspective). There is no portion control (guests may help themselves to as much as they want!) and they require extra staff to maintain them and keep them tidy. If there's meat to be cut or pasta to be prepared, for example, a carver and a chef are required. *Extra staff costs extra money.*

Skip the Appetizer

To cut sit-down dinner costs, skip the appetizer. What's wrong with starting the meal with a salad? No one will be the wiser.

Avoid Choice of Entree

While it's ever so generous and considerate to offer a choice to your guests, you're the one who's paying the tab. If you decide, for example, to offer either chicken or beef to your one hundred guests and seventy choose chicken, be advised that you will pay for one hundred beef dinners.

Don't Serve a Superfluous Dessert

Many caterers talk their clients into serving an extravagant dessert with dinner when there's a wedding cake! It's a waste of money. Bargain with the person in charge to exchange the dessert for an appetizer or for an entree upgrade.

After dinner, serve strawberries dipped in chocolate (one per guest) or a sorbet or, if that's too expensive, put a plate of good chocolate mints on each table. (The meal should always end with something sweet). Save the cake for dessert, that's what it's for.

Skip Saturday Night

Saturday night is a premium night in Wedding World; you'll pay more. Reserve Friday or Sunday night if you want an evening reception and always negotiate for a better price, which should be substantial (except at large, convention-type hotels where prices rarely vary).

Avoid the Summer Months

Summer months are steamy, and not just in terms of rising temperatures. They're the hottest wedding months of the year and demand the highest prices. Book your wedding off-season if you can, in spring or fall, and save money.

Avoid Holiday Receptions

Don't have a holiday wedding. They cost more because vendors inflate prices. But more important: Who wants to have a reception when a catering facility, restaurant, or caterer is more concerned with holiday business than with your wedding? Everyone takes their mother out for Mother's Day and every lover romances their sweetheart on Valentine's Day. Christ-mastime is typified by month-long parties and festivities, capped off by New Year's Eve. To avoid price hikes, confusion, and being lost in the shuffle, have your wedding at least three weeks before or three weeks after a holiday. And take note: Airfare and hotel rooms are at a premium and hotels require minimum stays.

Avoid Favors and All Those Extras

For the purposes of this book, we are not going to indulge in favors (that everyone leaves behind), or personalized cocktail napkins, menus, matches, or toasting goblets. *They are unnecessary.* If you total their cost, you'll find they cost hundreds of unnecessary dollars. Spend the money on your honeymoon.

Note: If you insist on favors, make them the edible kind, like chocolate, that end up in the guests' stomachs and not left on the guests' tables.

A really neat idea is *Matchbox-Chox*, chocolate for two in a matchbox (without the matches) that's printed with the bride's and groom's name and wedding date. (For more information, see appendix I.)

Part V: Your Options

Read Part V in its entirety. It will give you ideas and information that will be helpful to you, no matter what type of reception you're planning.
Apply all the previous information in this chapter to the following options. You have good, solid guidelines to follow and know how and where to save money. You're also aware of the precautionary measures you must take. It's now decision time. What type of reception is best for you, your wedding, and your budget? Don't rush. *Thoroughly analyze your options before making a choice.*

Option One: The Full-Service Catering Facility

By now, you've done your homework. You know the availability of country clubs, catering halls, hotels, private clubs, and restaurants. (For the purposes of this book, I'm going to refer to these establishments as full-service catering facilities or properties.) You know their price structure. Next, analyze what you can afford, based on one hundred or less guests.

The Best, Most Elegant, Most Economical Receptions

The Sit-Down Dinner

Many brides prefer sit-down dinners and they can be very economical if *packaged*. This means that everything from soup to nuts is included in one, per-head price. Open bars are usually included as is wine for dinner and a champagne toast. The package may also include a wedding cake. These packages are hard to beat.

The Cocktail–Hors d'oeuvre Reception

This is a great, fun way to celebrate. To be successful, plenty of good, varied hot and cold *finger* hors d'oeuvres must be served for the guests to feast upon. They should continue during the course of the reception until it's time for dessert—the wedding cake. *But don't confuse a cocktail–hors d'oeuvre reception with a buffet.* It's not. Christine Misiano thinks that the basic structure of a cocktail–hors d'oeuvre reception makes it tough for a bride and groom to host a traditional affair. Couples often mistake it for a buffet, which can lead to a reception that appears to be unstructured and haphazard.

A bride and groom, for example, still want to be introduced, have a first dance, have a bouquet and garter toss, and cut the cake, but where are their guests to sit through these festivities? (Cocktail–hors d'oeuvre receptions don't provide seating for all. The idea is to keep people up and mingling.) A bride, on her wedding day, wants all the tradition she can muster within the few short hours she has to be married and celebrate. But a cocktail–hors d'oeuvre reception makes it hard on the guests.

For one, think about the food that's served. A pasta station or a carving station, for example, features food that requires a knife and fork and a place to sit and eat. If there isn't one, what's a guest to do? Juggle a plate, a knife, a fork, and a glass—and try to eat and drink? For that reason, a *true* cocktail–hors d'oeuvre reception—one that's successful—will feature finger foods only requiring a napkin—*not a plate*. It also means that lots of hors d'oeuvres are served during the course of the evening, so that guests don't leave early because they're hungry.

And two, *think about the seating*. You don't really expect your guests to stand for three to four hours until the end of the affair when you cut the cake? Most caterers will admit that guests exit early at these types of receptions because of the seating. Is that what you want, when celebrating the most important day of your life? That's why it's important to understand that the structure of a cocktail–hors d'oeuvre reception may not be in your best interest—especially if you have your heart set on a traditional affair and all the customs that make it one. If you insist upon a cocktail–hors d'oeuvre reception, take the advice of your caterer or catering director, who can give you the best, most professional advice based upon their experience.

The Brunch or Lunch

An early- or late-morning wedding should be followed by brunch or lunch (depending on the time) served sit-down style to save money, which may be preceded by a light cocktail hour. Serve mimosas (a mixture of champagne and orange juice) or Bloody Marys. Have plenty of soft drinks and sparkling water. Offer your guests varied plates of cold fruits, vegetables and dip (crudite), and cheese and crackers.

Lunch or brunch should begin with salad or fruit (skip the appetizer to save money). Brunch may feature eggs Benedict or crepes and hash browns, and lunch could be stuffed chicken breast and a medley of fresh vegetables. Serve wine with brunch or lunch. Put a plate of light chocolate mints on the table when the meal is over. Serve the wedding cake for dessert.

The Midnight Breakfast

This is an exquisite, economical way to have a late-night wedding. A ceremony, for example, that begins at eight o'clock, is followed by an evening of cocktails and hors d'oeuvres that culminates in a midnight breakfast of fresh fruit cup, followed by waffles and ham, or eggs Benedict, topped off by wedding cake!

QUESTIONS YOU MUST ASK, INFORMATION YOU MUST KNOW

Copy *A Contract Checklist for Success* in this chapter and take it with you when interviewing catering directors. It will give you a solid guideline to follow. Inquire about each item on the list and take notes. All information on the checklist must be included in your contract.

OPTION TWO: THE DO-IT-YOURSELF CATERING FACILITY

These rental properties are available to the public and may include a historic home or building, a museum, or a park usually owned by the city, county, or state. Many private clubs and women's clubs also make their facilities available to brides and grooms, as do organizations like the Elks or American Legion. (If not a member, locate one who can sponsor you. Check into this option. It may be well worth it.) These properties give you the advantage of hiring your own caterer and buying your own liquor. *This type of facility can save you a bundle*. It's one of the most cost effective ways to host a reception, provided you plan it well.

QUESTIONS YOU MUST ASK, INFORMATION YOU MUST KNOW

Get a written estimate of all costs from the property.

The estimate should include:

1. Rental fees (of the property).
2. What the facility includes, for example, tables, chairs, china, crystal, dance floor.
3. The number of guests they can accommodate.
4. Date and time available and hours scheduled for the reception.
5. Overtime fees.
6. Restrictions (alcohol, for example, may not be permitted on some properties).
7. Clean-up fees and terms of security deposit.
8. Deposit—how much, when due, and terms for refunding.
9. Cancellation policy.
10. Liability. Who's responsible if someone is hurt on the property or a drunken guest leaves and gets involved in an accident?

Call their insurance company to make sure they have adequate coverage. Call yours also. It may be necessary to buy extra insurance.

11. Be sure the site can accommodate the electrical power needs generated by the caterer and entertainment.
12. Who's responsible for breakage or damage to the caterer's property?
13. Make sure that the facility is licensed by calling city and county licensing offices.

THE CATERER, YOU, AND THE PROPERTY

Before making a final decision on the property, interview a few caterers. (It's wise to choose those who are familiar with your facility.) *Meet with the caterer at the property.* This is critical. The property must meet their needs. It may be necessary to bring in extra ovens, for example, or more refrigeration equipment. This can be expensive. Take the advice of your caterer; it may be necessary to choose a different location.

Note: Ask your caterer to review the estimate and information provided by the property. Chances are there are things you haven't considered or aren't aware of! A caterer who has worked there before will know the property's limitations, like an air-conditioning unit that sometimes goes on the fritz. And remember, *all the items listed in the estimate should be a part of your contract.*

THE CATERER'S ESTIMATE

Get all estimates in writing from perspective caterers. The estimate should include:

1. The food (menu). List everything to be included. For the cocktail hour, food must be replenished until it ends. For a cocktail–hors d'oeuvre reception, food must be replenished until dessert is served.
2. Liquor charges and type of liquor—premium or call brands. *All unopened liquor must be returned for credit.* Try to buy the liquor yourself. But if it's not the caterer's policy, be sure to be specific about how you're being charged. List it in the contract. (For more information, see "Liquor and How to Buy It," in this chapter.)
3. Get an hourly rate for staffing, and the ratio of waiters per guest (it should be one for every fifteen guests for a sit-down affair). Confirm the number of captains in attendance (one for every seventy-five guests). Include the number of bartenders. There should be one for every fifty guests for the cocktail hour, one for every seventy guests for the reception.
4. Include all rental fees, staff charges, cost of valet parking (be sure they have insurance; get it in writing. There should be one attendant for every fifty guests and make certain that you are charged per car—not per person. Find out if you're being charged for a doorman (you should not be), set-up and tear-down fees, secu-rity deposit, taxes, service charges, and gratuities.
5. List the caterer's duties and responsibilities.
6. List all extra equipment charges and extra power source charges and who's responsible for obtaining them (if applicable).
7. Make sure the caterer is licensed and insured.
8. List liability. Who's responsible should there be an accident and the property is damaged or someone is hurt? Or someone leaves drunk and gets in an accident? Call the caterer's insurance agent to be sure they have adequate coverage. Call your insurance agent, also. It may be necessary to buy extra insurance.
9. List the total cost, including food and liquor fees, rental fees, staff fees, set-up and rip-down charges, overtime fees, and all taxes, service charges, and gratuities.
10. Who's responsible for damage or breakage of the caterer's property? If the caterer is using a rental company, who's responsible for damage and breakage? (Most times rental companies offer insurance. Make sure your caterer gets it—or you do if you're responsible.)
11. Have the caterer sign off that the price they give you is all-inclusive. Leave nothing to chance.

OPTION THREE: THE AT-HOME WEDDING

If you can accommodate an at-home wedding, it may be the most economical way to go. After all, you can hire your own caterer and buy your own liquor, which can generate thousands of dollars in savings. You will not pay for rental of a facility. If this is an option, review "The Caterer, You, and The Property" and "The Caterer's Estimate" before making a decision.

MAKE AN ANALYSIS

The at-home wedding or one held at a do-it-yourself catering facility may not be for you. It's important, therefore, to compare the advantages and disadvantages of this type of reception to one held at a full-service catering facility.

Make an appointment to visit five full-service properties. Get all pertinent information, meet with catering managers or directors, and make a conscientious tour of the facilities. Next, visit at least five caterers and do-it-yourself catering properties, from premium to down-right inexpensive. Pick their brains for ideas. Make copious notes (you may like the ideas of a premium caterer, for example, that can easily be implemented by one who's less expensive). Next, evaluate the difference in cost (and ambiance) between their facility and a wedding held at a home or a do-it-yourself catering facility.

Ask yourself the following questions and then make a determination:

1. Do the savings (if I have the affair at home) justify the wear and tear on the property?
2. How much am I saving in the way of food and liquor?
3. Does my home or catering facility create the right ambiance for my wedding or, if not, can it easily and economically be decorated to achieve that ambiance?
4. How much would I save in insurance and rental fees (china, dance floor, tables, etc.) that would be unnecessary at a full-service catering facility?
5. What does the catering facility include in the way of decorations?
6. What are the charges for additional services (for example, valet parking, cake cutting, or white-glove service)?
7. Who assumes responsibility if there's damage to the catering facility or my home? What if someone is injured? Who's responsible for a drunken guest?

Get out a sheet of paper. *List the advantages and disadvantages of each type of wedding.* List all costs. Which one is best for you? The decision is yours to make.

OTHER, LOW-COST OPTIONS

THE AFTERNOON PICNIC OR AT-THE-OCEAN WEDDING

Nothing can provide a more beautiful ambiance than lush, wooded grounds or the vast beauty of a deep blue ocean, providing you've made contingency plans in case of inclement weather. Park facilities (in forests or at the ocean) are usually owned by the city, county, or private organizations. They charge rental fees and must be reserved with a deposit (security deposits are also required). Call early and book well in advance. Get everything in writing. Next, hire a caterer, turn the responsibility over to them, and have a great time!

THE ELOPEMENT

Relatives and wedding planning got you down? Why not elope to a romantic tropical isle or a majestic mountain ski resort or take a cruise? You may be pleasantly surprised by the results—if you plan well. Interview a few good travel agents who specialize in weddings and can give you the best advice possible. Ask your immediate families to go along, if you'd like, and maybe your best man and maid of honor (with escorts). Make it a long weekend and then stay a few extra days without families and friends, to honeymoon.

THE POTLUCK SUPPER

For a small, family-friend wedding, this reception can be a warm, fun experience. The bride and groom have the celebration at their home or that of relatives or friends. Everyone helps decorate: little white Christmas lights illuminate the backyard trees (even though it's May); tons of votive candles twinkle, illuminating the red and white checkered squares of the rented tablecloths. Shallow wicker baskets filled with basil and tomato pasta (tied off with colored ribbons), wheels of cheeses and crackers, and polished fruit make for unique centerpieces. Bright red napkins, fanned in the water glasses, add to the festivity of the gaily decorated tables. All family members bring a dish: appetizers, salads, main course, and side dishes. There's plenty to drink. A one-man band, trio, or DJ is hired for entertainment and dancing. Wedding cake is served for dessert.

Note: It's essential that servers and a bartender are hired. Your family and friends should be enjoying the party as much as you are and should not be in the kitchen preparing the food, serving it, or cleaning up.

Part VI: The Value of Negotiation

NEGOTIATING YOUR WAY TO SAVINGS

In chapter 5, I taught you the value of research and how to shop for value and savings. Now let's put that knowledge to work—before you sign on that dotted line.

DO YOUR HOMEWORK

1. *Review all your materials and brochures.* Pick the places or caterers that are most appealing and competitively priced within your budget. (At this point, eliminate the highest priced and the lowest priced establishments and vendors.) Compare apples to apples—a sit-down dinner at Resort A to one at Resort B. A reception catered by Vendor I to one catered by Vendor II. Make appointments to meet with the person(s) in charge.
2. Discuss with each catering facility and vendor the advantages of using their establishment or services over their competition's. You should say, "What are you going to do for me that will convince me to have my reception here, or to use you as my caterer?" Take extensive notes.
3. Get all estimates in writing.
4. Go home and analyze the establishments and vendors you prefer. Evaluate the cost, what's included, which has the best ambiance, etc. Start to narrow your choice.
5. Make an appointment with your primary selections. Now's the time to negotiate. Say, for example, "Resort A (or Vendor I) is giving me free valet parking. Can you match that?" Or, "I like your resort better than Resort B's, but they're giving me roast beef for the same price you're giving me chicken. Can you do the same?" Or, "Vendor II is throwing in a whipped-cream cake, can you equal that?" Etc., etc., etc.
6. After you agree on terms and make your decision, leave a deposit and get a receipt.

And don't forget: Your wedding cake is dessert. Use dessert as a negotiating point. Exchange it for a champagne toast or more hors d'oeuvres.

Note: The larger your wedding, the bigger your bargaining power. Don't be afraid to be demanding. They can only say no, and you may end up with prime rib instead of chicken. *Get all estimates in writing.* What they say to get your business may not be the same when it comes to signing the contract.

Part VII: Liquor and How to Buy It

This is the most important part of this chapter. It will teach you how to save the most money on the most expensive item of your reception—the liquor.

CONTROLLING LIQUOR COSTS

Do not allow the caterer or property to control the consumption of liquor. They do it this way:

1. Charging for open bottles. Every open bottle, whether consumed or not, you pay for. They keep count.
2. Charging by the drink. Every drink that's consumed, you pay for. It's up to the caterer or facility to keep the tab.

Have you ever put your half-full glass down at a reception, walked away from the table, and noticed it's gone when you get back? Ever wonder why? When you pay by the drink or by the open bottle it's amazing how fast the liquor flies. The problem with either system is control—*there isn't any.* You must rely on the caterer or property to tell you how much liquor is consumed. This is unacceptable.

Note: If you find yourself in this predicament (the facility or caterer sells only by the bottle or by the drink), tell the person in charge to keep all empty and opened bottles so that you can count them after the wedding. (This might keep them more honest.) You must also tell them not to pick up any glasses unless empty. This may also help to keep the cost down.

PAY BY THE HEAD FOR WORRY FREE, ECONOMIC IMBIBING

Many catering facilities charge for liquor by the head. This means that one price is charged for every person of drinking age for a four- or five-hour reception (including the cocktail hour). If you can, buy liquor this way, even if half your family and friends are teetotalers. I've seen brides and grooms sweat every time their guests walk to the bar to get another drink. That mental cash register keeps ringing and ringing as the tab gets higher and higher. Don't let yourself in for this kind of stress or that kind of expenditure. Pay by the head and breathe easy!

A WORD ABOUT SO-CALLED TEETOTALERS

One of my clients was convinced by a catering director to buy her liquor by the drink; half her family and friends didn't drink and the other half were social drinkers. It's been my experience, however, that even light drinkers or alleged nondrinkers will imbibe at a wedding—*because it's free!* Therefore, I convinced my client to add this clause to her catering contract. It said, in effect, that she would pay for liquor by the drink, provided that the cost did not exceed the price if she had paid by the head.

I impressed upon my client that if the catering director was honest (and was sure that she should pay by the drink), she should have no problem with the clause. It was added to the contract. On Monday, following the wedding, my client burst into my store. "You saved me two thousand dollars. I can't believe that my family and friends could drink so much! Thank you! Thank you!"

THERE'S A CATCH-22. BE ON GUARD!

Buying by the head sounds too good to be true. You and your guests can imbibe to your hearts' content—and you only pay one flat fee per person—no matter how much is consumed. Who could ask for more? Here's the catch: After your ceremony, imagine one hundred guests dashing to the cocktail hour. They're dying for some food and drink, even a cool glass of water would do, but there's only one bartender. Your guests, instead of mingling and enjoying themselves, are standing in a long line, even to get a glass of ginger ale! Caterers know that the most liquor is consumed during the cocktail hour. By staffing one bartender for one hundred guests, they've kept their liquor cost under control—*at your expense*.

The Solution: Pay for extra bartenders. It will cost you a little more, but it will be well worth it.

HOW MANY BARTENDERS?

I suggest one bartender for every fifty people for the cocktail hour. After the cocktail hour, I suggest one for every seventy guests. For one hundred guests, however, two bartenders for the entire affair will suffice.

PREMIUM VS. WELL LIQUOR

Premium liquor is the good stuff—Dewar's Scotch, Tanqueray gin, Absolut vodka. *Well* liquor, on the other hand, is the kind you rarely hear of—Popov vodka, for example. When it comes to saving money, you can save a good deal by using well liquor. Discerning drinkers cringe at the idea—but money's money. The decision is up to you. If paying by the head, ask your caterer the difference in price between well liquor and premium brands. If it's negligible, go with the good stuff!

WINE SERVED WITH DINNER

It's an elegant touch to serve wine with dinner as long as you do it economically. To achieve this goal, close the bar during dinner (one hour) and bring on the wine. If you must purchase it through a caterer or full-service property, buy a medium grade of red and a medium grade of white wine. Allow two glasses per person during dinner. Then calculate the amount of wine you'll need.

Base your calculations on the number of guests. Do not allow the caterer to open more bottles than specified without your permission.

Number of Guests	Glasses per Person	Glasses per Bottle	Number of Bottles Required
100	2	5	40

THE CHAMPAGNE TOAST

The custom of the toast originated in France hundreds of years ago and it's still with us. Marie Antoinette, to drink her champagne in style, designed a long-stemmed glass, shallow and rounded, that followed the shape of her breast. This popular stemware is still in vogue today (although it's more correct to drink from a tulip-shaped or fluted glass. This longer, narrower design keeps the bubbles alive and the bouquet from escaping too rapidly). Champagne is wedding tradition and no bride or groom should be without it! It symbolizes gaiety, love, and life—a time for celebration. The champagne toast is a part of every wedding, no matter how small.

To keep the cost to a minimum, select *sparkling wine* rather than champagne. No one but wine connoisseurs will be the wiser. Then calculate how much you'll need. Once again, base your calculations on the number of guests. Do not allow the caterer to open more bottles than specified without your permission.

Number of Guests	Glasses per Person	Glasses per Bottle	Number of Bottles Required
100	1	6	17

WINE, CHAMPAGNE, AND THE PACKAGED RECEPTION

Many times, wine with dinner and a champagne toast is included in the cost of a packaged, sit-down dinner. If not, find out the cost and negotiate the best price with the catering director. Wine with dinner is an elegant touch, and the toast is tradition. Don't sacrifice either one. Ask the caterer (if wine and the toast are not included) if you can close your open bar for an hour during dinner and serve wine and sparkling wine (for a toast) instead.

A Word About Corking Charges

My sister-in-law held her daughter's wedding at a prestigious country club in New York. She asked the caterer if she could provide the wine (she was able to buy it at a huge discount). To her surprise, the corking charge was minimal and she saved a bundle.

Always ask if you can purchase your own wine and champagne for your reception (at a full-service facility). Most places allow it, but like my sister-in-law, you will pay a *corking charge*. (The fee the facility charges to open and serve your wine if you're not buying theirs.) Most times, this fee is exorbitant, making it more economical to purchase their wine, but it never hurts to ask, and it may even save you money.

No Cash Bars

Cash bars are the epitome of poor taste. If you use your head and schedule your reception for minimal, cost efficient liquor consumption, no one will be the wiser, and you'll save a bundle. Here's how:

• At the cocktail hour, serve sparkling wine or champagne. Have glasses on the bar for guests to help themselves and have them butlered (passed). For an added touch of elegance, put a fresh strawberry in each glass.

• When the cocktail hour ends, and the guests go into dinner, open the bar. Close it during the time that the bridal party and their families are introduced. This will save a half hour of liquor consumption.

• Close the bar when dinner is served. Wine will suffice and will save you an hour of bar time.

• Close the bar half an hour before the reception ends. People should not be drinking just before leaving the reception.

The Bottom Line: Your *open* bar has been open a grand total of two hours, whether the reception is held at a full-service or a do-it-yourself catering facility—or at your own home!

About Beer

A young, college-age, beer-drinking crowd— or family and friends who are beer drinkers, will appreciate a keg of beer (and so will you; it'll save you money). Have the caterer or facility buy a keg of beer and place it behind the bar. (If the wedding is at home or at a do-it-yourself catering facility, you can do the same.) Not only will it save you dollars, it will prevent guests from guzzling from bottles.

Caterers and Liquor

The idea of hiring a caterer is to save money. If you run into one who charges the same price for liquor as a full-service facility, look elsewhere. A caterer may get the liquor for you and charge a small percentage over cost for serving it. (Be sure you don't pay for unopened bottles;

these are returned for credit.) Or, the caterer may permit you to buy the liquor; all you pay for is their bartenders. (Wherever you purchase, be sure you're able to return unopened bottles for credit.)

IF YOU BUY YOUR OWN LIQUOR

Call liquor stores or state stores to get the best prices. Ask for discounts if you buy by the case and make sure you can return unopened bottles for cash. To determine how much you'll need, consult a good bartending book.

WHO'S DOM PÉRIGNON?

A blind monk by the name of Dom Pérignon invented champagne. He found that wine, kept for years in tightly sealed containers, fermented. After tasting his invention, he exclaimed, "I'm drinking the stars."[1] Thanks to him, we still are.

Part VIII: Receipts and Contracts

Unless money changes hands and you receive a receipt, your date is not reserved. Your receipt should contain the wedding date, the time scheduled for your reception, and the amount of the deposit. On the receipt, add the line, "Deposit is refundable if contract is not mutually agreed upon." Both parties should sign and date the receipt. Next, ask the caterer or catering director to draw up a contract.

THE CONTRACT — FOR ALL RECEPTIONS

The contract is legally binding and should be all-inclusive. It's your only recourse should something go amiss. Include in your contract all the items you've discussed with the caterer, catering facility, or full-service property. If they aren't included, add an addendum. Cross out items that don't meet with agreed upon terms. Initial all changes and additions and make sure the caterer does also.

A CONTRACT CHECKLIST FOR SUCCESS

Use this checklist to ensure the following items appear in your contract:

1. Date, time, and place of the affair.
2. Hours scheduled and overtime fee.
3. Room usage and contingency plans. For

example, the Blue Room for the ceremony; the Spice Room for the cocktail hour (should inclement weather force the festivities inside); the Green Room for dinner and dancing.

4. Liquor: how it's to be purchased, the brands, and the number of bartenders to be provided for the cocktail hour, sit-down dinner, or cocktail–hors d'oeuvre reception. The amount per hour for overtime, if you're paying by the head. (See "Liquor and How to Buy It" in this chapter.)

5. Food:

   a. For the cocktail hour, *food should be replenished until it ends*. Specify all foods to be served.

   b. For a cocktail–hors d'oeuvre reception, *food should be replenished until dessert is served*. Specify all foods to be served.

   c. For a sit-down dinner, specify all foods to be served and what's to be included in the package, for example, appetizer, salad, main course, etc.

   d. Number of servers (and specify that a captain or maître d' will be present—start to finish—to supervise the affair). For *excellent* service at a sit-down dinner, there should be one server per table of eight or ten (although one for every fifteen is acceptable). For cocktail–hors d'oeuvre receptions, one for every two tables of eight or ten. List carvers or pasta chefs required if applicable. If you're to have white-glove service, list it and the cost.

   e. The cake, if included. Its design, its flavor and color, the number of guests it will accommodate, and cake cutting charges, if any. (See chapter 18, "The Wedding Cake.")

6. Decorations. The decorations that the club, caterer, hotel, or facility provides should be noted in the contract.

7. Linens and Napkins. List the color in the contract.

8. Entertainment and its requirements. For example, an additional power source and whose responsibility it is to provide it.

9. The dance floor. It should be twenty-by-twenty feet for every one hundred guests. Adjust its size proportionately.

10. A free room should be extended to the bride and groom, if the reception is at a hotel. Put it in the contract. By the same token, if a block of rooms is reserved for out-of-town guests, the discounted rate and number of rooms should be included in the contract.

11. Restroom attendants should be provided for large weddings or if two weddings held at one location are sharing restroom facilities. List charges, if any.

12. Valet parking. One attendant for each fifty guests and the amount charged (and make sure they have insurance; get it in writing). Be sure that the cost is per car—not per person—and find out if you're being charged for a doorman; you should not be.

13. The cancellation policy. Make sure it appears in the contract. Add an addendum that states that the deposit money is transferable if the reception is canceled and another affair is booked within a one-year period. (This may be a birthday party or anniversary party, for example.) Or, that the deposit is refundable if the hotel books another affair for the same date, at the same time.

14. The guarantee. Most times, full-service facilities or caterers will ask that you guarantee the number of guests, meaning you pay even if your guests don't show. If required, guarantee a lower number of guests than anticipated and do it at the last possible moment the contract allows. You can always increase the number (within reason) if need be.

15. Taxes, gratuities, and service charges. List them in the contract.
16. The tasting. The contract must specify that you taste all foods to be served.
17. Dress of servers. Formal, for example, with white gloves.
18. Get the catering director's promise that he or she will stop by during the course of the festivities to ensure that everything is running smoothly.

The Caterer's Contract— There's More

1. Party rentals. Linens, tables, chairs, dance floor, dishes, flatware, etc.—even tents *should be the responsibility of the caterer.* List everything and the price charged. List specifics: color of china, type of flatware and serving dishes (silver-plate, for example), napkins, tablecloths, wooden folding chairs, etc.
2. Entertainment needs. At-home weddings require special electrical needs for the band or DJ. Be sure to specify whose responsibility it is to make the proper provisions and the cost.
3. Kitchen and electrical requirements. List what the caterer must provide in terms of extra ovens, refrigeration, etc., and the extra electrical power they require and the cost.
4. Liquor. Include how charged and return policy on unopened bottles. (See "Liquor and How to Buy It," this chapter.)
5. Set-up, tear-down, and clean-up, and security deposit. The time and number of staff allotted for each task and the cost if any.
6. Cost of servers and staff members.
7. Type of dress required for all staff members.
8. Insurance requirements and amount of coverage, both liability, and breakage or damage to the caterer's property and rented items, and liability for drunken guests.
9. List the name of the captain or maître d' who will coordinate the affair—start to finish. Get the caterer's word that they will stop in from time to time to ensure that everything's running smoothly.

Warning Words

I'm often asked to help when brides get in trouble with a caterer or vendor. The first thing I ask is to see their contract. The result: They usually get stuck. It amazes me that people will sign their name to just about anything without reading the big print let alone the fine variety. *Read your contract inside and out before signing it!* If you find things you don't agree with, negotiate them with the catering director or vendor. *Changes must be initialed by both parties.*

In Conclusion: Creating the Right Ambiance

To create an elegant reception, you must create a special ambiance. All it takes is a lot of thought, time, effort, and a little creativity. The result: *Elegance for a lot less!*

Your reception will define your personalities and taste (or lack thereof) to your guests. For that reason, make your wedding and reception an affair that you and your groom can be proud of—for all the years to come.

Chapter Ten

ENTERTAINMENT

(A Bite-the-Bullet Chapter)

The wine of Love is music,
And the feast of Love is song;
And when Love sits down to the banquet,
Love sits long.

—James Thomson, *The Vine,* Stanza 1

Nothing can make a party hop like great music. Nothing can break up a party faster than loud, obnoxious, or unfamiliar music or music that guests can't relate to. You want your friends and families to dance and have a great time at your wedding. For that reason, you have to find the *best* music that you can afford; music that will make your party hop—at the right price.

MUSIC, DANCING, AND THE PARTY

In the wedding newsgroups on the Internet, I often see comments like these: "My fiancé and I don't dance, so we don't think we'll have dancing," or, "I'd really like my family and friends to get to know each other again; my wedding is going to be like a family reunion. I think it would be wonderful if we didn't have music. I'd really like them to communicate."

Bologna! Weddings are a time of feasting and dancing—of celebration. Just because you don't dance, don't think your guests won't enjoy it. What are they supposed to do for four hours? Sit at a table and communicate? While that may be your idea of a fun time, it may not be theirs. You are their hosts. Their enjoyment must be your first priority.

Schedule Wisely, Budget Well

Directly after reserving your ceremony and reception sites, you must book your entertainment. Good entertainment reserves fast. Don't waste time. Today, because of the wonderful advances in technology, music is no longer expensive. Everyone can afford a great DJ and they abound. In this chapter, however, I'm going to give you some other economical alternatives. Once again, you must do your homework and thoroughly research the type of music that's best for you.

The Keys to Success: Experience, Expertise, Equipment, and Attitude

The experts I've interviewed all agree on one thing: *There's no substitute for experience and expertise.* Experience relates to the training you've had and years that you've practiced your profession. Expertise is how well you exercise that experience.

Top quality equipment, when it comes to music, is essential to get the best sound. Whether you hire a DJ, a band, or an orchestra, the equipment they use must be the best. *That's what you're paying for.*

And *attitude*—that speaks for itself. Michael Rose of Michael Rose Orchestras in Boca Raton, Florida, says that when he's performing, he's always watching the crowd, measuring their level of comfort. He makes sure the tempo of the music is correct (if not, people have trouble dancing). He watches *how* they talk at dinner. As Guy Lombardo once said to him, "If a couple leans over during dinner to speak to one another, the music's too loud."

To Michael, it's all a matter of *caring*, of making sure that every bride's reception is a success. *When you interview a prospective DJ or orchestra or band leader, make sure you have a sense that they care about you and your wedding—that you're not just a number.* If you think you are, look elsewhere.

Ethnic Music and Music Type

Many a bride, because of her heritage, wishes to feature ethnic music at her reception. But let me caution you. Unless all your guests share your heritage, it's not a wise choice. The music must relate to everyone! Don't forget that American music is the best known music in the world. *All* people are familiar with it, from rock to the blues to Sinatra. American music is a reception's Rosetta Stone. People love it, enjoy it, and relate to it.

Can Part-time, Hobby, or University Bands Save You Money?

Professional musicians are just that—*professional*. They play together regularly and have experience. They are also educated. Michael Rose and many of his musicians, for example, have a masters degree in music. And as professional musicians specializing in weddings, they also work regularly with caterers and understand the flow of a reception. *This is critical to ensure a smooth-sailing party.*

If your local college or university has a school of music, you may want to call to inquire as to whether they have an orchestra, string quartet, band, or group *who regularly play for ceremonies and receptions.* If they do, and the musicians are skilled with lots of wedding experience, they may be able to save you a ton of money (their fee is usually much less than professionals). Get references and hear them live or on video before booking.

Part I: The Disc Jockey

A Good DJ Is Ten Times Better Than a Bad Band

In terms of saving money, your best bet is hiring a great DJ. The advantages are enormous: The original artists perform the music; the quality, because music is played from a disc, is superb; and you don't have to worry about interruptions (DJs shouldn't take breaks). What more could a bride and groom, who want the best entertainment for their wedding at a palatable price, ask for?

The DJ as a Specialist

Most experienced DJs are specialists and make their own niche within the wedding format. Some, for example, may be great MCs and others dance experts, teaching the guests line dancing or the popular dances of the day. Others may be ethnic wedding experts, experienced in Jewish or Latino weddings. Others may specialize in the big-band sound, Top 40 tunes, or high tech. Some might offer a sophisticated, low-key style for the more refined bride and groom.

Whine and Dine

The complaints I hear the most about DJs are about their style: "They're so loud!" or, "They never shut up!" or, "They act like stand-up comedians!" If this type of behavior is unsuitable to you, make your demands known and put them in writing (in your contract).

The only way to determine a DJ's style is to preview their performance. This is accomplished, most times, by seeing a videotape. *Insist upon it!* If you don't like their style, look elsewhere. If you like their performance, however, but would change their introduction of the bridal party, tell them and put your instructions in your contract. *You only have yourself to blame* if, at your reception, you're dining and whining about your DJ!

Choose What's Best for You Based on the Expert's Advice

Kenny Mondo, owner of Kenny Mondo's Professional Disc Jockeys in West Palm Beach, Florida, is a wedding professional and a celebrity disc jockey. He has played for the likes of Peter, Paul & Mary, Aretha Franklin, and Tony Bennett. He has been a DJ for over twenty years and his company of disc jockeys is the largest in Florida.

Kenny says that the best wedding entertainment features a mix of music that relates to all age groups. The ideal is to choose about one hundred artists from the DJ's list and let him or her decide when and how they're to be played—Sinatra for dinner, for example and something faster and more upbeat for dancing. If you advised Kenny that you only wanted heavy metal played at your reception, he'd answer that it's unacceptable and would result in your guests' early exit. That's the last thing you want.

Recently, a videographer told me about a wedding he attended. All that was played was rap music, making the reception a disaster. No one danced (how could they?) and most of the people left after dinner. According to Kenny, most older people leave within the first three hours, so vary and mix the music in the beginning. Later, once the older guests exit, you can feature the music you prefer.

Breaks Are Unacceptable

According to Kenny, DJ's should not take breaks because they must not chance missing the action. A DJ should not be outside eating, drinking, or having a smoke during the reception. *Your contract must state that continuous music be played* (meaning there's only one five-minute break every hour), and that a tape be played during the DJ's break.

Kenny says there's no excuse for DJs to eat (or drink alcoholic beverages) *during* the reception, nor should a bride and groom feed them. Receptions normally last four to five hours. DJs should arrive at least one hour beforehand to set up and they can bring a sandwich if they'd like to eat *before the reception begins*. Put it in your contract.

Equipment Is Us!

Quality equipment means quality sound. Therefore, it's essential that the DJ you employ has the best equipment money can buy. Ask what their system is worth. Great sound systems cost thousands of dollars (and so should the system your DJ is using). When you hire a professional DJ, you are paying for the best sound possible.

Another key question: How many times per week do you perform? DJs who perform two or three times weekly will have good quality, dependable equipment. And they will be career DJs. *Don't hire a part-timer.*

Your DJ must have two CD players (or turntables, but be aware that CDs provide the best sound), and a tape deck, because many times guests come with tapes and make requests: "Hi, could you play this?" Kenny stresses, however, that tape decks should not be used exclusively because their sound isn't the greatest. But, he says, they're essential if there's a breakdown. Even though his DJs come prepared with full back-up equipment, they still need time to make a change should it falter. That's when a tape deck saves the day!

To Save Money: Use Your DJ to Provide Your Ceremony Music

If your ceremony and reception are in the same location, you can use your DJ to provide your ceremony music. They may, for example, play classical music or instrumentals as the guests are being seated. Separate selections will be chosen for the bridal party's march. Music for the ceremony and the processional and the recessional will be chosen at the discretion of the bride and groom based on the advice of the DJ and the officiant.

The point is: *You'll save money if your DJ*

provides your ceremony music. You'll only pay for an additional hour of their services.

Tip: Most DJs carry wireless microphones. (It's essential for the officiant to be wired for the guests to hear the vows.) Kenny also places a microphone stand in front of the bride and groom so that guests can hear them. If you have over seventy guests, it's critical that the participants be wired. Be sure to ask your DJ.

MUSIC FOR THE COCKTAIL HOUR

A DJ who's playing at a ceremony cannot play at the cocktail hour (because of break-down and set-up time). Neither can they play at a cocktail hour if they have to set up for the reception. So what do you do for the cocktail hour? Kenny suggests a good quality boom box or portable CD system (for seventy people or less). He stresses *good quality!* It will do the job—economically. (For information on how to contact *Kenny Mondo's Professional Disc Jockeys,* see appendix I.)

THE CRITERIA (AND TIPS) FOR CHOOSING A DJ

- The DJ should regularly perform at weddings
- Get caterers' recommendations
- Make sure the DJ has backup for *all* his equipment (and a tape deck)
- Make sure the DJ has a quality sound system

- Meet with the DJ a week or two before the wedding. Put everything in writing: song selections, names of all members of the bridal party and families who are to be introduced, the sequence of events, etc.
- Make sure the DJ is formally dressed (put this in your contract)

YOUR CONTRACT MUST CONTAIN

- The cancellation policy (deposit should be transferable if the wedding is canceled within a reasonable time period)
- Hours to be played and overtime fee
- The date and time of the affair

- Name of the DJ performing
- Amount of coverage (ceremony and reception, for example)
- Price and overtime fee
- Type of music (continuous)

Part II: The Orchestra and All It Has to Offer!

A RETURN TO THE BIG-BAND ERA

When Michael Rose began his orchestra, it was not considered to be a wedding band; nor was his type of music fashionable for receptions. People preferred bands that played popular music. But a few years ago all that changed. While entertaining at a prestigious hotel in South Florida, younger people began approaching him for information. Their reasoning: They wanted something different, different from the typical rock bands that had become the norm. They wanted something exceptional for their reception, but not as loud. And they also wanted music to please their parents. His wedding business took off! Michael attributes this revival to a generation who appreciates the likes of Cole Porter and George Gershwin—a generation who's come to understand classic American music.

THE BIG-BAND SOUND AND ECONOMICS

Michael Rose's orchestra is famous. He recently opened the social season at Donald Trump's prestigious Palm Beach club, Mar-A-Lago. Needless to say, his band is top-notch. Yet, he's spent the past three years in a very time-consuming endeavor aimed at benefitting the consumer. He's converted his big-band library; it's now digital. What does that mean to you? Plenty in terms of entertainment options and your budget.

There was once a time when a big band (thirteen pieces) was required to produce a big-band sound. And it was expensive. But no longer! *You can attain that big-band sound with only four pieces*, and the most important component—*digital sequencing*. These pieces include: a keyboard player (who may also be a vocalist), a trumpet player, a drummer, and a saxophone player. With the proper equipment, these four pieces will be adequate to provide the right sound, even in a large room. Imagine the savings!

Now it's possible to return to that remarkable nostalgic era made famous by the likes of Benny Goodman and to do it economically. Technology has made it possible. The advantage: Every bride can now afford to have that phenomenal big-band sound! Talk about *putting on the ritz*!

The advantages of digital sequencing are enormous. Due to highly sophisticated equipment, Michael can digitally sequence his own exceptional arrangements into the computer. Whether it be a quartet or a seven- or a nine-piece group, its sound can be accurately emulated. These sequences are then used in conjunction with a live performance.

If Michael plays with a small group featuring a trumpet, a saxophone, and a trombone, for example, he will use digital sequencing to provide the background music, muting the horns in the sequence segment. Therefore, *the audience hears the horns on stage, performing live*. He stresses that this is not karaoke, but his own unique arrangements.

Michael has digitally sequenced three thousand of his arrangements, note-by-note, into his computer. Each is played by either him or his musicians. When a bride reserves Michael for her reception, he sends her a copy of the arrangements and asks her to highlight those that she and the groom would prefer. If there's a selection she'd like but it's not listed, she can request it. Michael will then arrange and digitally sequence that selection in time for the reception. Years ago, big bands were limited by the selections they could play. After all, how many arrangements can one orchestra know? A bride, in turn, was limited by her know-how. But now, the sky's the limit.

When Michael plays at a function, his laptop sits in front of him. On it are three screens. On the first, the titles are displayed. On the second is the instrumentation. (He checks the musicians who are performing live, and then mutes those particular instruments in the digital sequence.) And on the third is an orchestral picture of the entire arrangement. He then downloads the selection, gives the count to the live musicians, and begins to play. All this is done in a matter of seconds, and the resulting sound is so amazing that Michael says his four-piece band leaves the crowd in awe. But there's one critical factor to ensure its quality: *It requires expensive, state-of-the-art sound equipment.*

CAUTION: THE NUMBER OF GUESTS AND THE SIZE OF THE ROOM

Four pieces, backed by digital sequencing, works great in the right size room. But it doesn't work in a stadium-size ballroom packed with two hundred guests. A wedding of 150 people or more must be entertained by six to seven musicians to properly project the sound.

WHAT ABOUT THE CEREMONY?

For the budget-conscious, Michael suggests a string quartet or a keyboard or a combination of flute and violin for an indoor ceremony. For an outdoor ceremony, it's best to exercise some caution. Music gets lost outdoors and may require amplification. Be sure to hear the music at the location before deciding on the pieces you'll need (based on the advice of your entertainer).

THE COCKTAIL HOUR—SAVING MONEY

Cocktail hours are noisy. Therefore, it might be best to skip the music (and save the money). But if you think music is essential, most times a piano is adequate. If there are a lot of guests or the room is large, however, you'll need amplification. Be sure to discuss this factor with your orchestra leader.

Mix and Match to Make Your Wedding Unique

What about a keyboard player for the ceremony and a violin or two playing romantic music that brings the guests to tears? How about a cocktail hour that includes those same violins, flanked by an accordion player, who together circulate and play among your guests? Doesn't this add variety and spice to that ever-featured (and sometimes boring) string quartet? And finally, for the reception, how about a DJ, or a four-piece big band?

This is a remarkable mix of music: the solemnity of violins and piano for the ceremony; the more upbeat sound of an accordion for the cocktail hour; and a DJ or big band for all-out partying! All these options are available—without breaking the bank!

The Tailor-Made Band for the Discerning Bride

A good band leader, with many musical options at his disposal, is in the unique position to tailor make a band for a bride (and to meet most of her budget requirements). Michael gives this advice: *Be honest about your budget.* Once an orchestra leader knows your financial limitations, he can structure the best sound (and pieces) for your ceremony, cocktail hour, and reception. Let the band leader determine what's best for you! (For information on how to contact Michael Rose and his orchestra, see appendix I.)

Michael has one of the top orchestras in the country, yet he strives to make it affordable for all his clients. A volume of work keeps his stable of musicians busy, and they prefer it that way. Most times, he adds, brides mistakenly think that the big-band sound is unaffordable. It isn't! Don't be afraid to approach a band leader and ask what he or she can do for you.

Part III: Bands

Bands that are highly skilled, highly trained, and play together on a regular basis are expensive. There's no way around it. If you want a good band, you'll have to book it far in advance, and you can expect to pay dearly.

Most experts agree that while a synthesizer (or sequencer) adds dimension (because it gives a band a broader repertoire of musical selections), it should in no way act as a substitute for the members who play live. Talented, skilled musicians make a good band; there's no substitute. That's what you're paying for!

Gary Farr, president of Samantha Farr and Secret Formula, an upscale, popular band based in Hollywood, Florida, says that today's brides are looking for a different sound. There are now many requests for sixties, seventies (with lots of horns), and nineties music (alternative), and the big-band sound. A good band is versatile.

THE RIGHT SOUND

A good band requires five or six pieces or more. The core should include vocalist, keyboard, drums, guitar, sax, and bass. Some of these musicians may play other instruments or be vocalists. Booking a band with less is sacrificing the sound and the quality. Gary says that people often ask for three to four pieces, on the stipulation that they get the same quantity of music and the same sound as his seven-piece band. He advises: "Get a great DJ who will give you the kind of music and the sound you want. A three- or four-piece band won't meet or deliver your expectations."

TO SAVE MONEY

To save money, book a band on an off-night, off-day, or off-season. Saturday night is out. Also, don't book your wedding on a holiday weekend. For the ceremony and cocktail hour, utilize one or two members of the band—for example, a keyboard and a flute player (if your ceremony and reception are at the same location). It's much more economical than hiring additional musicians.

Beware of Booking Agents: You'll Pay More.

Bands must be booked directly to save money. If you go through an agency, you'll pay an agency fee (on top of the band's fee). *No matter how you book your band, it's essential that the band members' names are listed on your contract.* This will ensure that the same people you booked will show up at your wedding. This is a must! Gary says that he would only hire a *set* band—one that plays together regularly.

CONTINUOUS MUSIC IS A MUST

A good band plays *continuous* music (one five-minute break is taken every hour), with at least one musician left on stage to keep the music flowing. *This must be in your contract.* If the music stops, so does the party.

Tip: Gary says that the bride and groom must get up on the dance floor to get the party hopping! If the couple doesn't dance, their guests may feel strange about dancing. Even if you don't dance, get up for the first few numbers. (For information on how to contact Samantha Farr and Secret Formula, see appendix I.)

THE POINT

Unless you can afford a good band, don't book one. Nothing will make guests exit earlier than bad music. If you're on a budget, hire a great DJ.

THE ONE-MAN BAND

Because of technology and synthesizers, a one-man band can sound like a lot more pieces and be a terrific alternative to a DJ, especially if the person is also a great vocalist. A one-man band is also relatively inexpensive. There is a draw-back, however. A one-man band is only good for small rooms and small weddings—less than fifty people. If you're thinking of a one-man band, have them audition at your reception site. You might be pleasantly surprised.

Chapter Eleven

PHOTOGRAPHY

Two Divergent Schools of Thought . . . and the Tie That Binds
(A Bite-the-Bullet Chapter)

Sometimes, you're better off spending a little more than you planned, instead of a little less than you should. —Monte Zucker

When choosing a photographer, my emphasis is on finding someone who is better than good—one who is talented and who will make your wedding photos memorable and everlasting. After your wedding, you will anxiously visit your photographer to see your proofs or your wedding images. It should be a wonderful time, one to look forward to with joy in your heart! When you first gaze upon your photos, you should cry *in happiness*, not in heartbreak.

But after their wedding, the complaint I hear from most brides is about their photography. The reason: *They shop price.* Quality and talent don't enter the picture (and that's what

pictures are all about!). This is not the way to book your wedding photographer. And if you do, you may be asking for trouble.

This is one wedding component that may require more of an expenditure than you bargained for. Shop diligently and hard and then juggle your budget to secure the photographer who will turn your wedding day photos into treasured memories. As top photographer Monte Zucker states, "A bride and groom are going to be concerned with *price* only at the time they book the package, but they're going to be concerned with the *quality* of the product for the rest of their marriage."

MY FOCUS

Today's wedding photography is dominated by two distinct schools of thought: classic wedding portraiture and photojournalism. It was

my idea, therefore, to go to the experts and hear their philosophy. What transpired was a reversal of my thinking. I found my interviews to be a total learning experience. Their ideas and concepts influenced me and changed my ideas and perceptions. These experts also gave me invaluable tips about wedding photography, saving money, and securing a wedding photographer, no matter which school of thought you prefer.

A Traditional Approach: Monte Zucker— Great Art and Classic Romanticism

Monte Zucker is one of the finest wedding portrait artists in the world. He believes in classic traditional wedding portraiture: the bride posed romantically and elegantly, with the proper light falling on and flattering her face and her pose; the proper angle to maximize her best look; the most natural makeup to enhance her features. Literally, photos—like art—for posterity.

When I interviewed Monte, he asked me a simple question: "Do you have a photo of your parents' wedding?" I didn't (my parents eloped), but I often think of the picture of my in-laws' wedding. In fact, it so impressed me that I included it in my first book, *For the Bride*. That photo is mesmerizing. *I was then struck by the enormity of his question*. If one was to have their wedding photojournalistically captured (the camera tells the story start-to-finish, but the pictures are natural—nothing is posed), what would have happened to that priceless picture of my in-laws' wedding?

Monte's simple question was not simple at all. A wedding is a historical event in the life of a family. It should be documented in pictures. Beautiful, classic photos should be taken, even if you're a fan of the photojournalistic school of thought. Just think of how they'll be treasured by children, grandchildren, and beyond. I was beginning to think differently about the *value* of wedding photography. I began to look past the pictures and into the future, into the eyes of future generations who would treasure them forever.

That's why Monte insists that a bride's parents be present when he meets with an engaged couple to discuss their wedding day photography and its objectives (even if the couple is paying for their own wedding). To Monte, the parents' needs and wants are as paramount as the bride's and groom's; they should not fall by the wayside. The couple, for example, may want photojournalistic photos, but their parents may want more traditional shots. *Both points of view should be addressed and respected*. A wedding is a family affair and *communication* between the parents and the bride and groom is essential.

Monte, believe it or not, is also a proponent of photojournalism. He believes in a mix of the two schools of thought to achieve wonderful, unique, well-rounded wedding photography. The key, however, is not to let one style eclipse the other. *That is the tie that binds*. There must be balance in wedding photos. The educated bride and groom, therefore, will maintain a level of objectivity when shopping for the type of wedding photography—and the type of photographer—who's best for them.

A Photographer's Skill

Classical wedding portraiture requires training, skill, and experience. These are the factors that allow the photographer to create art through the lens of a camera. (Sometimes, when looking at Monte's pictures, you forget they're photos. The composition is so perfect, the lighting so ethereal, the poses so romantic, they look like paintings.)

The training, skill, and experience that a photographer acquires provides him with the building blocks to create art, and there's no substitute for it. In Monte's eyes, a photographer cannot be consistently creative unless he or she has a basic understanding of everything that goes into creating a photograph.

A trained eye will allow a photographer to be able to analyze your face, your figure, your personality, and your desires. He or she will know how to photograph you at your most flattering angle to achieve the best expressions. He or she will be able to give you images of yourself and of those you love the most that will far exceed your expectations. On the other hand, a photographer with little experience and/or technique may create a lot of images for you but not ones that capture your ideal or your dream of how you picture yourself on your wedding day.

Monte makes this analogy: An accomplished photographer is no different than a focused athlete who works hard, practices, trains with his coach and teacher, and then makes it to the Olympics. A photographer who wants to obtain a superior level of skill and expertise must do the same.

Unfortunately, Monte says, many *undisciplined* photographers think being a photojournalist is enough. Why should they, for example, put out the effort to learn and study about classic wedding portraiture when they can photograph everyone as they are, without leaving the comfort zone of their own inability to pose and use light effectively? Let's take a second look at this argument.

How can an untrained photojournalist, for example, position himself or herself in the best place to take advantage of natural lighting conditions and backgrounds that are as important to her or her type of photography as they are to more traditional photography? In addi-

tion, how can they look for the best facial angles, if they haven't first studied facial structure? As Monte states, "Good photojournalism is still capturing people at their best, because people want to remember themselves looking fabulous on their wedding day." The quality of the work of an untrained photojournalist cannot match the quality of a photographer who has mastered the basics and beyond.

It's Monte's assertion that this training—or lack thereof—can make or break a photojournalist. A photographer trained in classical portrait photography can *also* be a photojournalist; he has the basics from which to build his skill. But can an untrained photojournalist *also* be a classic wedding photographer? *Ask your intended photographers what they've done in the way of training and education, and how much wedding experience they have.* Their answer will tell you much about their qualifications and the quality of their photography.

THE PROS AND CONS

When analyzing the pros and cons of photojournalism and classic wedding portraiture, it's best to ask yourself these questions:

1. Do I want my wedding day photographed as it is, snapshot style?
2. Do I want formal shots included?
3. Do I want some of each?

Let's make an analysis: Let's imagine it's your wedding day and it's time to cut the cake. You stand beside it, join hands with your husband, grasp the cake knife and start to cut, but just then he inadvertently leans over and blocks your face! The photojournalist snaps the picture. But the traditional photographer stops the action, changes the groom's angle, and then snaps. Which do you prefer? *It's a matter of choice and one that must be discussed in detail with a skilled photographer.*

Monte suggests that you avoid stress on the wedding day by planning every detail with the photographer well in advance of the wedding date. Know what the photographer will and won't do. Know which pictures will be taken and be sure to let him know which pictures don't interest you.

Monte's Rule One: Find a photographer who will give you what you want—in the style that you can live with and enjoy—but *don't forget the basics!* Analyze the type of photography that best suits you. (And take your parents' input into consideration.)

THE EXPERT PHOTOGRAPHER AND CONTROL

Brides reserve the best professionals they can for their wedding, based on referrals from family and friends and their budget. The people they employ are experienced professionals. Then why do brides often dictate to the experts they've hired, *without asking questions or listening to their advice?* Take note: *You are paying for information, advice, and service.* You've hired a professional to tell you the best way to achieve your goal and how to avoid disaster. Listen to the experts you've hired. *If you don't, you're wasting your time, money, and letting yourself in for needless aggravation.*

A visit to a photographer must be a learning experience. Are you learning about their style? Their expertise? About photography? How they're going to approach your wedding? Are they telling you what to expect from your photos and what to expect on your wedding day? *Or are you dictating to them?*

Monte's Rule Two: When shopping for a photographer, make sure that you and the photographer understand each other implicitly. Make sure he or she imparts a feeling of confidence

to you. They should be able to advise you on what's best for you and your wedding (based on your input). They should direct and educate you. If you don't agree with their suggestions or feel they're vacillating or they don't give you good, sound advice or you haven't learned from them, it might be best to keep looking. And, last, but just as important, analyze your comfort level! Do you feel good when you're with this photographer?

QUESTIONS FROM THE HEART

When you interview a photographer, Monte suggests asking a few well-directed questions:

1. What is your philosophy? What are your thoughts about what you want to capture at my wedding? What is your plan for my wedding day?
2. How much do you expect me to spend to get what I need? And how much would you like me to spend for you to give all your time and attention to it?

These questions will expose the photographer's thoughts and ideas—*his expectations.* Now ask yourself: Do they match mine? If not, keep looking.

WHAT FORMAT? WHAT SIZE? WHAT COLOR?

Monte's the master of the square-format (cameras that produce square photos) and for that reason, he loves his Hasselblad. But he also incorporates 35mm photography and he's gung ho about digital imaging—the wave of the future (more about this later).

For interest, he features different size photos in his albums. And he finds black-and-white film exciting, provided the photographer knows what they're doing. Most photographers, he says, don't understand the true proprieties of this complex film, which can dramatically project a complete range of beautiful tones, from light to dark. But photographers who put black-and-white film in a camera and shoot it the same way they do color should be a signal to you that they are not technically prepared to give you the quality or results that you may be expecting.

A good photographer, knowledgeable and experienced in black-and-white technique, understands lighting ratios and knows that it will be necessary to go lighter and darker in tones to achieve the desired effect. (In color, on the other hand, you must keep all the tones fairly close together.) When I asked Monte how one could determine the quality of a black-and-white photo, he answered: "If it's exciting. If it's dramatic!"

The whole objective of black-and-white photos can be summed up in one word: *Drama* (that most photographers can't capture in color). If you look at a black-and-white photo and it's just a typical, run-of-the mill-picture, why bother?

Weddings are happy, exciting, *colorful* occasions. If you'd like black-and-white, Monte suggests mixing a few black-and-white photos with a majority of color ones. It makes for a fascinating blend.

Monte's Rule Three: When searching for a talented, skilled photographer, look for one who can offer you choices in your selection of your album's details. These should include:

- Leather-bound albums with various styled pages
- The opportunity to have different size photos
- Black-and-white or color photos, or a combination of both
- Traditional or photojournalist, or a combination of both

- An album (or profile) that requires easy care and provides for the long life of your photos

MONTE'S IDEAL

I asked Monte to characterize his ideal album. He said it would include the following:

- Memorable portraits of family members and others who are important to the families, not just the bride and groom
- Formal portraits of the bride and groom
- Photos that capture the emotions of the day
- Photos that interpret the day *as you wish to remember it*
- Exciting photos, start to finish

Keep all your options open. Interview photographers, take notes, learn! Then begin to analyze, formulate opinions, and make decisions. Don't sign a contract until you have time to think about your decision.

WHAT ABOUT SPECIAL EFFECTS AND FILTERS?

What does the excessive use of special effects mean? According to the professionals, it could mean a cover-up (for lack of skill). As Monte says: "A photographer should not use special effects in place of good quality imaging." And for him, "special effects" go far beyond trick photography. It's an abstract concept, but one whose properties should be inherent in all photos. He sums it up in three words: "Dignity, simplicity, and elegance." *To Monte, these are the only special effects that count.*

Monte suggests the use of a filter to soften a face or to add a different dimension to a photo, but just like special effects, filters can be overdone and draw attention to the effects rather than to the image itself.

How Important Is Equipment?

Monte says that ability far outweighs the type of equipment utilized by the photographer. He showed me photos taken with an inexpensive Canon point-and-shoot camera, and I have to admit that the quality was amazing. To underscore his point, he makes this analogy: If you're an accomplished writer, you can achieve your task by writing longhand or by using a typewriter or by utilizing a computer. By the same token, if you learn basic photographic technique, allowing you to say anything that you want to say (photographically), the question remains: *Do you have anything to say?* In other words: Can you make meaningful and lasting impressions with your camera; images that will be treasured for a lifetime?

A Primal Test

Many photographers offer free sittings to entice future clients. THIS IS NOT OPTIONAL. IF THEY DON'T MAKE THE OFFER, YOU SUGGEST A SITTING—EVEN IF YOU HAVE TO PAY FOR IT! Once you're photographed, you'll be able to see, at a glance, if the photographer has captured your essence on film and the look you're trying to achieve. You'll know immediately if you like what you see. If you don't, move on. A prewedding sitting is the best indicator of a photographer's work and the best prewedding gift you can give yourself. Even if it costs a few dollars, isn't peace of mind worth it?

And Before You Go—How About Your Makeup?

Monte insists on a trial run with a makeup artist before the wedding day. So why not schedule one before your prewedding session with your photographer? Not only will you determine if you like your photographer, you'll also know if you like your makeup. It's an easy way to weed out inept vendors before you sign on that dotted line.

Be very cautious about who you select to do your makeup. Let an overzealous makeup artist get her hands on an unsuspecting bride—and *wow!* Pollyanna is transformed into Cleopatra. Don't let this happen to you. As Monte says: "Makeup must be realistic and natural, and the person doing it should be trained for the camera." He advises against unnatural makeup colors, like blue and green, that draw attention to the color of the eyes and are distracting. It's best to go with soft accent colors like brown and taupe, which accentuate the look (and work well for all brides).

Monte's warning: Makeup artists must do their work expediently and get the bride to the church on time (so to speak)! He refuses to work with tardy makeup artists who can throw an entire day's schedule askew by being late.

Tip: Ask the makeup artist for recent references, and *call them!* Ask the brides if the makeup artist was punctual! Select the one who is not only talented but will guarantee punctuality. There's nothing worse than being late for your own wedding.

An Assistant Is Essential (and Maybe Another Photographer)

Monte shoots with an assistant, one who knows what's going on in his mind and what to do in advance. *This person is invaluable because he saves him time and wasted effort* (and what's more important at a wedding?). When Monte shoots, for example, he simply says to his assistant, "Can you move that light an inch or two?" It makes everything easier and faster.

If photojournalism is your goal, Monte suggests a second photographer, one who gives a different perspective, no matter how large or small the wedding. But it all depends on how much you're willing to invest in your photographs.

FOR PEACE OF MIND

Who makes you feel better than a trusted friend? No one. That's why Monte advises that you find a photographer with whom you are compatible, and one whom you can trust to fulfill your expectations and meet your goals. It's also crucial to find that one person who can accomplish those goals with as few problems and stress as possible.

The photographer you interview must explain all the options that are available to you. You must feel (for your own comfort) that the photographer knows better than you do, because what you think you want may not be what you want later on.

Tip: Monte says it's essential for a bride and groom or their families to call the photographer's references. No one is more qualified to give you an opinion than a bridal couple or family who has recently worked with the photographer you're considering.

MONTE'S TIPS FOR EXCITING PHOTOS

• *Seat everyone together.* Don't have bride's side and groom's side seating (which sometimes results in a lopsided room). Why not have both families and both sets of friends sit together at the ceremony? When the ushers seat the guests, they should say, for example: We'd like all our family and friends to be seated together.

• *Integrate the bridesmaids and the ushers.* For more interesting photos, mix them together and have them stand (together) on either side of the altar.

• *Change positions with the officiant.* During the ceremony, the bride and groom normally stand with their backs to the guests. When they exchange rings, however, have them reverse positions with the officiant, who will then stand in front of them (with his back to the guests).

• *The parents should follow the bride and groom down the aisle* (not the bridal party). This gives them the opportunity of greeting, hugging, and kissing the couple while everyone's on an emotional high. This makes for wonderful candid photos.

• *Choose the best, most exciting photos for your album,* ones that tell your story—start to finish.

A WORD ABOUT RETOUCHING

According to Monte, retouching of all closeup portraits is *a must!* Good portrait lighting increases the visibility of facial lines, such as lines around the eyes, neck, etc. Be sure you discuss retouching with your photographer and the price of the service is included in your contract.

SAVING $$$—ACCORDING TO MONTE

Employ a skilled portrait photographer for a couple of hours to shoot the ceremony and take classic, beautiful photos and family shots. Have friends and family take the candids at the wedding and reception.

MONTE'S WEB

Monte is currently on the World Wide Web. His website is a wealth of education, knowledge, and interest and a photographer's (and amateur's) delight. And he'll be more than glad to help you with any questions you may have about wedding photography. (For more information, see appendix I.)

The Master Captures the Moment (only!) in Photos: Denis Reggie

Denis Reggie is the master of photojournalism. His picture of John Kennedy Jr. romantically kissing Carolyn Bessette's hand as they leave the tiny chapel on Cumberland Island will always be in our hearts and minds.

When I interviewed Denis, I asked why he had turned the tide on traditional wedding portraiture. He said simply that a bride deserved something different. For over twenty years, wedding photography has been mostly defined as a portrait concept. He wanted more!

To Denis, the idea of rigidly posing a bride at her wedding or the continual prompting by the photographer to move a head or to ask for a wave or a smile is abhorrent. In his opinion, unless at the bride's request, the photographer should *not* be creating the moment or forming the subject into his interpretation or putting the subject within that arrangement (ergo, changing the flow of the wedding). It's what is called *proactive*; the photographer, in essence, makes the news. It's the antithesis of being *reactive*, and that's the basis of Denis's wedding photojournalism.

How the Concept Was Born

After college, Denis attended the wedding of an ex-girlfriend and observed how the photographer posed her and her friends and family (even on the dance floor!). He thought that a great injustice had been done, *because all the photos in her album would feature subjects who were aware of the camera*. Her album would not be documentary in any form.

Denis thinks that traditional wedding photography, if you take it to the extreme, is fiction. The wedding photographer makes people do things they otherwise wouldn't do. He asked himself this question: *What if I shot a wedding more as a sports, fine arts, or documentary photographer?*

Denis, in his early years, played football and later went on to photograph the sport. When shooting, he describes himself on the sidelines, armed with a long lens—one who looks at the play but realizes that it's not going to go his way. But he also knows that with the proper operating skills, he will sense where the play will go and will make sure he's in the right place at the right time, *without controlling the event. He is there to document. His job is to be the historian*—to capture, to preserve the moment. It's this philosophy that enabled him to capture the spontaneity of love at a wedding. It made him famous.

Photojournalism Costs More

High-tech equipment and film make photojournalism expensive. The best cameras, for example, must be able to function in almost no light and they're costly. The same holds true with the film. And the number of photos taken is mind-boggling! Denis may shoot between 800 and 1,000 photos at a wedding, from start to finish. Moral of the story: If you want a photojournalist, expect to pay more.

The photojournalist's skill depends greatly on his expertise—and his intuition. As Denis says, he must be a skilled observer, watching the eyes of his subjects to sense, feel, and anticipate—*to document and capture reality*. A true photojournalist must be content enough to let people be themselves. He must not require them to look at the camera: "Heads together now! Give me a smile. Don't move!" That's proactive.

Today's bride, in Denis's opinion, wants a more natural portrayal of her wedding, and hence the boom in photojournalism. The photographer who shoots the wedding is no longer seen as the leader of the event—but the follower. The photojournalist captures the action from the sidelines, says little, and quietly—from the shadows—finds people at their best. The photojournalist believes that the best photos of people are the ones done when they're not actively aware of the camera.

PORTRAITURE IN DENIS'S PHOTOJOURNALISM

Denis, however, in his own wedding "coverages," doesn't shun portraiture altogether. For the purpose of posterity, he feels that some key images need to be brought together and posed. It comprises about 5 percent of his work.

Denis's Five Key Posed Portraits

1. The bride
2. The couple
3. The couple with both sets of parents
4. The couple with their attendants
5. A family grouping or two

The bride's portrait may be taken minutes before the ceremony, the rest in a ten-minute session afterward, perhaps on arrival at the reception site. *And he means ten minutes*—not an hour, not two hours. Denis sees traditional wedding albums as "who" books because their goal is to tell the observer "who" was at the

wedding. But a photojournalistic album answers those other basic questions: What, why, when, and where.

Denis thinks the advantages of photojournalism are enormous. The bride doesn't have to stand for a long series of posed photos before the ceremony or see the groom. She may have a receiving line if she chooses, and both she and the groom can enjoy the cocktail hour.

A BEHIND-THE-SCENES APPROACH

A photojournalist will start the wedding day early. From the time the bride arrives at her hotel or her mom's house to get ready, the photographer will be there. Maybe she still has a few place cards to write; maybe she wants to play with her dog to relax (while her hair is in curlers); maybe she starts to cry when she sees her dad. These are the types of images the photojournalist is there to capture.

A FANTASY OR A REALITY BRIDE— WHICH ARE YOU?

In Denis's mind, there are two distinctive types of brides with very different goals. The first: The bride who sees her wedding as the fulfillment of a fantasy. A portrait photographer, in effect, is a co-conspirator in arranging images supportive of her dream; he meets her needs. This woman and her opinions are to be respected. It's up to that photographer to arrange photographs that achieve her goal.

The second: The bride who perhaps has seen more of the world, is more exposed, and knows what she wants. Staging images is not her goal, because she's presumably living her life the way she wants to. This woman's aim is reality and the photojournalist's mission is to become the historian, the artist who *finds* her at her best. A skilled photojournalist (as an artist) understands lighting, the face, the moment. It's up to him/her to capture the bride in the most flattering way.

Whatever type of bride you are, it's up to you to find the photographer who respects your goals, your dreams of fantasy, or your striving for reality. *Photographic style must meet the mind-set of the bride.*

PHOTOS: THEIR SIZE, COLOR, AND FORMAT

A photojournalistic album typically features a mix of different size photos. Because this wedding is shot more like a magazine documentary, *A Day In The Life of Mary and Bob*, not all the shots have to be full page to be appreciated. A photo of a few little rose petals on the ground or the squeeze of the bride's and groom's hands in the receiving line or a close-up of the ring are all powerful images. Do they need to be full-page? No.

The best photojournalistic albums tell their tale with a blending of small and large groupings of photos, laid out with interest, and flowing from left to right. A full, exciting album is composed of groupings of images that relate visually and tell a story. Due influence is given to those images that warrant it: a picture filled with lots of faces, for example, might be a large photo; a subtle detail, on the other hand, doesn't need to be big to be valued. A proper, well-laid-out, varied selection of photos requires creativity on the part of the photographer as he assumes the role of layout designer.

Denis mixes black-and-white with color. He enjoys, for example, capturing the bride dressing before the ceremony in black-and-white. He likens the moment to *The Wizard of Oz*. When in Kansas, the film portrays Dorothy's life, conceptually, in black-and-white, but when she falls over the rainbow, a whole new colorful world opens up to her. Denis finds that 25 to 30 percent of his clients request their entire wedding shot in black-and-white.

As for equipment, Denis loves his Hasselblads and his 35mm cameras; he uses the best tools for any given situation. He also talks in awe of today's advanced technology—of top-notch 35mm cameras and the quality film that enables them to produce excellent pictures. But, he stresses, *talent is the key.* "Someone could have the best tools in the world and be a poor photographer. It's the artist, not the brush, that makes the real difference."

THE BRIDE AS EDITOR

Denis often takes between 800 to 1,000 photos at a wedding. After they're developed, he edits and sequences the selection and then asks the bride to pick her favorites, in essence asking the bride to be his editor. The number of photos isn't important. If she chooses many, he may adjust the print size to fill the album. He may do some in black-and-white and some in color. Based on her favorite photos, he creatively designs the layout of the album. He plans it in a way that beautifully—and with proper interest and artistic balance—tells the story far beyond the typical album (which tells the story with one photo per page).

TIPS FROM DENIS

• Always hire an experienced, *professional* wedding photographer; this is not a day for a shutterbug friend or family member; there's no chance to reshoot.

• As a photojournalist, he prefers reality to special effects. As he states, "Life is good enough."

• Still wedding photography should typically encompass 10 to 12 percent of your wedding budget.

• The photographer's payment plan and package contents must be fully evident—

Denis offers plans that are fully inclusive. By having an inclusive plan, you can eliminate the element of surprise after the wedding. (See "Your Budget and the Up-Sell or the Prepaid Package," this chapter). Pictures that you select for your albums do not have to be based on whether you can afford them; they should already be a part of your all-inclusive plan. Accordingly, decisions can come from your heart—and *artistry can supersede the finances.*

A Photojournalistic Approach to Makeup

Denis Reggie believes that a bride must look natural; she doesn't need to be hyper-made-up to accentuate her look. She may even have a trusted friend or relative do the makeup, but she shouldn't do it herself! It's too nerve wracking. Besides, it's good to have third-person objectivity. And remember: *Less is more.* Denis says if you can afford a professional, hire one. But, once again, work with a person who understands that makeup should merely *complement.* You must look like you when you walk down that aisle. You should not look like you're on stage.

Denis's Internet Connection

Denis has established the *Wedding Photographers Network* on the Internet, which lists thousands of wedding photographers, in conjunction with *The Knot*, the Web's number one wedding site. Its purpose: To give information to brides about photography and to help them find photographers in the town (or area) where they live. It will address all budgets and the major photographic styles. In other words, a bride may say: "I live in Canton, Ohio. I want a mix of both traditional and photojournalistic photography and as far as price, I want to stay toward the low end." The website will then provide her with a list of photographers who meet her criteria.

A bride will even be able to see examples of the photographer's work and read about their philosophy. It will allow her to research the photographer and decide whether she wants to pursue him or her further. *It will also allow the bride to educate herself.* It will end her frustration with trying to decide where to go to find a photographer, the one who will fulfill her dreams. (For more information, see appendix I.)

An Up-and-Coming Master Is the Tie That Binds: Tim Roberts

Top wedding photographer Tim Roberts shoots with a mix of both photographic styles, believes in both, and is equally comfortable with photojournalism or classic wedding portraiture. He sees merit and value in both methodologies. In the past few years, however, Tim has had to lean more toward photojournalism due to his clients, who want a more natural, less posed approach. He attributes this trend to Denis Reggie and the massive press he generates.

Tim also recognizes, however, that many of his clients who basically want the reality of photojournalism also want to be beautifully portrayed. To achieve stunning portraiture, however, you need proper lighting. And the most flattering, most effective type of light is *studio light.* To Tim, the argument for one type of photography over another verges on the *technical.* No one is going to be as flattered by an on-camera flash or a battery operated, handheld strobe as they are by a large soft box with a reflector (that thing in the photographer's studio that looks like an umbrella).

Tim also uses filters, because he knows that a client, especially a bride, wants to look her best. Filters can help soften a face and make lines and wrinkles appear softer. But they don't dominate his work. He's well aware that today's trend is toward realism.

A Hit-and-Miss Proposition

Tim is boggled when he thinks of the photojournalist's efforts: *He must take many, many photos to make one work.* He gives an example of the photojournalist who shoots the newly married couple on the dance floor. The bride and groom look terrific, while the bride's father, who's standing next to them, is yawning with his eyes closed. His point: Sometimes candids don't work and sometimes they do. It's a hit-and-miss proposition.

Tim's solution is to take candid photos to document the event, but to also include beautiful portraits to guarantee that everyone looks their best and that everyone is included. Tim's style is a healthy mix and one that fully satisfies the needs of his clients.

An Educated Photographer— Your Best Bet for Success

Tim is a photographer trained in the basics and in the classical approach. He understands the tilt, the lighting, and the body language of fine portraiture and his work shows it; his candid photos exemplify his training and experience. *Your best bet, therefore, is to find a photographer who's trained in both styles of photography.*

Keep an Open Mind

Tim says that a bride's greatest detriment is shopping (for a photographer) with a closed mind. His clients, in the past couple of years, have gone so far to the left (photojournalism) that they refuse to see the value of the right (traditional wedding portraiture).

Tim says he will sometimes lose a client who's locked into photojournalism if he tries to educate her about classical wedding photography and its value. The trend for photojournalism has gone so far, he says, that some photographers are advertising as many as five cameras to shoot the wedding and reception. What you're actually getting, he states, is one trained cameraman working with a bunch of untrained part-timers with less than professional equipment. This is not the way to shop for—or secure—wedding photography or a photographer.

That's why it's critical to shop with an open mind, to educate yourself about the type of photography you prefer, and to make an informed decision based upon sound advice. It's important to voice your wants, but *it's critical to listen to the expertise of the photographer.* You don't want to look back on your pictures, five, ten, or even twenty years from now and ask yourself: What was I thinking?

The Format Tim Prefers

Tim prefers the square photo because of the balance it affords him. And he, like the other experts, relies on his trusty Hasselblad. Because the camera produces a large negative, it makes retouching easier. He is also now using 35mm cameras and sees their value in photojournalism.

Tim loves the square-shaped photos produced by his Hasselblad, and he's developed his own unique style within that medium. He composes his images within the camera and rarely crops them after they're developed. His albums feature either 10″ × 10″, 8″ × 8″, or 5″ × 5″ photos.

He also enjoys the drama and excitement of

black-and-white. Advances in film technology allow him to shoot an entire wedding in color and then make stunning black-and-white prints from the color negatives. This gives the client the advantage of choice: they may have any or all of their photos in either black-and-white or color.

TIP FROM TIM: APPOINT A GROUP LIAISON AND SAVE TIME

It seems that brides are always complaining about photographers who take inordinate amounts of time shooting their family photos after the ceremony. It infringes on their reception time, leaving precious little time to spend with their friends and family.

Tim has helped solve this problem by spending an hour or two with the bride and groom, a week or two before the wedding, reviewing all family groupings. *Everything is in writing.* (You make sure your photographer does the same.) He also insists that the couple appoint a group liaison—someone who knows the members of both families and their friends—who can get them organized after the ceremony in a speedy, efficient way. *This is a must!* It's not up to the photographer to go after Uncle Will, who snuck off to the cocktail hour for a quick nip. *That wastes time!*

Tim estimates that family-group photos will take approximately twenty to thirty minutes after the ceremony and personals (photos of the bride and groom) will take about the same amount of time (provided the families cooperate). The photographer may then want to shoot the couple in romantic settings afforded by dramatic indoor or outdoor locations.

TIM'S SOUND ADVICE

Tim says you must use your common sense when hiring a photographer. And put your wedding photos in perspective! *Weigh their value against the value of your other wedding components.* If wine isn't served in time for the toast, for example, it's forgivable. If the cake collapses when a waiter accidentally bumps the cake table, it's a disaster for sure, but one that won't forever mar the wedding festivities. What troubles Tim, however, is that people spend thousands of dollars on their wedding and then take a chance with their photos. In his opinion, they are risking their investment (and their memories).

Your photos are the only tangible by-product you'll have of the most important day of your life. What if they're ruined by an inept photographer? Your pictures are your memories; treat them with respect. In Tim's opinion, *the photos are the most important wedding component.* Give them the time and attention they deserve—and budget wisely! Educate yourself before signing a contract. (What he says makes sense.)

MORE TIPS FROM TIM

• You must find a studio that's a stickler for documentation. *Everything must be in writing,* from start times to who's included in the family groupings—even directions to the ceremony and reception sites. *Everything must also be itemized.* When you buy a package, make sure there's a concise list of what's included.

Look for a photographer who's extremely specific and a studio that asks for documentation from you—to document the schedule and the arrangements. Ask the photographer how he will plan the wedding day and make sure he schedules it with you. It should be in writing. *This will protect you!* A photographer must not only be a great cameraman, he must be extremely well organized and detailed. These skills should be evident in the first interview. If you don't feel he or she is concise or in control, look elsewhere.

Makeup for Success

Tim, like our other experts, says that makeup is essential for the best photos and *it must be natural.* He also says it must be done professionally to achieve the best quality photographs (and the best look).

Like Monte Zucker, Tim believes in a prewedding session with the photographer as well as the makeup artist, but he takes it a step further: A prewedding session will also educate the photographer: From his or her standpoint, it will guide them to make the proper analysis of her facial structure and to decide in advance what kinds of lighting and angles will most flatter her. It's an important learning experience—and one that may save a bride a lot of headaches (and retouching).

Tim's Money-Saving Tip—a Different Approach

Tim says that the best way to reduce his price is for his clients to treat him with respect and kindness; to make sure that they are as considerate of him as he is of them. To offer him a meal (sandwiches are just fine) if he's working longer than six hours and to treat him with courtesy. According to Tim, the best thing that you can do is to make your photographer a part of your family for your wedding day. It will be rewarded in kind—and effort. (For more information, see appendix I.)

And Finally . . . the Experts Agree: Tips for Choosing a Photographer and Saving Money

1. You should have a sense of the photographer's professionalism, reliability, and work quality. You can make this determination when you interview the photographer and by checking references (not only recently married brides but caterers, florists, and party planners who work regularly with photographers).
2. Shop diligently—look at the competition's work closely.
3. Make sure the photographer carries backup for *all* his equipment.
4. If you'd like to reserve your pictures for posterity, ask if your photographer can digitize your photos (record them on a disc). If your album burns in a fire or is lost, you will always have a copy of your photos.
5. Hire only a professional wedding photographer.
6. To save money, explore various album options. Simple albums are plentiful; leather-bound albums are the finest available and are costly.
7. A fresh talent may offer you a better value. Others may find comfort in an experienced, premium photographer. Shop and research diligently.

To End this Chapter: Trends, Debates, and Warning Words

What's New in Photography?

Right now, you can buy a camera that shoots an image and logs it digitally into the camera. There is no film. Once the picture is taken, the camera displays it—in color—on a screen located on its reverse side. At once, the photo appears and you can immediately determine if you've taken a good one or not. Good-bye, Polaroid!

Once you return home, you plug the camera into your computer. The photo appears. You can then blow it up, reduce it, adjust the color, and touch it up (bye-bye wrinkles and bags). You can even remove people from the photographs and transmit them to far-off places. Just imagine the bride and groom standing in front of the Taj Mahal or swinging on monkey vines in the Amazon like Tarzan and Jane. Your only obstacle is your imagination. This technology will take you anywhere you want to go.

Tim Roberts envisions a time when a bride, who doesn't want her photographs taken before the ceremony, will be photographed (sans groom) with her family and bridal party. And a groom who will be photographed (sans bride) with his family and bridal party. After the ceremony, the photographer will take a few quick shots of the couple together. But once he's back in his studio, *wow*! He'll mix and match the groups into various combinations (and photos) any way the bride and groom and their families choose—along with the help of his trusty computer.

How this technology will affect professional photography can only be imagined. Photos will be retouched, blown up, developed (so to speak), and printed within a matter of minutes. Printers are now available that are capable of printing oil directly onto canvas; the resulting photos can look like art rather than pictures. There will be no cost for film or lab fees.

The photographer will be in total control. His photos won't leave his studio until they're relinquished to the bride and groom. They, in turn, may choose to have a traditional album or have their photos presented to them on a computer disc to watch on their computer or TV screen. It's only a matter of time before all TVs are digital. *The photographer you interview should be aware of digital imaging and educated about it.* If the one you interview downplays its importance, it might be better to look elsewhere. You want to find the most up-to-date photographer you can.

Albums vs. CD Rom

When video was first introduced, it captured action live with motion and sound, making it more efficient than a still photograph. It was said at the time that video would replace still photography; it didn't. People still like to see that special moment captured in a split second by the photographer. They love to hold, touch, and feel their albums. There will always be a place for still photos, framed in a beautiful album.

But there's also room for discs. What's wrong with having your photos on CD Rom, plugging them into your computer (and later your TV) and watching your photos come to life on a screen? In my opinion, there's merit to both mediums.

The Great Debate: Photos Before or After the Wedding?

Many classic photographers wish to spend hours with the bride, groom, and their families before the ceremony to take their photos. If the pictures are taken afterward, however, time becomes the watchword. Pictures must be taken quickly while trying to include everyone! Normally, these photos take about thirty minutes (if the families cooperate) and about thirty minutes for the bride and groom's personals.

It's up to you to decide: Before or after? Many brides don't like to see the groom beforehand. Others say they'll look their best and won't be rushed if the photos are taken before the ceremony. It's all up to you, based on the advice of your photographer.

But now there's a new solution to the problem! Photographers may advise that the groom's photos be taken with his family a few hours beforehand. Then the bride's with her family. After the ceremony, everyone gets together for a few family shots and the bride and groom for their personals. The advantages are tremendous: One, the bride doesn't see the groom beforehand. Two, most of the families' portraits and the bride's portraits are taken early when everyone looks their best and everybody is relaxed. And three, everyone can enjoy the party (once the ceremony ends)!

Let me say, however, that both Monte and Tim will schedule the photos any way the bride chooses. But it's my advice, based on my experience, that a good photographer should be able to schedule these pictures succinctly and do them expertly, no matter what your preference may be.

THE NEVER-ENDING NEGATIVE DEBATE

When a photographer shoots your wedding, he owns the copyright on the photos. That's why you can't take your proofs to the nearest photo lab and have them copied. If you want more pictures, you must go back to your photographer and pay for them. That's how a photographer makes money—it's his or her livelihood.

Many upscale photographers like Denis give the bride all the negatives after the wedding is shot and their album completed. Monte gives his back one year after the bride's album is delivered. Other photographers don't give them back, and that's their prerogative. (*Note:* That's how most photographers make their money, and they shouldn't be condemned for the practice.)

If you want the negatives, or want to purchase the negatives, you must find a photographer who agrees to it. *This is a pertinent issue that must be discussed with the photographer ahead of time, and one that must be included in your contract.* If you insist upon ownership of the negatives and the photographer resists, it's time to move on.

WORDS OF CAUTION ABOUT EQUIPMENT

The experts in this chapter agree that a photographer's ability is a greater asset than the equipment that's utilized, but let me caution you. Technology has made great advances in the past decade; cameras are not what they used to be. Personally, I would not employ a photographer who did not have up-to-date equipment. Let me take this one step further. If I were paying a premium price, I would not only require that he or she have the most up-to-date equipment, but the best equipment. That's one factor that separates the professionals from the point-and-shoots.

I often tell the story of the bride who employed the photographer whose camera was so old that it failed to signal him that it malfunctioned. He didn't know it and she had no photos of her wedding. Is that a chance you want to take?

Your Budget and the Up-Sell or the Prepaid Package

Some photographers sell their packages for a minimal fee, which may include, for example, their time and an album or two. They make money when the client previews the proofs and buys more photos than they had originally planned. This is called an *up-sell*, and it can catch you by surprise if you're not careful. I've known many brides who spent thousands of dollars more than they budgeted for—*and more than the package they originally paid for*—because they just couldn't resist those beautiful photos! *It's a practice that can throw your finances into disarray* (if you don't exercise caution). Once you sign on that dotted line, those photos are yours, even if you have to go on the easy-payment plan to pay the bill.

I once sent a client to Tim. She came back and said he was too expensive, way over her budget. Instead, she chose a mediocre photographer who was one-third the price. In the end, after she bought all the extra photos she wanted, she spent a thousand dollars more than Tim's all-inclusive package.

For this reason, I think it's better to buy a *prepaid, all-inclusive* package. Everything is sold up front. The number of albums, wallet-size photos, portraits, etc. are all included in one price (depending on the type of package you book). It's up to you to determine exactly what you and your families want and need. *You must then properly budget to pay for it,* but there are no surprises or easy-payment plans after the fact.

In Conclusion . . .

This chapter is based upon the experts' advice. It's up to you to adhere to their rules, heed their wisdom, and take advantage of their knowledge. The information in this chapter should help you find the best photographer you can and make an educated decision about him or her and the style of photography that's best for you. It's information that will save you money and heartache in the long run, and forever safeguard those memories. And just think! You may even find a new and up-and-coming master at an affordable price (if you shop and research hard enough)!

Chapter Twelve

VIDEOGRAPHY

(A Bite-the-Bullet Chapter)

If one picture is worth a thousand words, then a video is an encyclopedia.
—Steve Almes, president, ARC Video

Video is one of your top four priorities. It may be necessary to spend more money than you anticipated to achieve the quality and the professionalism required. Shop well and research vendors in all price ranges. Find out what makes one more expensive than another. Educate yourself by interviewing videographers. Take the time to analyze a few of their tapes for quality and to ensure they're not cookie-cutter videographers (more about this later). *Schedule your time and budget wisely.* But first, let's dispel some misconceptions.

DON'T DO IT?

I have never seen a wedding component more maligned or more misunderstood than this one. I have never seen a component that elicits more negativity or one that's approached with more ignorance. I have never seen a component that causes more trepidation or one whose predominant determining factor is the budget. I have never seen a component that evokes more regret, after the fact, from those who decided against it.

Why? There is no other component that can give you more joy or impart more feelings of love or nostalgia. No other component can transport you back in time, a virtual time machine of memories and the love and laughter and heartfelt joy of family and friends. There is no other component that with a push of a button can make your wedding day, and all the people in it, come alive—whether it's five, ten, or fifty years hence! All in all, there is not one other wedding component that has the properties or capabilities of this one. Why would you think twice about it?

A HISTORY AND AN ATTITUDE

Before video, many brides took movies of their wedding using 8mm film. In the sixties and seventies, the movie-fad faded. But in the eighties, with video becoming more readily available, it moved to the forefront. It was then that some saw the possibility of filming weddings as *documentaries*—the biggest news in the life of a family.

Let's think of your wedding as *news*! Of course, it's not going to make the cover of *Time*, but it is one of the most significant events to happen within your families; it deserves the same attention as the wedding of John Kennedy Jr. and Carolyn Bessette.

THE PROBLEM WITH VIDEO IS NOT A PROBLEM

When a bride tells me she's rejecting video because, "They're always in your face; they're bothersome," I know that she has never seen a *good* video. Good videographers, just like good photographers, are *unobtrusive*; you don't know they're there.

When you view a wedding tape, are the people squinting because of an unbearable light that's shined in their face? Do they look harassed by the mike that's pushed near their mouth? Are they embarrassed by an obnoxious videographer who's asking them to comment on the bride and groom's happiness? If you answered yes to these questions, you're watching a tape shot by an untrained, unskilled, overbearing videographer.

IT'S ALL SO EASY

Brides seem to have great difficulty evaluating video. Why? There are no gray areas. Let's compare it to a movie. Think of your favorite *romantic* film. Ask yourself these questions:

- Is the picture clear? Is it jumpy?
- Are there any dead spots?
- Are you aware of the special effects (unless the movie is a fantasy)?
- How's the lighting?
- How's the sound?
- How long does it last?
- Does it keep you entertained?
- Do you feel emotion?

Since we're asking these questions about your *favorite* movie, let's answer them. If the picture wasn't clear and there were dead spots or it jumped, and the lighting was poor and you had trouble hearing the main characters, would it still be your favorite movie? At the same time, does it pull at your heartstrings? And how about the way it's filmed? Is it a realistic portrayal or does it remind you more of *Star Wars*? And the last thing to ask: Is it boring? Of course not! If it were too long and the plot bored you, it wouldn't be your favorite movie. So *why is a wedding video any different*? Why is it so difficult to look at one and make an analysis?

DON'T ASK FOR REFERRALS

When it comes to video, I'm going to break the rule. Don't ask for referrals from friends. Most people will tell you that their video is the best ever. But how do you know unless you take the time to watch the videos of recently married friends, relatives, and business associates? Once you do, you can make your own determination (based upon the above criteria).

It's critical, however, to ask for referrals about the reliability of the videographer, their attitude, and style. Were they on time? Were they organized? Were they intrusive? Were they obnoxious? These are important factors to know before you hire them.

DON'T ASK A PHOTOGRAPHER

The biggest mistake that brides make is to equate videography with photography. Why? What's the correlation? I see only two common factors: both are visual and both feature pictures. The relationship ends there.

Photography and videography are two distinct art forms. You would not call McDonald's to ask for a caterer. McDonald's specializes in hamburgers and fries. What in the world do they know about catering? It's the same when you call a photographer and ask him to refer a videographer. *Photography is his specialty.* The buck stops there.

Photographers and videographers are trained differently because their medium is different. Still pictures and moving ones are two separate entities. Each medium takes years of training, experience, and the development of expertise to master (and let's not forget talent). I correlate the person who conquers both professions to one who holds both a medical and a law degree. These careers are as far apart as the North and South Poles. The same with photos and videos; it's a unique person who can master both mediums.

VIDEO: A COMPLICATED, MULTIFACETED CRAFT

A videographer is much more than a cameraman. Let's take another look at your favorite movie. What does it take to put that movie together? Besides a great script, it requires a talented team of professionals: actors, a director, a cinematographer, a producer, an audio technician, a gaffer (lighting technician), and countless others. Each of these people is a specialist in their field. And the one factor that brings it all together? The editing. *It makes the event!*

A bride, when hiring a videographer, must remember that this *single individual* is a master of all these specialties. Imagine the training and experience and talent they must have to enable them to properly and professionally create your video? To take hours of raw tape and turn it into a fast-paced, well-orchestrated, well-timed docudrama of your wedding day? *It's not easy.*

TRAINING

A videographer must be trained in his craft. The technology is relatively new, but almost every college and university offers classes in TV and movie production. The importance of this training has nothing to do with your videographer's expertise when it comes to shooting your wedding, but it has everything to do with teaching them the basics of their craft. This is essential.

You must ask a videographer about their background during your interview. Their training is important, but the years they've been producing wedding videos is even more weighty. A cameraman, for example, who shoots the news for CNN but has never shot a wedding will likely produce a lousy wedding video. Shooting weddings successfully is a highly specialized profession.

FULL-TIME OR PART-TIME?

A full-time videographer earns a living shooting video; he is a professional. The fact that he's in business for a number of years should tell you that he's proficient. A full-timer also has a vested interest in keeping you happy as a customer, to maintain a better level and quality of equipment, and to dedicate the time necessary for proper editing.

A part-time videographer, on the other hand, always has his regular job to fall back on. You are not his bread and butter. It's my advice, therefore, to hire a full-time professional, one who has the time to devote himself solely to his job and to you.

EQUIPMENT

There's one piece of equipment that can make a huge difference in the final product—*the camera*. A single chip camera is very different from a three-chip model. The disparity lies in the clarity of the picture, the sound, and the cost. When you pay for a videographer, make sure he uses a three-chip camera. That's one factor that makes his videography superior to an amateur's. When you hire a professional, you're also paying for premium equipment.

Videographers must have backup for all their equipment. And there must be two videographers to shoot your ceremony. This is essential! What happens if the camera breaks down during the vows? Even if he has backup, when can the videographer make the replacement? He cannot stop the ceremony. A second videographer solves the problem.

Two cameras also give you two different perspectives, which can make the final product much more interesting. The videographer who's positioned alongside the altar is going to shoot a much different picture than the one who's positioned at the end of the aisle. Imagine the two perspectives blended into one?

To make it easier and to cut costs, many videographers will man one camera and let a second run on its own. The problem: The unmanned camera may be nudged, bumped, or knocked out of direction or focus. Another drawback: This camera is pointed in one direction, with the lens set one way. For that reason, it's best to have two cameras operated by two videographers, who have the option of zooming in and out to get different angles and shots. To keep costs down, *you may employ only one videographer to film the reception*—provided they bring a color monitor to constantly check the tape. *This is a must.*

AUDIO

Fifty percent of a good video is good audio. In order to accomplish it, the videographer must use a variety of microphones. Roy Chapman, Chairman of WEVA International (Wedding & Event Videographers Association) and long-time videographer, says a good way to test a videographer's skill and experience is to ask, "How many microphones will you be using at my ceremony?"

To have good, professional audio, the officiant and the groom have to be miked (with a wireless microphone). The readers (or the pulpit) must be also miked, if applicable. A cantor or soloist must be individually miked for best results. If not, they may sound like they're in a wind tunnel. When you listen to a video, it should exhibit *even sound presence*; it should not fade in and out.

AND DON'T FORGET TALENT

Steve Almes, president of ARC Video Productions in Boca Raton, Florida, says that you can't discount talent. It's something that's inborn and enhanced by training and experience, *but it's the one factor that makes each wedding interpretation different.* Jeff Smith, his senior videographer, correlates it to students in an art class. Each one sketches the bowl of fruit on the table, but each sketch is distinct; no two look alike. It's the same with video. (For more information, please see appendix I.)

For that reason, *look at a few sample tapes*

from each videographer. If they employ the same music, the same special effects, the same format (opening and close, for example), something is missing—namely personalized attention. Each bride and groom should have their own specialized video based on their wants, needs, and input, not a cookie-cutter rendition.

The Cost: Photography vs. Videography

An experienced, professional videographer may average about thirty hours, start to finish, to shoot and edit your wedding properly. *That's why your video should cost no less than your photography.* In fact, if you were to analyze it, there's no doubt that it should cost more.

A photographer shoots a wedding, sends the film out to be developed, removes bad pictures, crops them if necessary, puts the shots in order, and lets the bride select the ones for her album. (She, with his input, becomes his editor.) He then puts the finished product together in an album.

For the videographer, shooting the wedding is only the beginning. Afterward, he must edit the tape. He must, if requested, add baby and honeymoon photos. He must merge the video from two cameras into one. He must add the bride's and groom's favorite music (at just the right times). He must include the right people. He must remove dead spots, enhance the sound, cut unnecessary footage. He must season it with just the right amount of special effects for added interest.

He must make the video flow, make it entertaining and fun, and cut its length to about one-and-a-half hours. This skill requires talent, experience, expertise. *To be successful, he must be as talented an editor as he is a cameraman.* Now let's correlate the experience and skill of the videographer and the time he spends to complete the product, to the price. If you spent an average thirty hours on a wedding, would you charge only five hundred dollars? Think about it.

If You Had to Choose

Because of budget limitations, you may have to choose between photography and video. What should you do? Let's examine the problem. Roy Chapman poses this question to his clients: Assume you could have either a photo album of your grandparents' wedding day or a video. Which would you prefer? If your budget makes you choose, scale down your photography. Hire the photographer for a couple of hours to take the ceremony shots and the family groupings afterward. Put your money in your video.

Warning Words

The experts agree that it's essential to ask the videographer *how long their camera is running.* (It should run start to finish). Because many videographers hire unskilled "videotapers" to shoot weddings, this question is pivotal. Videotapers are merely given a list of what to shoot and are instructed to turn the camera on and off at opportune times.

This technique is also called *in-camera editing.* Be forewarned: *There is no such thing!* If your prospective videographer says that he's going to do an in-camera edit and hand you the tape(s) at the end of the evening—*run!*

Don't confuse a videotaper with a videographer. A person, for example, who does in-camera editing is a videotaper. *Style or talent does not enter their picture.* The term videographer, on the other hand, implies the addition of *artistry*. This artistry turns raw tape into a work of art called a wedding video.

THE BRIDE AND GROOM'S RESPONSIBILITY

Recently, a bride's rabbi sent a letter to her photographer and videographer (two weeks prior to the wedding), explaining that he would not permit flash or camera lighting during the ceremony and that no photos could be taken from the front. *What?* The wedding was held at a hotel. There were no religious restrictions other than his own whims. This made life miserable for the photographer and videographer, who tried to do the best they could.

This type of experience frustrates Roy Chapman. He states, "The bride and groom are the 'executive producers.' It's up to them to obtain any official permission that's necessary for video. And it must be done at the beginning of the wedding planning process."

In other words, the vendor is not contracting with the church or synagogue. *The bride and groom are.* In this example, the couple should have talked with their rabbi beforehand. While he might not have wanted photos or videos (maybe he felt they're intrusive)—*it's their wedding!*

Don't let this happen to you. Discuss with clergy (or the officiant) the importance of your day (and the value of the people you've hired). *Make your demands known up front and don't wait until the last minute.* Experts say that the bride often thinks this responsibility is the videographer's. It's not.

THE VIDEOGRAPHER'S STYLE AND FOCUS

Each videographer has their own style—their way of doing things. Steve Almes, for example, doesn't conduct interviews unless the bride requests it. If a bride insists, however, he advises the bride and groom to select a person or two who's familiar with their families—who's outgoing and affable—to conduct them instead. It makes the person interviewed feel comfortable and at ease and makes for great video.

A good videographer will focus on the primary people (family, bridal party, close friends) attending your wedding. Tell the videographer where your families and close friends are seated and let them go to work! Don't make the videographer shoot each table; it's a waste of precious time and effort. They should be focusing on you and your families.

THE REHEARSAL AND WEDDING DAY COVERAGE

Professional, highly disciplined videographers will *always* try to attend the rehearsal. It enables them to see the physical setup of the place and to find out the best way to position themselves and their equipment. It enables them to discuss all plans with the officiant and to go over restrictions. They are also able to meet the families and know who's who. All of these factors help to make for relatively stress-free shooting on the wedding day.

On the day itself, a good videographer will be there at least two hours before the ceremony to set up and will remain until the end of the reception. However, the amount of coverage you receive depends upon the package you reserve, and your budget.

HOW LONG SHOULD IT LAST

A well-produced wedding video should last no longer than one-and-a-half to two hours. It should cover the length of the ceremony and important reception highlights: father-daughter dance, cake cutting, etc. (If a videographer says their tapes run an average of three to four hours, look elsewhere. They're not doing their job.)

A NEW FORMAT

Recently, a new concept has been introduced called the *thirty-minute edit*. Pioneered by top videographers Robert Ehrlich, Art Polin, and others, it's basically a well-edited version of the wedding day's events cut to thirty minutes. The experts point out that most TV sitcoms last thirty minutes (including commercials) and are able to tell an entertaining, fast-paced story. Why can't a wedding video do the same?

This is not an easy task. To capture the poignant moments of the ceremony, and include *just* the right people, and cover the *main* highlights of the reception—without missing critical action—is an art. A videographer who suggests the thirty-minute edit will generally provide the bride and groom with raw footage (called an *archive tape*) of the entire event.

Think about it. How often can you watch a two-hour tape of your wedding? And, even if you enjoy watching it, consider your friends. They'll thoroughly enjoy a thirty-minute tape, but asking them to sit through a two-hour video is asking too much.

When you visit friends to watch their tapes, doesn't it often go like this: "Speed it up, Fred. Mary and Joe don't want to watch Aunt Sue," or, "We've seen enough dancing, get to the cake cutting." But imagine if the whole tape were only thirty minutes, beginning to end? Think how often you and your families would show it and how much more you'd enjoy it!

THE HIGHLIGHTS TAPE

Many videographers offer their clients a *highlights tape* (in addition to their one-and-a-half- to two-hour edited video). This ten- to fifteen-minute tape highlights the wedding start to finish. They cost more, but I think they're worth every cent. Just like the thirty-minute edit, they're fun, fast, and easy to watch.

Feed the Videographer!

The wedding day is a long one. It's tough to be on your feet for hours on end, lugging equipment while supporting a camera on your shoulder. Take note: The way to a videographer's heart is through their stomach! You may inform the caterer that you would like sandwiches for your videographer(s). (It's not necessary that they receive the same meal as your guests.) A table should be set up in the back of the reception room and they should be served along with your guests. (They must remain in the room, however, so that they won't miss any action.)

What's New in Technology

Digital technology is changing the nature of videography. Digital cameras create sharper, clearer pictures. For videographers, digital editing equipment opens the doors to limitless creativity. They are no longer "cutting and pasting" or forced to fill in holes with special effects (as they are with analog technology). They can, for example, move and superimpose frames, change groups of people, add plush settings and baby photos at the push of a button. Within a few years, all videographers will utilize digital equipment. If yours does, it's an added plus. Ask prospective videographers about it, because they should be up-to-date with the latest trends.

This technology also enables videotape to be put on disc, either CD Rom or even the new DVD (Digital Video Disc). DVD is the wave of the future. Each disc holds four hours of video and the resolution is twice as high as that of a regular VHS tape. The quality is superb!

Although no one knows for sure the shelf life of videotape, they do know that discs are timeless. It's advisable to have your video put on disc. That way it's safeguarded. If your videographer isn't able to make the transfer, ask him to refer you to someone who can.

To Save Money

1. If you're on a tight budget, avoid *love stories* and highlights tapes and the recap. (Love stories are special videos, done before the wedding, that tell the tale of the bride and groom's meeting, relationship, engagement, etc.) Highlights tapes, although I feel they're essential, cost extra money. You can always have them made at a later date, when you have extra income. Recaps require a lot of editing time, and cost more!

2. Have two videographers for the ceremony, one for the reception (insist he bring a color monitor).

3. Cut baby and honeymoon photos, special music, and special effects. It cuts editing time—and time is money.

4. Many videographers will discount if your wedding is on an off-day or during an off-season—a Friday or a weekday during the spring or fall, for example.

Precautionary Measures

1. Ask the videographer if the work you're previewing is their own. *This is a must.*

2. Make sure you interview the main videographer who will shoot your wedding.

3. It is essential that a videographer shoot your entire wedding ceremony, and it's best that he or she be at your reception from beginning to end, but that depends upon your budget and the package you reserve.

4. Once the videographer is booked, it's essential to have a prewedding conference. The style, format, and emphasis that you want should be put in writing. The names of family members should also be included. (Don't forget, a videographer may shoot many weddings per month. If everything is on paper, it eliminates confusion.)

5. *Don't shop price! Shop quality!* In order to see what's available and to educate yourself, *shop all price ranges.* Find out what makes one videographer different from another. *Then make an educated decision.*

The Contract

1. List the name(s) of the videographer shooting your wedding.

2. List the coverage that's included. (Ceremony and reception, for example.)

3. List the date, time, and place of the affair. Note the time period that the videographer is to attend (for example, two hours before the ceremony until the exit of the bride and groom).

4. Note that the videographers are to bring color monitors and full back-up equipment, which they must carry with them. *They must not leave it in their car.*

5. Include the specifics of the package (for example, the number of tapes it's to include and when to expect delivery).

6. Be specific about the *style* of the videographer and where you want the emphasis (based upon your input and their advice).

7. List the price, the cancellation policy, the deposit amount paid, when the balance is due, and acceptable form of payment. (All deposits should be transferable if the wedding is canceled within a reasonable time before the date of the affair. All deposits should be refundable if another wedding [of the same value] is booked in its place.)

Beware — the Copyright and Reproduction

Your videographer owns the rights to your video and he is protected by the copyright laws of the United States. He is the only one who may legally reproduce it. If you do, you will be acting illegally. But even more important, *you will be sacrificing the quality of the tape.* A videographer makes duplications from a *master tape (or disc), using super VHS or higher quality video.* That's why additional tapes (obtained from the videographer) are always sharp and clear. Copies, however, made from copies, leave much to be desired.

About WEVA International

WEVA International is a wonderful nonprofit organization of professional videographers worldwide. And its services are available to the consumer (namely, brides). If you need a referral for a videographer, no matter where you live, just call WEVA International for assistance. Or, if you'd like to know more about videography, call them for information. (For information on how to contact WEVA International, see appendix I.)

And Finally: To Video or Not to Video? That Is the Question

Recently, I attended a wedding that began in a most unusual fashion. The bride and groom had each been escorted up the aisle by their parents and stood tentatively in front of the officiant. He looked down upon them warmly, greeted their guests, and said that he knew how anxious the couple was and how fast the day was progressing. He added that after it was over, they would wonder how a day could pass so quickly. Their wedding would be nothing more than a wonderful, loving blur in their memories.

But lo and behold! he continued, to save the day, they had a video! For years and years, they would be able to view their tape over and over again, to relive their joy and happiness, and the joy and happiness of their families. Imagine the wonder on their children's faces when they first view it! And think what it will mean to their families generations from now. To video or not to video? *Don't think twice!*

Chapter Thirteen

FLOWERS AND DECORATIONS

(A Bite-the-Bullet Chapter)

Oh, my Luve's like a red, red rose
That's newly sprung in June;

—Robert Burns, "A Red, Red Rose"

Part I: Flowers

FLOWERS, PHOTOS, AND MEMORIES

Why all the hoopla about flowers? The trend, it seems, is for brides and their maids to carry silk bouquets. Or for the bride to carry fresh flowers while her bridesmaids carry a single rose or bloom. It's obviously best to spend as little as possible on flowers and to put your money elsewhere, right? *Wrong!* Fresh flowers and weddings are tradition. Just like a bride, they have a beauty all their own. Besides, they are cheerful and genuine and fragrant. *Your wedding is the one time in your life when you should carry fresh flowers.*

Many brides think that silk flowers are less expensive than fresh but that's not the case. Good quality silks, the kind that look real, cost about three times more than their fresh counterparts. *To save money, use fresh flowers!*

Flowers make weddings special, but just as important, they make wedding day photos elegant, memorable, and outstanding. Today, when I look at the picture of my mother-in-law's bridal party, I am awed by the flowers, their abundance, and their design. I've often wondered if I would take a second look at that picture if the flowers had taken a back seat, if the bride carried a small cascade and the bridesmaids a single rose? I doubt it.

In my old bridal books, photos of weddings and their glorious flowers abound. In Emily Post's *Weddings* (written in an age when an entire formal wedding cost a total $4,000), the flowers are breathtaking. They cascade from staircases and drop in rich, heavy swags from candelabra. In fact, the flowers in the rooms pictured seem to grow in magic gardens—more fantasy than reality—just like the type you see in movies like *Father of the Bride*. Today, the flowers in Emily's book would cost much more than the $4,000 she budgeted for an entire wedding. Today, *flowers are expensive.*

Your photos provide the only tangible memories you'll have of your wedding day. To make those pictures unforgettable, enhance them with an abundance of fresh flowers, which will make them stunning and memorable. For that reason, don't discount their value. Shop wisely and well and give your flowers all the time and attention they deserve.

REFERRALS ONLY!

Ask recently married friends, relatives, and business associates for the names of reliable florists (in all price ranges) who they used successfully. Shop only at places that have been referred to you.

SAVE MONEY WHILE OBTAINING *THE LOOK*

The Look is defined as creating the *illusion* of having an abundance of elegantly styled fresh flowers that look like they cost thousands of dollars. To achieve *The Look*, you will invest the majority of your flower dollars in your bridal party flowers and in a couple of fresh-flower bouquets for the ceremony. The rest you'll improvise; I'll teach you how (later in this chapter).

Bridal party flowers have clout; they're the ones that will be featured, *forever*, in your wedding photos. These pictures—the ones taken before, during, and after the ceremony—are the ones that will dominate your wedding albums. *They are your memories*. Make your flowers something you can be proud of and something your children will look back on with pride.

SAVE MORE MONEY: KEEP THE BRIDAL PARTY SMALL

In the chapter, "The Double Budget and Tips for Successful Shopping and Saving Money," I advise keeping the bridal party small to keep your budget and your stress levels in line. To have the bridal party flowers of your dreams, it's essential. Don't delude yourself into thinking a single bloom is *elegant* when everyone knows (yourself included) that you chose a single-flower bouquet due to budget restrictions. (If you decide to use a single flower, however, see "About Bridesmaids' Bouquets," this chapter.)

WARNING: DO-IT-YOURSELF FLOWERS? NEVER

Don't attempt to do your own bridal party flowers. Flowers are extremely perishable, require preservatives to stay and look their best, and need to be stored in water, in a cold place, normally a cooler. Proper floral design also requires professional florists' supplies and a florist who exhibits talent, training, and years of experience. Flowers also take up a lot of space (they are purchased in bunches) and are dirty to work with.

Flowers may look easy to style, but even that fresh, just-cut-from-the-garden look that so many brides ask for requires talent, experience, and expertise to create. *To keep your stress levels low and to make your wedding as beautiful and as elegant as possible, leave the bridal party flowers to the professionals.*

BEFORE YOU SHOP—HOW ARE FLOWERS PRICED?

Flowers are priced based upon their type, their size, and their quantity. For example, a bouquet of twenty Teneke roses (a large, premium variety) with greens and baby's breath will cost much more than a bouquet of twenty bridal-white roses (a small, inexpensive variety) with greens and baby's breath. In the same vein, a bouquet of ten Catalaya orchids will cost much more than a bouquet of twenty Teneke roses.

To save money: Stay away from orchids, lilies, stephanotis, and gardenias. The cost is prohibitive.

Floral costs are also contingent upon the florist's *name.* Just like people who spend exorbitant money for products labeled Gucci, a florist with a name will also command a higher price. His overhead may also demand that he charge more. That's why it's critical to be a savvy shopper. *You should be able to find the flowers you want in the design you want at a price you can afford.*

BUDGETING FOR FLOWERS

WHAT YOU NEED FOR THE BRIDAL PARTY

a. Bride's bouquet and toss-away bouquet (if desired)
b. Bridemaids' bouquets (including flower girl[s])
c. Groomsmen's boutonnieres (including ring bearer)
d. Corsages for mothers and grandmothers (and stepparents)
e. Boutonnieres for fathers and grandfathers (and stepparents)
f. Boutonnieres and/or corsages for clergy and vocalist(s) or organist (provided they're not paid participants)

g. Boutonnieres and/or corsages for wedding helpers (i.e. the person who minds the guest book or hands out the wedding programs)
h. Boutonnieres and/or corsages for immediate family members who are not wedding participants (this is a matter of budget and choice)

FOR THE CEREMONY SITE

a. One or two fresh-flower arrangements— one to be placed on the altar or one for either side of the altar
b. A bouquet for the Virgin Mary (for Catholic ceremonies)

The Bride's Flowers: What You Must Know Before You Shop!

Even a Daisy Can Be Formal—If It's Styled Formally

All fresh flowers are uniquely beautiful, even daisies. Many brides tell me of their frustration with florists: "He says I have to use lilies for my bouquet or it won't be formal enough," or, "I love daisies, why can't I have them for my bouquet?" You can, provided that you educate yourself with the basic rules of good floral design and relate those rules to you and your gown. After you do, you must shop with diligence to find the right florist who will implement your ideas.

Your Wedding Gown

If your gown's bodice is its focal point, carry a *cascade*, a bouquet that drops downward, or a *colonial* (round) bouquet. If the skirt is the gown's focal point, carry a *presentation* bouquet, a spray of flowers that's held in the crook of the arm, or a colonial bouquet.

Note: Although Calla lilies are expensive, they are so large that a few of them will make for an impressive, cost-effective bridal bouquet.

The Bouquet and Your Size

• *If you're small, your bouquet should be, too.* It should never overpower you. I once handled the wedding of a petite bride who had a magnificent Yumi Katsura gown. She told me of her desire to carry a huge, magnificent cascade, one that fell from her waist to the hem of her skirt. I dissuaded her. Why would you want the flowers to hide that magnificent dress? Why would you want the bouquet to dwarf you? She ended up with a nosegay of full-blown Osiana

roses. It was the perfect complement to her size and her gown.

• *If you're large, you should have a large bouquet.* I once consulted for a bride who was a size 24. When Tim, my partner in our floral business, saw her, his immediate response was, "I'm going to make the bouquet so large it will hide her body." And that's exactly what he did. She later told me that people, looking at her photos, thought she had lost twenty pounds for her wedding. The flowers transformed her. The oversize cascade hid her waistline and was in proportion to the full, billowing skirt of her very large traditional gown. I've never seen a happier bride.

The Key to Success: The flowers must be in proportion to your size and the style of your gown. If the florist does not ask to see a picture of your gown, or a color swatch, or if they don't discuss the style of your dress and the design of your bouquet in relation to your size, it is wise to shop for another florist.

And Color

A bridal bouquet should *not* be a focal point. Did you ever look at a photo of a bride, dressed totally in white, holding a bright red bouquet? What is your eye drawn to? The bouquet. It shouldn't be. For that reason, it's best to go with white flowers or pastels. White flowers are not pure white. You may, for example, look at a white rose and think: Why, that rose looks a little green (or pink or yellow). A white rose exhibits many different *shades* of color.

Flowers also have different textures. The petals of a white rose, for example, are smooth; a white Fuji mum, on the other hand, is feathery; and baby's breath resembles small tufts of cotton. Put all of these diverse shades and textures together and you can imagine how engaging a white bouquet can be!

FLOWER COLOR AND THE GLITZ FACTOR

If your gown is ornate, it's best to go with a white bouquet. Even pastel flowers can be overpowering if the dress is glitzy. When in doubt, go white.

If the dress is characterized by simple elegance, you may use white or pastel blooms. And if you have to have those hot, jewel tones in your flowers, this is the gown for it!

ABOUT BRIDESMAIDS' BOUQUETS

- Pick a bouquet that complements the style of the dress. (Follow the tips under "Your Wedding Gown.")
- Choose floral colors that complement the dress color. When in doubt go white or use a multicolored bouquet.
- If you must use a single flower (due to budget restrictions), make sure that flower has substance, i.e. that it's surrounded by ribbons, lace, or has a pearl drop (a string of faux-pearls that attaches to the flower and drops to the hemline of the skirt).

HOW TO SHOP TO SAVE DOLLARS — OR OBTAINING THE LOOK FOR LESS!

STEP 1: DON'T SHOP PRICE

Let's leave the budget behind us for a moment. The most expensive florists are usually found in the most exclusive parts of town—in upscale neighborhoods where the overhead is high. Most times, these shops feature terrific, innovative designers and carry flowers in all varieties, from the typical to the unique. Don't let their name or their prices scare you! Take advantage of their expertise; learn by what they have to offer. (I'm not saying that a less pricey shop has less to offer. What I am saying is: Shop *all* your options.)

Visit these shops to see great design, to hear about what's new in weddings, to view many different types of flowers. Make an appointment and discuss your wedding with the florist. Be honest with them. Tell them you're only interested in bridal party flowers and a couple of bouquets for the ceremony site (more about that later). And you're not interested in expensive varieties of flowers: lilies, orchids, stephanotis, or gardenias. The florist will show you different combinations of flower types and colors. They will also explain their design ideas for your wedding. Pick their brains. Ask lots of questions. Take notes. *Be appreciative of their efforts*. Get an estimate of the cost, in writing. (It might take the florist a few days or more to get an estimate to you. Be patient.)

STEP 2: THE WEDDING DAY VISIT

In order to choose the proper florist, it's essential that you visit them on a day they're preparing for a wedding. Examine their work closely. Here's what to look for:

- *Bouquets should contain many flowers.* When you look at a bouquet, you should see the flowers first, not the greens.
- *Bouquets should have dimension.* They

should not be flat. When you evaluate a bouquet, look at it from the side. Make sure it's rounded and has an interesting shape. The flowers should look like they're "popping" artistically from the bouquet.

- *The flowers must be fresh.* Look closely at the flowers to ensure that they don't have brown or yellow edges or aren't wilted.

- *The design should be interesting and pleasing to the eye.*

- *Boutonnieres and corsages must be fresh and pleasing in their design.*

Step 3: Visit Midscale Shops

After visiting a few upscale shops, visit a few that are less so. Once again, discuss ideas and take notes. Make sure that you visit the shops on days they're preparing for a wedding.

Step 4: Make an Analysis

After visiting a few florists and seeing their work, it's time to evaluate what you've seen and to study your estimates. Maybe a florist at a less exclusive shop is just as talented as the one at his more expensive counterpart's. Or maybe the cost between the more expensive shop and the less expensive shop is negligible (and the expensive shop offers so much more). Or maybe one florist can implement the ideas of another for less. Or maybe one shop is willing to go overboard for you.

Warning: Don't trust a florist who says he can beat the estimate of another, *unless he's willing to put all details in writing.* Let me give you an example. Florist A says he will make you a rose cascade for much less than Florist B. But Florist A doesn't disclose that he's using a dozen bridal whites instead of the twenty Tenekes that Florist B is using. *Of course he can do it for less!* And rightfully so. *You are not saving money by reserving Florist A.* Make sure the *same number* and the same varieties of flowers are used in the bouquets, etc. *Compare apples to apples* before making any decisions. *Get it in writing.*

Part II: Decorations

Do-It-Yourself Decorating? Now That's a Different Story!

There's no reason why you can't plan your own decorating and have your family and friends implement it, if they're willing and able. *It's unadvisable for the bride and groom to do any decorating the day before the wedding or on the wedding day.* You may prepare the decorations in advance, but leave the actual decorating to family and friends. It's the bride and groom's job to relax and rest for the wedding and reception—nothing more.

An Important Word About Decorating

This chapter is divided into sections based on where your ceremony will take place. Because there are so many different ideas under each subheading (that may be adapted to your ceremony, no matter what your religion), it's best to read Part II in its entirety. Use your imagination! Mix and match the parts of this chapter to make your wedding dreams come true!

A Word About Mirrors, Votive Candles, Rental Trees, and More

In the next part of this chapter, I frequently mention the use of mirrors, candles, candelabra, rental trees, and more. Nothing spruces up or transforms a room like inexpensive rental trees (available through most florists). Most are trimmed with small white twinkle lights and can turn a drab room into a wonderland. (For a morning or an afternoon wedding in a *naturally lit room*, omit the lights.)

Even a mundane centerpiece can look more formal and elegant by placing it on a round or square mirror (depending on the shape of your tables). If your caterer or catering facility doesn't provide them, they are available through party-rental stores.

And ah, candlelight. What's more romantic? What can make a room look more ethereal? Nothing I know of. Many caterers and catering facilities offer votive candles (stubby candles that are held in small, round glass containers) to their brides. If not, they are available through party rental stores.

Warning: If you rent mirrors, candelabra, candles, etc. from party rental stores, make sure you make arrangements for a friend or family member to retrieve them for you from the reception site and return them to the store.

Discuss your "rentals" with your caterer or person in charge. Tell them when they'll be delivered, who will be delivering them, and when they'll be picked up the next day. (Your florist will handle the delivery and pickup of the rental trees.)

Aisle Runners

Centuries ago, aisle runners were used so that the bride's feet would not touch the ground where evil spirits lurked. The tradition has survived the centuries, although we use aisle runners today out of respect for the bride and to achieve a more elegant effect at the ceremony.

Many churches restrict the use of aisle runners; people can easily trip over them. Be sure to check with clergy before you reserve one (most times, they're available through your florist, or they may be purchased at your craft or party supply store). Cloth runners are expensive, so most florists use the paper variety.

Flowers and Decorations for the Ceremony Site

I. The Church Ceremony

Most churches permit altar flowers, but little more. In Protestant ceremonies, a bouquet may be placed directly on the altar. In Catholic ceremonies, they're placed on either side of the altar (meaning you'll need two arrangements). These may be taken to the reception afterward, *depending on the policy of the church.*

Most churches are strict and limit decorating. (Please check with clergy before making any decorating decisions and before visiting with your florist.) I once had an experience with an Episcopal priest who wouldn't let me place flowers anywhere near the altar (even though the bride had supposedly cleared it with him beforehand). His comment, "This is a church, not a flower shop!"

Most churches do permit bows on the pews, provided they're put on with pew clips (a plastic gizmo that slips over the pew and secures the bow). Ask your church or your florist for pew clips. *Never use tape of any kind.*

Many churches also provide candelabra, which come in many different shapes and sizes. They are a wonderful way to decorate inexpensively and provide beauty, romance, and elegance. They can make a dull room come to life. The big, multistemmed variety that hold many candles are usually placed on either side of the altar.

Candelabra may be used in place of altar flowers and are an elegant, economical substitute. The single variety, which holds only one candle, may be placed strategically down both sides of the aisle and lit by the ushers before the bridal party begins the processional. They create an impressive aisle for the bride and her party.

To further enhance their look, make white-satin or ivory bows with long streamers. (Make the bows in the color of your bridal party, *if the color doesn't clash with the decor of the church.* When in doubt, go white or ivory.) Attach the bows to the candelabra with pipe cleaners and let the streamers puddle on the floor. It's an added touch that makes the candelabra more festive, elegant, and bridal. If your church doesn't have candelabra and permits their use (with professional, nondrip candles), they are available at party rental stores.

II. Decorating at Temples

Synagogues are much more liberal when it comes to decorating, and so it becomes a matter of budget. *What can I afford to do?* There's also the matter of the chuppa. If you're Jewish, you can't get married without one.

The Chuppa

Many synagogues provide chuppot (be sure to ask clergy). They may not look like much, but they can be decorated. An elegant look can be created economically by draping swags of inexpensive tulle (in white or ivory) around the top. Secure the tulle to the chuppa with long pipe cleaners. Next, form billows of tulle and place them down the poles, once again securing with pipe cleaners. Make about sixteen large bows (ahead of time) and place at the top corners of the chuppa and in the places (on the poles) where the pipe cleaners secure the billows of tulle. (You may also use inexpensive polyester satin, found at fabric outlet stores. Ask for a better price if you buy by the bolt. The same when purchasing tulle.)

You may hire your florist to decorate the chuppa, or your friends or family may decorate it the night before or the day of the wedding, depending on the temple's schedule. (And whatever you do, be sure to practice beforehand.)

Many people also decide to use handheld chuppot. This entails four friends or family members, who each hold one of the four chuppa poles. Over the top, there's usually draped a *tallis* (Jewish prayer shawl). This is traditional, correct, and inexpensive.

We've also devised our own chuppa by renting two arches from a party rental store, putting them about six feet apart, one in front of the other, and then draping the top in tulle and placing swags of tulle along the sides at the top. We then formed billows of tulle, draped them down the sides, and secured them with pipe cleaners. (Once again, you may also use inexpensive polyester satin.)

Or Why Not Make One?

It's easy to make a chuppa (even if you don't sew) and just think: You'll be creating an heirloom! Using pinking shears, which prevents the fabric from fraying, and at the same time, makes a decorative edge, and glue, you can make your own. Our chuppa is about eight-by-eight feet, allowing enough room for all who need to, to stand inside. You may, however, cut it to the size you prefer. Make adjustments accordingly.

The cloth you use for your chuppa may be anything your heart desires. Visit the fabric stores and select cloth that matches your bridal party colors (but make sure they don't clash with the colors of the temple), or use white or ivory fabric (always a safe bet). Or hand paint one with watercolor pens using Biblical scripture related to marriage. Or cut Hebrew symbols from multicolored pieces of felt and paste them on. Have friends and family help you. (What a great idea for a shower!) The choice is yours.

Note: The underside and outside of the flaps will be visible during the ceremony, not the top. Concentrate your efforts on the flaps.

Step 1: Making the top: For an eight-by-eight foot chuppa, buy nine yards of fabric (forty-eight or fifty-four inches wide). The fabric will be folded in the middle. On the floor, lay it out length-wise and, with your pinking shears, cut a piece that's eight feet long. Then cut another eight-foot long piece. Unfold both pieces of fabric and put the two pieces together to form a piece that's eight-by-eight feet. Sew or glue the two pieces together. (Use Beacon's Fabri Tac, available at fabric and craft stores.)

Step 2: Making the flaps: Take the remaining fabric and, using your pinking shears, cut another piece eight feet long and unfold. (You will now have a piece of fabric that's eight feet long by either forty-eight or fifty-four inches wide.) Cut the piece of fabric into four pieces, length-wise (twelve inches wide × eight feet long). You now have four flaps. Attach each flap to each side of the chuppa top (if you don't sew, glue them).

Step 3: Cut four small holes in the top piece, one at the end of each corner. Dab the holes with glue so that the fabric won't rip or fray. Allow to dry.

Step 4: Buy five-foot-long wooden dowel rods at a builder's outlet and paint them the color of your choice. At the top of each pole, hammer in a decorative nail (with a large head) about one-half inch from the top of the pole. The holes you cut in the top of the chuppa should slide easily over the tops of the nails. Voila! You've got a fabulous chuppa, one your children and grandchildren will treasure. (For more information, get my video, *The Chuppa: Creating an Heirloom.* See appendix I.)

Make It Part of the Ceremony

Since we don't have much to spend on decorations, let's go for drama! Why not have the chuppa carried into the ceremony as part of the processional? Imagine four of your closest family and friends making their way up the aisle, holding the chuppa aloft, slowly ascending the stairs to the bimah (the platform found at the end of the sanctuary), as they reverently take their place awaiting the bridal party and the ceremony to begin. Talk about impressive!

The Bimah

The *bimah* is where the ceremony takes place and is the focal point of the sanctuary, much the same way that a stage is the focal point of a theater. It's important, therefore, that it look impressive. The best way to achieve *The Look* is with inexpensive rental trees (decorated with tiny white lights). They work miracles and can turn any room into a fantasy. Have the florist put a row of trees along the back wall. The trees will frame the chuppa. On either side of the chuppa, have the florist place a huge arrangement of full-blown gladioli (in the color(s) of your choice) and greens. They are inexpensive and dramatic. Or rent two large candelabra and place one on either side of the chuppa. Or do both.

Along the Aisle

Go to the party rental store and rent single candelabra that will be placed strategically along the aisle, from the first row of seats to the last. Position them across from one another. Six to eight should do the trick (less perhaps, if the aisle is short).

Ahead of time, make bows for the candelabra in the color of your bridal party or chuppa (unless it clashes with temple decor.

When in doubt go with white or ivory). Attach long pipe cleaners to the bows, which will allow them to be easily attached to the candelabra.

The Ultimate Look

To achieve the ultimate look of elegance, swag tulle from one candelabra to the next, the entire length of the aisle. Attach the tulle to the candelabra with pipe cleaners. Next, put down an aisle runner (available at craft shops). With pins, pin the runner to the carpet at the beginning of the aisle (closest to the bimah). Tape down the end of the runner (over the pins) with heavy, white fabric tape. This will secure it. Now extend the runner down the aisle. When you reach the end (don't extend it past the last row of seats), cut it and tape it down (pins aren't necessary) with double-sided tape. The aisle runner should end where the first set of candelabra begin.

The next step is to block off the aisle with tulle. Cut a swag of tulle and string it across the aisle. Attach it to the first set of candelabra with pipe cleaners. When guests enter, they behold a magnificent aisle ready for the bride's walk, and a bimah filled with rental trees glistening in white light and floral arrangements filled full of gladioli or flaming candelabra. (The ushers who greet the guests seat them from the sides of the aisle.) Directly before the processional begins, the tulle drape is removed. Two ushers with lit tapers, in succession and starting at the top of the aisle, light the candelabra. Once they're lit, they take their place with the other groomsmen and the processional begins.

III. Ceremonies Held at Catering Halls, Hotels, etc.

No matter what your religion, if the ceremony is not conducted in a sanctuary, you can probably decorate to your heart's content, *provided you have the time.* Check with the person in charge to find out if there are time or decorating restrictions.

If the room is dull, use lots of those inexpensive rental trees with their sparkling white lights. For a morning or afternoon wedding in a naturally lit room, omit the lights.

In a non-Jewish wedding, you might consider an arch (also available from party rental stores). Along the back wall (if necessary) place the rental trees. Decorate the arch with swags of tulle and bows. On either side, place candelabra. Have your florist make oversize arrangements of full-blown gladioli, or use both.

Along the Aisle

Rent stanchions from a party rental store (six to eight should suffice, depending on the length of the aisle). Place them strategically along the aisle on both sides, from the first row of seats to the last. Drape swags of tulle from one to the other and secure with heavy, white fabric tape. Next, add a bow (tape to the top of the stanchion) and let the streamers puddle elegantly on the floor.

On top of the stanchions place potted plants or luxuriant ferns or ivy plants that have been placed in foil hats. (These are available from florists' supply stores. Check the Yellow Pages.) These hats are not shiny, come in many colors, and are inexpensive. While at the florists' supply store, buy a can of *leaf shine.* This stuff works miracles. Just spray it on. No matter how dirty the plant, the grit will disappear and the greens will glow! For the ultimate look, lay and secure an aisle runner, rope off the aisle and seat guests from the side.

After the Ceremony

If your ceremony and reception are in the same location, you may have the flowers, decorations, and the rental trees moved from the ceremony room to the reception room (during the cocktail hour). Make arrangements with the catering director, the person in charge, or your florist. *Put it in your contract(s).*

The Reception

I. The Cocktail Hour

Don't spend a lot of money on decorations for the cocktail hour. The caterer or catering facility should be able to provide you with little lanterns, votive candles, or mirrors to place on the tables. Be sure to ask the person in charge. (*Note:* There should be limited seating at the cocktail hour, only a few tables and chairs for the elderly. The idea is to mingle and get acquainted.)

II. Centerpieces

Centerpieces are essential if an elegant wedding is your goal. They make the guests' tables special and provide ambiance. The best way to achieve *The Look* economically is with non-floral centerpieces. *No one said that centerpieces have to contain flowers.* You can achieve elegance without them and still make a statement!

Sample 1: Candelabra, mirror, votive candles, and matching napkin stuffers.

*Sample 2: Gold or silver fruit, mirror, votive candles, table runner,
and matching napkin stuffers.*

Here Are a Few Ideas

1. *Candles and Mirrors:* Nothing is more elegant and romantic than candlelight reflecting on a mirror. Go to an outlet or craft store and buy single candle holders (allow three or four per table).

Note: Candle holders may be spray painted in the color of your choice. Next, buy tall candles in varying heights, for example, twenty-four, twenty-eight, thirty, or thirty-six inch.

Put a mirror on each table (either round or square). Place the three (or four) candle holders on the mirror, close to the center. Put the candles in the holders. Next, place three (or four) votive candles around the tall candles (on the outskirts of the mirror). And if you'd like, scatter a few glass "pebbles" (found at craft or floral supply stores) on the mirror.

Warning: Any time you are using tall candles in holders, it's essential to buy candle "putty" at craft stores. It fills the gaps between the holder and the candle and keeps them erect.

Before the guests enter, the catering director or maître d' will light the candles. You've just created a magnificent centerpiece for little money and turned the room into a romantic, candlelit wonderland!

2. *Candelabra and Mirrors* (sample 1). Party rental stores rent candelabra (normally silver-plate). Place a mirror on each guest table. Put the candelabra on top of each mirror. Place tapers in the candelabra. Put three votive candles on each mirror at the base of the candelabra. String some silk greens through the prongs of the candelabra to give it a more elegant look.

3. *Bowls, Gold or Silver Fruit and Mirrors* (sample 2). In the fall, nothing makes for a more elegant centerpiece than fruit. Rent silver-plate or crystal bowls from a party rental store. Fill each bowl two-thirds full with newspaper (crystal bowls with gold or silver foil). Place fresh fruit (grapes, apples, and pears) in a shallow box. Make sure the fruit is room temperature. Spray with gold or silver paint (found at craft stores). Wait until dry.

Mound the fruit decoratively in the bowls. Add a few large green silk leaves if you'd like. (The centerpieces may be made a couple of days in advance and kept in a cool room. They should be finished before transporting to the reception.) When you arrive at the reception, place each bowl on a mirror that's been placed on each table. Put three votive candles on each mirror. The candles will be lit before the guests enter. (For a morning or afternoon wedding in a naturally lit room, omit the candles.)

4. *Floral Centerpieces and Mirrors.* For afternoon weddings, there's nothing prettier than a potted flower that sits in a wicker basket (or a foil hat) placed on a mirror. Call your garden outlet store and reserve the flowers that you'll need. There are many different types of flowers available, even Gerbera daisies. Buy wicker baskets from a garden or craft store. You may select different types or all one type. Spray them the color you'd like (the color should complement the decor of the reception room).

Retrieve the flowers from the garden outlet a day or two before the wedding. Keep them in a cool room. If need be, stuff the baskets with newspapers to provide a base for the plants. Place the flowers in the baskets and take them to the reception. Once again, place each centerpiece on a mirror (available through party rental stores). If you'd prefer, place some silk green leaves around the mirror to provide a warmer ambiance.

The Ultimate Look: Table Runners and Napkin Stuffers

Let's say that your reception room is dull beige. The caterer only has white tablecloths. It's fall, so you've decided to rent crystal bowls and fill them with fresh fruit (sprayed gold) and place them on mirrors surrounded by votive candles (sample 2).

To brighten the table and make it more elegant and festive you add a gold lace runner that extends down the center of the table and drapes over the sides. To top off the look, you add matching gold lace napkin stuffers. *Wow!* What you've just done to the look of your table and your room!

To Make Table Runners

For a six-foot round table, cut a piece of fabric nine feet by fourteen inches with pinking shears. Angle the ends. It's finished! (See sample 2.)

Note: To adjust for table size, measure the length of the table and add on three feet. If the table was eight feet long (or wide), for example, the runner would be eleven feet by fourteen inches. (The ends should drape over the table, at least fifteen inches on each side.)

To Make the Ends Decorative

A. *The Tassel* (*sample 2*). (You'll need two tassels per runner.)
  1. Buy fringe from a fabric outlet (found in the trim section; it's sold by the yard) in the color of your choice.
  2. Cut a six-inch piece. Roll it up (from the top); it will resemble a tassel. Glue or sew the top to secure.
  3. Glue the "tassel" onto the pointed end of the angled runner, on the wrong side of the runner.

B. *The Rolled Rose.* (You'll need two roses per runner.)
  1. Cut a piece of lightweight fabric twelve inches by four inches in the color of your choice.
  2. Starting at the long end, simply roll the fabric to the other end. It will resemble a rosebud. Glue, staple, or sew the end to secure.
  3. Glue or sew the "rose" onto the angled tip of the runner (on the wrong side of the runner). Glue a few silk leaves (white or green) around the rose. What a look!

Matching Napkin Stuffers (samples 1 and 2)

For an added touch, I've made napkin stuffers that may either pick up the bridal party colors or the colors of the room's decor. In sample 2, the napkin stuffers are made from the same fabric as the table runners.

To Make

1. Buy fabric, either forty-eight or fifty-four inches wide, that looks almost as good on the *right* side as it does on the *wrong* side, in the color of your choice. (Each yard of fabric will make six napkins.)
2. Using a regular napkin (approximately 15.5 inches × 15.5 inches) as a prototype, lay it on the fabric, draw around it with a marking pencil, and, with your pinking shears, cut out as many as you need. They're finished!
3. Give them to your catering director or caterer, who will stuff them in the glasses or arrange them on the tables, *folded with their regular napkins*. (In sample 2, I used regular white napkins folded with napkin stuffers to give a two-toned look.) Or, you may use the stuffers as your napkins.

Note: A day or so before the wedding, have the table runners and the napkins delivered to the reception site. *Make sure they're personally given to the person in charge.* You don't want them to be misplaced.

When the caterer sets the table, he or she will place one runner down the center, over the tablecloth(s). He or she will then take the napkin stuffers and fan them in the water glasses or fold them (with or without their own napkins) and place them on the tables. The tables are then set as usual and the centerpieces added. Just imagine the look you've created (sample 2). Super elegant tables, magnificent centerpieces, and an ambiance that your guests will not soon forget. (For more information, get my video, *Tempting Tables: Yours for the Making.* See appendix I.)

OTHER CENTERPIECE IDEAS

1. *Ferns and/or Ivy, Mirrors, and Candles.* These plants make beautiful centerpieces. Buy them from a garden outlet store and place them in foil hats in the color you prefer. Before going to the reception site, spray the plants with leaf shine (available at garden stores and outlets or florists' supply stores). Once you arrive, put mirrors on the tables and the plants on the mirrors. Surround the plants with votive candles.
2. *For Christmastime Receptions.* Let your imagination run wild. Visit Christmas stores and discount department stores and buy what you need *after Christmas*, when everything is half-price or better! Perhaps you can make centerpieces by gluing together large plastic snowflakes of varying sizes. Perhaps you can buy Santa Clauses (about ten to twelve inches high) or sleighs or reindeer or a combination of different items, if they don't have enough of one type.

   All of these pieces can be sprayed lightly with glue (it comes in cans, available at your craft store), and sprinkled with glitter (in the color of your choice). Imagine Santa Clauses or reindeer or snowflakes or sleighs placed on mirrors, surrounded by votive candles, glittering their warmth and hospitality to your guests! (For an added extra, sprinkle some glitter on the mirrors.)
3. *Christmas Flower Centerpieces.* Nothing is prettier than a poinsettia on the table, and it doesn't have to be red. Poinsettias come in white, pink, and even in a hybrid—pink and white. Place each in a foil hat. Place on a mirror and surround with votive candles (available through party rental stores).

Note: Reserve your poinsettias early (through your garden outlet store). In that way, you're assured of getting the best plants. For more info, please get my video *Show-stopping Centerpieces (Aren't Costly).* (See appendix I.)

TABLECLOTHS AND MORE

Nothing makes a wedding more elegant than floor-length tablecloths, and you don't have to rent them. Ask your catering director to use two tablecloths per table instead of one. That should solve the problem (even if it costs a little more).

Tablecloths and overlays are expensive to rent (if your caterer's selection of cloths don't fit the bill). If white cloths are your only option, you can coordinate the look you want by making decorative table runners and matching napkins. Make sure that the fabrics you select coordinate with the colors of your reception room.

AROUND THE ROOM

Many brides ask me what they can do about their dull—even ugly—reception rooms. Once again, those inexpensive rental trees can solve the problem. Even in daylight, they can make a room look warm and appealing.

Another alternative is tulle. I've draped inexpensive tulle from sconces on the walls and climbed up ladders and draped it from chandeliers. Combined with the rental trees, centerpieces, table runners, and napkins, tulle can make for a super elegant room, economically. And nothing can hide a room's shortcomings like an evening affair. Dim the lights, turn on the lights on the rental trees, put plenty of candles on the tables and your guests will think they're at the Ritz.

Chair Covers

If your reception room chairs are eyesores, it might be necessary to rent new ones. Chair covers are very expensive. It might be more economical to rent the chairs than the covers. Call your party rental stores and check the cost.

AND FINALLY—A WORD ABOUT VULGARITY

Decorating is meant to enhance the beauty of your wedding. It should be as subtle, elegant, and tasteful as possible. I think this chapter demonstrates that you can achieve elegance and beauty with very little money (*no matter how much you have to spend*). All you need is some ingenuity and a lot of common sense.

Chapter Fourteen

THE HONEYMOON

Yes, this is Love, the steadfast and the true,
The immortal glory which has never set;
The best, the brightest boon the heart e'er knew:
Of all life's sweets the very sweetest yet!
—Charles Swain, "I Will Tell Thee What It Is to Love"

Part I: Preliminary Information

A MEETING OF THE MINDS

Before you begin, decide *together* where you want to go, no surprises! A honeymoon is a once-in-a-lifetime event. Both of you must be comfortable and happy. A honeymoon, and its destination, must be a mutual decision.

GO TO A HONEYMOON SPECIALIST

Contact a travel agent who specializes in honeymoons. They are your best source of accurate information. They should thoroughly interview you to determine your goals and expectations (while you are interviewing them). They should also give you many options based upon your budget. Ask for referrals of their most recent honeymoon clients. *Call these couples* and ask if they were happy with the travel agent and the service they provided.

BE BUDGET HONEST

Be honest with your travel agent when discussing your budget. Tell them what you plan on spending. Include food, alcohol, lodging, tips, gifts . . . *the total amount.* If they know what you're working with, they can best advise you on where, when, and how to get the best value for your dollar.

It takes hours and hours to research honeymoon locations. If they look for places (in a certain price range) and then you change your budget, all that work goes down the drain. Be certain of your budget before visiting a travel agent.

Use Frequent-Flier Miles and Start Early

Many people use their frequent-flier miles to save money when planning a honeymoon, as well they should. The secret to success is to plan early—*at least a year in advance*. Any good travel agent will tell you that seats reserved for frequent-flier customers are limited. When they're gone, they're gone. Using frequent-flier miles can save you hundreds, even thousands of dollars. Plan well so that you can take advantage of their savings.

Part II: Places and the Best Time and Value

The Best, Most Cost-Effective Season

The best time to reserve a wedding date, to save dollars, is *off-season*. The same holds true for your honeymoon. Summer, in the Caribbean, for example, is off-season; winter is off-season in Europe. Hot times (to be avoided) are Christmas and holidays, when travel and lodging are expensive.

The Best Value—and the *Big* Skippable!

Marcy Forster, co-owner of *Atrium Travel* in Boca Raton, Florida says that *all-inclusive properties* are the best value. In other words, those that offer food, lodging, and activities for *one price* (airfare and liquor are extra). This includes properties like *adults-only* Club Med, Sandals, and off-season Caribbean cruises. The *big* skippable is Hawaii, which remains a top honeymoon spot. It's very expensive, no matter when you go, or how.

To me, Hawaii elicits thoughts of islands, palm trees, tall waterfalls, and majestic mountains and the ocean all rolled into one. You can get the same type of ambiance at some Caribbean islands—for a lot less money.

More Value, More Places

- *Mexico*. The Princess and Las Brisas Hotels in Acapulco are considered a good value. Airfare to Mexico is reasonable.
- *Canada*. There are lovely places to travel throughout Canada (in late spring, summer, and early fall). The country is beautiful and the cities have much to offer—many with a European flair. (Because of the devaluation of the Canadian dollar, it's a terrific value.)
- *Europe*. The rates go down in October (and go back up around Christmas). They are also low in April. The fall and spring are good months to go.
- *The California Wine Country*. Make plans well in advance. Book reservations at bed and breakfasts, visit wineries, and tour to your hearts' content.
- *The California Coast Drive* (from Los An-

geles to San Francisco). Book well in advance. Fly to L.A., then rent a car and drive. Stay at bed and breakfasts.

• *Florida*. Some Florida resorts have great honeymoon packages. The Breakers, for example, or The Ritz-Carlton on the west coast have great opportunities for honeymooners (and imagine the savings off-season).

FOR THE ADVENTUROUS

Joe Vendi, owner of Travel Is Fun in Kendall, Florida, and in business for forty years, says that the adventurous may want to try Eastern Europe, particularly the wondrous cities of Prague and Budapest. He also suggests Portugal, called one of the last great European bargains. But he advises caution. The hotels, even the premium variety, may be less than luxurious, and many things that we take for granted—like elevators—may not be in the best repair or even exist.

South America, for the enterprising, may also be an option. Chile and Argentina are wonderful and their seasons are the opposite of ours. When it's winter here, it's summer there. Check with your travel agent and research your options thoroughly. Just like Eastern Europe and Portugal, however, lodging, etc. may be less than luxurious. (For information on travel agents, see appendix I.)

Part III: Safeguards

USE CREDIT CARDS—ONLY!

Always use your credit card (especially since honeymoon reservations must be made so far in advance). If you don't have one, borrow your parents' or your grandparents'. This is the only protection you have should a vendor, airline, travel agent, etc. go under. Use them the entire time you travel.

Recently, on an investigative news program, there was a segment about travel. The focus was honeymoon couples who had given cash or checks to travel agents. In one case, the agent went under and the couple lost thousands of dollars. In the other, a tour company used by the agent went out of business. This couple, too, lost their deposit. *The couples who used their credit card, however, did not lose their money.*

GET CANCELLATION INSURANCE TO SAFEGUARD YOUR INVESTMENT

The cost is minimal and will be well worth it if anything occurs that may cancel your trip. (This insurance does not cover pre-existing medical conditions and will require a doctor's excuse if the trip is cancelled.) Most times, this insurance is offered by cruise and tour companies. Be sure to ask your travel agent. Or you may purchase your own. Don't chance losing your deposit. Buy insurance. (For more information, see appendix I.)

Beware the Honeymoon Registry

Many travel agents are establishing bridal registries for engaged couples. Friends, relatives, and business associates send money to the travel agent (in lieu of gifts), who puts it in the bank for the bride and groom's honeymoon. *Don't do it!* Never entrust any vendor with *your* money. You have no way of knowing how much was sent (especially if someone were irresponsible enough to send cash). And what happens if the agency goes out of business? If you want money for your honeymoon, pass the news through the grapevine or have a honeymoon shower (more about this later). Put it in your own account.

Travel Documents (and Money)

If traveling within the United States, travel with a valid driver's license and one other form of identification (a credit card). A passport is required when traveling outside the United States except in Canada, Mexico, and some Caribbean countries (although you will need proof of citizenship).

Tip: Make a copy of the inside cover of your passport. If it's lost or stolen, you'll have the necessary information to help authorities trace it.

Tip: Brides must have all travel reservations made in their maiden name. The name on their driver's license must match the name on their passport and airline ticket.

Tip: Travel with traveler's checks and credit cards. Don't carry much cash, which may get lost or stolen.

Part IV: The Honeymoon Shower

For those experiencing financial difficulty, or for something different from a traditional shower, ask your maid of honor to throw a honeymoon shower. The invitations will spread the word:

Ms. Susan Jones
requests the pleasure of your company
at a Honeymoon Bridal Shower
in honor of
Linda Smith
Saturday, the tenth of July
at two o'clock
15 Medford Lane
Albany, New York

R.s.v.p. by July first
Susan Jones (987) 345-9876

After receiving a honeymoon shower invitation, many will call to ask, "What is a honeymoon shower?" and, "What should I bring?" When it comes to showers, you can be a little more forward than you can when sending a wedding invitation. The maid of honor's response may be, for example, "A gift of money would be the best gift, but that's up to you. Linda and Tom are dying to go to the Caribbean. I thought it would be nice if I threw a shower to help make their dreams come true."

Part V: A Fun Alternative

For those who like to gamble and save money (how about that for a contradiction in terms?), give the Aloha Travel Auction a spin. Presented online by *The Knot* and *Honeymoon* magazine, it gives participants the chance to bid in honeymoon travel auctions at locations featuring top-notch resorts, including cruises and romantic weekend getaways from all over the world, and *for a fraction of the retail cost.* (For details, see appendix I.)

Chapter Fifteen

INVITATIONS

I'll send out one hundred fifty invitations. None of the out-of-towners will come.

—My clients

In terms of *saving money*, this is the most important chapter in this book. The reason: The number of invitations you send out will determine the number of guests who will attend your wedding and reception. *You must control your guest list to control your budget.* For that reason, *don't be careless with your invitations!*

DETERMINING THE GUEST LIST

IF YOU'RE THE HOST

Once you determine the total number of guests you can afford (see chapter 4, "The Double Budget and Tips for Successful Shopping and Saving Money") to invite, you can determine the total number of invitations you'll need. For example, you may decide to invite eighty guests. This translates into about forty invitations (remember: most people come in couples). You may choose to keep thirty invitations for yourself (sixty guests) and extend five invitations to each of your families (total: twenty

people). It's now their choice as to whom they'd like to invite. They may decide to ask distant family that you decided to skip or their friends. I think this is important: You want everyone to feel happy and comfortable at your wedding. Friends and family make that possible.

IF THE BRIDE'S FAMILY ARE HOSTS

This is a problem area so take note! Don't ask for the groom's family's list without setting parameters. If you don't, you're asking for trouble. "We only have twenty-five couples on our list, but when we got his family's, it contained one hundred fifty names. What are we going to do?" is a lament I've heard too often. The result: The bride and her family are infuriated, insulted, and face a financial crisis. This is a no-win situation and can only cause hard feelings on both sides. Yet it's such a simple situation to avoid, *before the fact*.

Once the bride's parents decide on the total number of guests they can afford, they should meet with their daughter and her fiancé. At that time, it should be decided on *how* the invitations are to be divided. If the total number of guests is one hundred, for example, the parents may decide to keep thirty invitations (about sixty people) for themselves, and give the rest to the bride and groom.

At this point, you and your fiancé may decide to keep ten invitations (about twenty people) *and extend the rest to his family*. It's now up to the future groom to call his parents. He may say, "You know, Mom and Dad, Sue's parents are hosting the wedding. The invitations have been divided among her family, Sue and me, and you. Therefore, you can invite ten couples (or twenty guests). Please send us your list once it's completed so that we can check for duplicates."

Set the ground rules! Don't ever give carte blanche. If the groom's family insist on inviting more friends or relatives, have your fiancé explain that if they do, they will be responsible for all extra costs including invitations, food, liquor, flowers, centerpieces, and all applicable taxes and gratuities. That should nip the problem in the bud.

IF BOTH FAMILIES ARE HOSTING

This is easy: Determine the total number of guests, then divide the number of invitations equally among the bride and groom and their families.

AND, USE YOUR COMMON SENSE

If the groom's family is large, for example, and the bride's family is small, the groom's family should pick up the excess cost (for the number of guests that exceeds the number the bride's family is inviting). Keep things fair!

THE BIGGEST MISTAKE THAT HOSTS MAKE

Don't send out more invitations than your budgeted number of guests; that's the biggest mistake you can make. Every day I hear from my clients, "We're sending out one hundred fifty invitations, but none of the out-of-town people will show." When I ask my clients how many people they're *actually* expecting, the usual answer is, "Oh, about one hundred to one hundred twenty-five." Don't court disaster. If 150 invitations are sent out, 300 people could *possibly* show. *Never assume that people will not attend.* Every day I hear the cries of brides who did not heed my advice. Don't be foolish with your guestlist. *Control it; don't let it control you!*

STEP 1: WHO'S INVITED?

Let's say the bride and groom are hosting the wedding. They decide to keep thirty invitations (sixty people) for themselves. They extend ten invitations to each of their families (forty people). *The total number of invited guests is one hundred.* As hosts, the bride and groom inform their families that they will issue the wedding invitations to the bridal party and both their immediate families (including first cousins). They will also include the invitation to clergy or the officiant.

STEP 2: MAKING THE LISTS

The *hosts* make three lists. They place each guest's name (with spouse or date) under the appropriate list.

On *List I*, place the names of:

- Immediate families (of the bride and groom). Include parents and grandparents, steprelatives, brothers and sisters, uncles, aunts, and first cousins with spouses or dates.
- The bridal party. Include spouses and dates and parents of the ring bearer and flower girl(s).
- Clergy or officiant (and spouse, if applicable).

Once List I is completed, the hosts count the invitations. In this example, the bride and groom count the number of people on List I and determine that they've used twenty invitations (forty people). They also know that these people are sure bets; they're a part of their wedding party and their immediate families. They will attend.

On *List II*, place the names of:

- Close family friends of the bride and groom
- Close friends of the bride and groom
- Close business associates of the bride and groom
- Close business associates of the families

The hosts make an analysis: They only have ten invitations remaining. Their parents, with their allotment of invitations, will invite their close family friends and business associates. Therefore, the bride and groom decide to invite twenty of *their* closest friends and business associates. They've now used all of their invitations. They continue with List III.

On *List III*, place the names of:

- Those who did not make List II
- Distant relatives and friends

- Casual acquaintances in the workplace or community

Note: People who don't make the guest list will receive announcements.

STEP 3: THE LISTS ARE SENT TO THE HOSTS

In this case, the families send their lists to the bride and groom, who will check for duplicates. If there's a duplicate with their list, the family who issued the invitation will be asked for another name. The hosts address the invitations and send them out. *They send out only the total allotted number of invitations* (in this case, fifty). *They assume that everyone will attend.* They wait for the responses to come back.

STEP 4: TALLYING RESPONSES

When a negative response comes back, the hosts will check the lists, find out who issued the invitation, and ask for another name. They will then send out another invitation. *Once the quota is full, no more invitations will be sent. This system controls your guest list.* It leaves nothing to chance. Once the guest list is full, the hosts will ask the families for a list of names of those people whom they would like to receive announcements.

THAT ALL-IMPORTANT RESPOND CARD

A respond card (with self-addressed, stamped envelope) is sent to each guest along with their invitation. The purpose of a respond card is to compel a guest to respond within a specific time frame.

Unfortunately, many people don't bother to respond one way or the other. This puts the hosts in an awkward position. *Do I call them?*

And if I do, *What do I say? Yes!* You call them. If they're rude enough not to respond, you can be rude enough to put them on the spot, but nicely: "Hi Sue, did you by any chance get an invitation to my wedding? I thought it might have been lost in the mail." Then wait for the response. If they decline, send out another invitation, hopefully to someone who will be more appreciative and considerate. It's perfectly appropriate for guests to receive an invitation up to two weeks before the respond date.

How Many Guests?

The respond card is also designed to inform you of how many people will be attending. This factor must also be controlled. For example, *Never, Never* ask for the number of guests on a card, or you may be surprised by the results. One of my brides had a card returned to her with the number 8 penciled in. She was dumbfounded; I had warned her.

Always use these two wonderful little words:

Accepts_____ Regrets_____

The guests *check* the appropriate response and mail back. They do not have the option of entering a number.

If you make your own invitations (more about this later), you can use your computer to print the name of the guest(s) on the card. This eliminates the opportunity for them to add more guests than you intended, for example:

> *Mr. and Mrs. Joseph Jones*
> *request the pleasure of the company of*
> *Mr. and Mrs. Michael Smith and Emily*
> *at their wedding reception*
> ____Accepts   ____Regrets

The Old Fire Code Excuse

Many guests take it upon themselves to invite guests that you hadn't planned on inviting, i.e. they decide to bring their children. If this happens, call and say, "Gee, Sue, I'd love the kids to come, but unfortunately the club is restricted by fire codes. The room's capacity is one hundred people and we've reached the quota. I am, however, providing a baby-sitter at my sister's home. Just drop the kids off there and pick them up afterward." Problem solved, no hard feelings.

How Is the Respond Date Determined?

Most caterers want a final headcount seventy-two hours in advance. Let's say the wedding date is June 30. Therefore, the caterer will want a final headcount on June 27. To give yourself ample time to contact those who don't bother to respond, make the respond date June 17. This gives you ten days to call those who haven't replied. It's critical that you find out whether or not these people will be attending. *Leave nothing to chance!*

When Should Invitations Be Sent?

Wedding invitations are sent out eight to ten weeks before the respond date to out-of-town guests. This gives them plenty of time to make hotel reservations and arrange for travel. If the wedding falls near a holiday, making travel plans and reservations more difficult to book, they may be sent out a few weeks earlier. *This is the only exception to the rule.* Wedding invitations to local guests are sent out two to four weeks before the respond date.

Don't send invitations out ahead of the

specified time! People (other than family) may lose the invitations or vacillate—"I have all this time, no sense in deciding now." *The tighter the time frame, the quicker the response.* Don't assume people will answer faster because you give them extra time. It doesn't happen that way.

Don't Ever Pay Retail

All invitations are discounted. Your goal is to find the vendors who discount them. I discount invitations to my clients, for example, and I know many stationery stores, bridal salons, and formal-wear stores that do also. Today, anyone who pays retail for invitations is not using their head.

Don't Discount Their Value

Many people regard invitations as a necessary evil. I don't know how many times I've heard, "Any old invitation will do. People just look at them and throw them away." I disagree completely. Your wedding invitation should be carefully selected. It sets the tone for your wedding and should reflect its formality. It should also reflect the personality of you and your fiancé. A beautiful, fine, or unique invitation is a joy to receive. The recipient knows that any couple who put so much thought, effort, and time into their invitation will do the same with their wedding. It only makes sense.

Follow the Rules

The wording of your invitation should follow the rules of etiquette, whether your wedding is formal, semiformal, or informal. You should know how to address them properly and how to properly address your guests. It's all a part of being knowledgeable, thorough, and doing things the right way.

I have developed a software program for use on your personal computer. It teaches you how to develop and maintain your guest list. It also includes traditional and classic invitation wordings and the rules of etiquette. It explains how invitations should be addressed and how to properly address your guests. It includes and defines all those other little cards that go along with invitations. It retains your guest list with addresses, maintains a log of your gifts, and lets you record thank you notes. It also provides a chart for reception seating.

It is also designed for those who would like to make their own invitations with the help of their computer and a little of their own ingenuity. (For information about my software, *Invitations: Inventing Elegance,* please see appendix I.)

Why Are Some Invitations Expensive?

Invitations can cost thousands of dollars. These costly cards are made of the finest papers and are most times engraved (an expensive process that produces raised lettering). Often they're decorated with ribbons, pearls, and fabrics like moire or silk. They may even be layered, with the invitation itself covered by a sheet of sheer rice paper or plastic. They are glitzy!

Classic, costly invitations, the kind Crane is known for, are engraved on fine paper and are simple and elegant. The most formal are white, ivory, or ecru and are engraved in black ink. Today, a discerning bride may choose either type of invitation. It depends solely on her taste. Either is correct for a formal wedding.

A Budget-Saving Bonanza

Classic, traditional invitations are my choice for the budget-conscious bride. Let me tell you why: The average person can't tell the difference between the inexpensive ones from Regency that are thermographed (an inexpensive printing process that produces raised lettering) and the expensive ones from Crane. For all intents and purposes, *they look the same.* They are also traditional and correct!

Many brides think these invitations are too plain, but for a formal or semiformal wedding, they're the ticket. They're elegant, timeless, and tasteful. (And, no one knows whether they're expensive or not!) All invitation companies make classic, traditional invitations in all price ranges. They may not look like much, but they are *simply* beautiful. *Pick a company that makes them inexpensively. They are a sure way to save money* and stay in touch with tradition.

In my opinion, nothing says, *"Cheap!"* like an invitation bedecked with colored flowers. Or how about the ones with the cowgirl and cowboy? Or the little green frogs on the lily pads? Or how about Cinderella's castle? These invitations are *not* classic. When you look back on them twenty years from now, you may wonder what you were drinking when you made your selection.

What You Need

1. *Invitations.*
2. *Return address on envelope flap.* This is your return address, printed on the outside envelope of the invitation.
3. *Reception card.* This tells your guests the name and address of the reception site and the time it's to take place. It should also tell your guests what type of reception you're hosting, for example:

> Hors d'oeuvre Reception
> immediately following ceremony

4. *Respond card set.* This is a card (that comes with a printed, return envelope) that guests fill in and return to you. It tells you whether they'll be attending and how many to expect. It may also include a choice of entree.
5. *Informal Personal Note Folders.* This is another name for thank you notes with one important distinction. They are not printed with the words "Thank you" on the outside or a corny, thank you verse on the inside. The outside may contain your monogram, once classically the bride's, since she was the one who sent the notes, but times have changed. A monogram may combine both your names, or you may simply have *Mr. and Mrs. Charles Smith* printed on the outside. The inside of the card is plain and is used to write a personal note to each guest who sent you a gift. (Send the cards within three weeks of receiving a gift.)
6. Buy *twenty-five extra invitations and all the little cards that go with them.* This is your insurance policy. The cost for an additional twenty-five is minimal (invitations and cards are sold in increments of twenty-five). But if you run out and need an additional twenty-five, you'll soon find that the reprinting cost is monumental. Don't be pennywise and pound foolish.
7. *Announcements.* Announcements inform people of your marriage *without obligating them to send a gift.* They are addressed beforehand and sent out the day following the wedding.

WHAT YOU DON'T NEED— SAVING $$$$

1. *Colored ink*. Most stock invitation companies charge more per item for colored ink. It's not necessary.
2. *Envelope liners*. Pretty, but hardly essential.
3. *Printed napkins, swizzle sticks, matches*, and all those other little goodies found at the back of invitation catalogs. Don't waste your hard-earned dollars on these unnecessary and frivolous items. And remember: It's up to the caterer or catering facility to provide napkins. That's what you're paying them for.
4. *Printed place cards*. You can find packages of place cards at party stores for much less than the printed variety found in invitation catalogs. Or, you can make your own. (See "And Place Cards," this chapter.)

A WORD ABOUT MAIL-ORDER INVITATIONS

Mail-order invitations are featured in bridal magazines. They copy most stock invitations (the type found in inexpensive invitation catalogs), but are even *less expensive*. The difference is that they're normally lesser quality, both in paper stock and in thermography.

I think you can do better. Shop and compare the mail-order variety to the kind found in invitation catalogs in retail stores. I think you'll find the catalog variety to be better quality. Find a vendor who discounts their invitations and then place your order. You may pay a few dollars more (even with the discount), but the difference in quality will be well worth it.

THE ULTIMATE—BUT MOST ELEGANT— MONEY SAVER

What I say may shock you, but if you have a computer and a little ingenuity you can *make* gorgeous invitations, for even *less* than mail order!

Step 1: Visit stationery stores and look at expensive invitation catalogs. Get a feel for the big-card invitations that are so popular today. Some are plain, but others may be trimmed with laces and pearls and fabrics, while others may even be layered (one layer of paper is put atop another for a dramatic effect).

Step 2: Decide on the type of invitation that best suits you. You may want to create a simple, traditional paneled invitation. You can find boxes of these, with matching cards, at stationery outlet stores (check the Yellow Pages).

They are inexpensive. You can word them and format them on your computer and print them out as easy as 1,2,3.

You may decide to print your invitations on beautiful, elegant stationery (the kind that comes with matching envelopes). Small note cards may also be purchased in corresponding or contrasting colors with envelopes and without, which can be dubbed for reception and respond cards. Or, you may decide to go all out and make the layered variety. The choice is yours.

In this chapter, you'll find examples of invitations that I've made along with some corresponding place cards. They were simple to make; they just took a little time. (For information get my video, *Making Irresistible*

Invitations (Inexpensively and Elegantly), see appendix I.)

HOW I DID IT

I visited a large craft store and was amazed by what I found. They offered loose stationery in all colors, sizes, and shapes, and in different qualities. I bought a smattering of different varieties, all good quality (heavy paper a *must*) and all inexpensive. Then I went to the do-it-yourself picture-framing section of the store and bought mat board in different colors and textures (one even looks like suede). I also bought an inexpensive mat cutter, and I went to the decoupage section and bought a brayer (a rubber roller) and some decoupage glue. Then I went to my favorite fabric outlet and bought a couple of yards of cheap lace and some ready-made bows and dried flowers. I also purchased a container of Beacon Fabri Tac glue and acrylic sealer (matte finish). I also bought an inexpensive paper cutter at an office warehouse store. I was ready to begin!

WHAT YOU'LL NEED (LAYERED INVITATIONS)

- Paper towels, wax paper, toothpicks
- Paper cutter
- Decorations of your choice, for example:
  Silk flowers
  Ribbon
- Decoupage glue
- Decoupage brayer (rubber roller)
- Scissors, pencil, ruler
- Mat board cutter
- Clear acrylic sealer
- Beacon's Fabri Tac glue
- Water, plate, small sponge

Photo 1.   COMPUTER GENERATED INVITATIONS

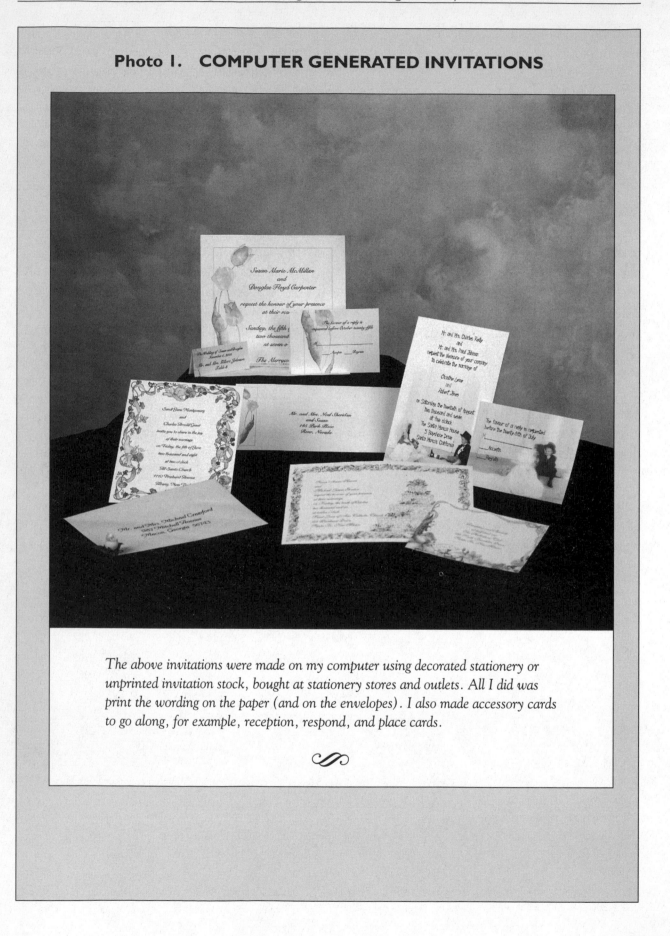

The above invitations were made on my computer using decorated stationery or unprinted invitation stock, bought at stationery stores and outlets. All I did was print the wording on the paper (and on the envelopes). I also made accessory cards to go along, for example, reception, respond, and place cards.

Photo 2.   COMPUTER GENERATED, LAYERED INVITATIONS

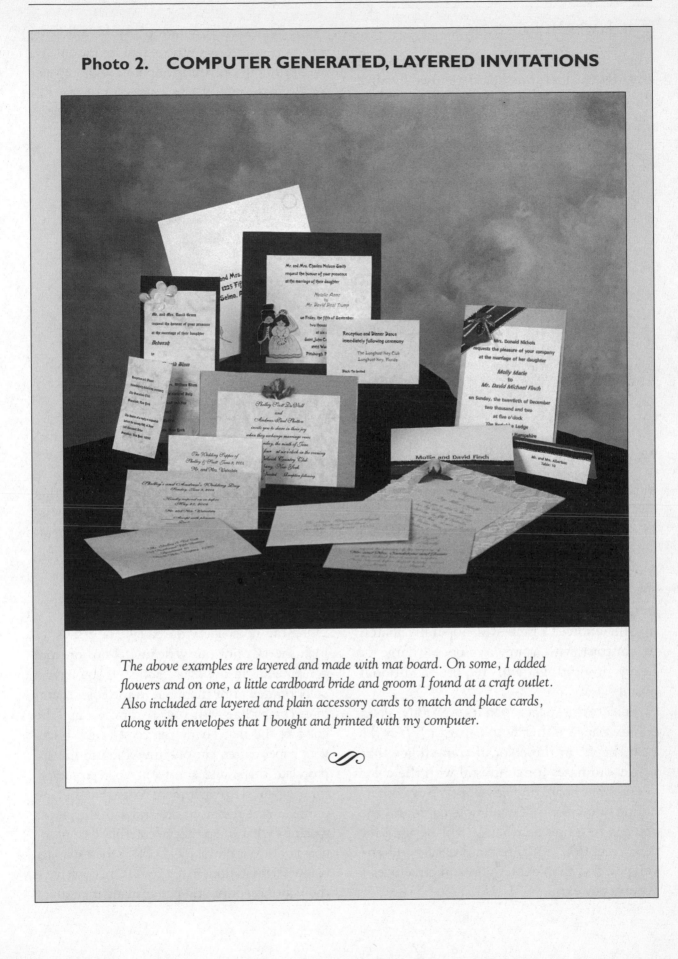

*The above examples are layered and made with mat board. On some, I added
flowers and on one, a little cardboard bride and groom I found at a craft outlet.
Also included are layered and plain accessory cards to match and place cards,
along with envelopes that I bought and printed with my computer.*

THE LAYERED INVITATION

These invitations can be made in any size to fit any size envelope. Mat board was used for all of the examples in photo 2.

Note: The word "invitation" in the following instructions, refers to the actual invitation you will print out on your computer, on notepaper or 8½ by 11 inch sheets, using WordPerfect or another word processing program, for example:

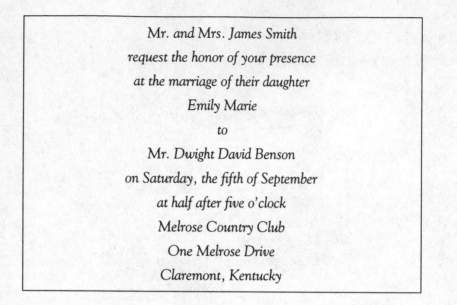

Mr. and Mrs. James Smith
request the honor of your presence
at the marriage of their daughter
Emily Marie
to
Mr. Dwight David Benson
on Saturday, the fifth of September
at half after five o'clock
Melrose Country Club
One Melrose Drive
Claremont, Kentucky

MAKING THE LAYERED INVITATION

Before you begin choose your envelopes, paper, and mat board. Buy the invitation envelopes in the size and color of your choice. These will determine the size of your invitation. Always buy twenty-five extra. Next, select the mat board you'll use. Buy the lightest weight mat board you can find, in the color of your choice, which will hopefully match or contrast with your envelopes. (Large or heavy invitations will require additional postage.)

Select the paper you'll use. Buy good quality paper, either note paper or 8½ × 11 inch sheets, in the color of your choice that best coordinates (or contrasts) with the color of your mat board and envelopes. Buy coordinating or contrasting small note cards and envelopes to go along. (These will be used for your reception cards, respond cards, and envelopes, and thank you notes and envelopes.) Always buy extra.

Step 1: Make a Prototype

From a piece of cardboard, cut a prototype that will easily fit into the envelopes you've selected for your invitations. Use your paper cutter to ensure that the prototype is cut straight.

Step 2: Print Out and Cut the Invitations

Using the notepaper you bought or 8½ × 11 inch sheets, print out your invitations on your computer, as in the figure above. If you have a color printer, print them out in the color that is most compatible with your paper color and the color of the mat board you've selected. Using your paper cutter, cut one invitation to the appropriate shape and size to fit your prototype. (You will need to experiment to see that they are printed in the right font size and with the proper spacing so that when they're cut, they'll comfortably fit on your prototype. Look at the examples of layered invitations in photo 2.) Once you have the right size, print and cut as many invitations as you'll need. (All other cards—reception, respond, thank yous, etc.—and envelopes should also be printed on your computer.)

Step 3: Marking and Cutting the Mat Board

Turn the mat board on the wrong side and, using your prototype and ruler, mark off the mat board. Mark as many mat boards as it takes to provide you with the number of invitations you'll need. With your mat board cutter (a heavy-duty razorblade knife) and ruler, cut out the mat board. (The mat board provides the first layer of your invitations.)

Step 4: Gluing Lace, Covering, and Braying

In one example (see photo 2), I covered the mat board with inexpensive lace fabric (you can use any fabric you choose). Cut a piece of lace a little larger than the mat board. Next, mix a little decoupage glue on a saucer with some water to thin it and dab it on the wrong side of the lace. Put the lace on the mat board, glue side down, and cover it with a piece of wax paper and a paper towel. Using your decoupage brayer, roll the lace onto the mat board.

Note: If you were applying your invitation directly to the mat board, you would simply dab the back of the invitation with a little water-glue mixture and roll it onto the mat board (which was covered by wax paper and a paper towel) with your brayer. Continue with the following steps.

Step 5: Drying

Put a clean piece of wax paper and a paper towel over the mat board and put it under a phone book (or other heavy book) to dry for a few hours. You may stack up to five invitations at once under one book, one on top of the other, each covered with a piece of wax paper and a paper towel. (This will prevent the mat board from bowing.)

Step 6: After They Dry, Trimming and Applying Invitations

After the lace is dry and glued to the mat board, turn it over and, with scissors, trim it to fit the mat board. Next, take an invitation, dab the wrong side lightly with the glue-water mixture, position it on the lace-covered mat board, cover with wax paper, and lightly and gently roll the invitation on with your brayer. Allow this to dry.

Step 7: Add Flowers, Ribbon, or Other Trim

Attach ribbons and flowers (spray dried flowers with clear acrylic before using), etc. to the invitation with Beacon Fabri Tac glue (don't use too much). When attaching the ribbon, allow the ends to extend over the mat board. Allow this to dry completely before trimming the ribbon to the size of the mat board. You now have a beautiful layered invitation. (See examples, photo 2.)

Troubleshooting

If the invitation or the fabric lifts from the mat board, take a toothpick, put some decoupage glue on the end, and run under the edge of the invitation or fabric. Press down with your finger. Don't be afraid to wipe excess glue off the invitation with a clean, damp sponge. Cover with wax paper and a paper towel and place under the phone book to dry.

ABOUT ENVELOPES—HAVING TROUBLE?

I was able to buy loose envelopes in all sizes at the craft store and stationery store. For unusual sizes and colors, I bought boxes of Christmas cards after the big day, for 75 percent off, and used the envelopes. They cost peanuts.

AND ALL THOSE OTHER LITTLE CARDS

I put most of my time and effort into the invitations and bought small matching or contrasting cards and envelopes (for reception and respond cards and envelopes) in the stationery department at the craft store. You may, however, decide to create your own. Or, you may decide to get really artsy and decorate these cards, too (I did in photo 2). The choice is yours.

THE TRADITIONAL CARD INVITATION

These can be found at stationery outlet stores and are inexpensive. They come with matching envelopes and small cards (with or without envelopes) that can be used for reception and respond cards, and envelopes, and thank you notes and envelopes. Print them on your computer.

THE STATIONERY INVITATION

It's easy to purchase a box of pretty stationery with matching envelopes. On a sheet of paper, print the invitation to the ceremony. Cut a sheet of stationery smaller to make a reception or a respond card. Then buy plain, small note cards (in matching or contrasting colors) to use for thank you notes and envelopes (see photo 1).

THE UNPRINTED INVITATION

Believe it or not, you can buy invitations and all those other little cards, unprinted. It's costly, but not as costly as buying the printed variety (see photo 1).

AND PLACE CARDS

With my sample invitations, I've included some matching place cards. Look at my examples and let your imagination soar (photos 1 and 2). I made the layered ones by gluing ribbon and flowers to plain, heavy paper that I cut to the appropriate size. Make them any way you wish. They're fun and easy to do!

ABOUT TIME AND MONEY

Naturally, the stationery invitation or traditional stock invitation are the easiest to make (all you do is print them). They take the least amount of time and cost the least. The fancy (unprinted) variety can be more expensive, but if you don't have the time and want something pretty and upscale, they may be the answer to your prayers. The layered variety takes time and effort, no doubt about it, but they are easy to do. Even with the expense of buying a paper cutter, mat board, glue, and flowers, these gorgeous invitations are inexpensive to make. Watch for sales at the craft and fabric stores; *buy only when there's a sale!*

THE SCHEDULE—IF MAKING YOUR OWN

Invitations printed on your computer from card stock or on stationery or on unprinted invitation stock should only take a few days. Always make extra.

Fancy invitations are different. Allow yourself one day to make ten. If you did ten on a Saturday or Sunday, and were making fifty, you would need five weeks. It's also wise to make five extra. Then allow another day to set up the computer and print all those other little cards (always print extras), and another day to do the envelopes. Schedule your time so that you and your fiancé can have fun making the invitations together on the weekends. Don't let it become a burden. And who knows? If you work great together and set up an invitation assembly line, you may easily be able to do more than ten per day. Have fun and good luck!

Chapter Sixteen

WEDDING GOWNS AND BRIDESMAIDS' DRESSES

I . . . chose my wife, as she did her wedding-gown, not for a fine glossy surface, but such qualities as would wear well.

—Oliver Goldsmith, *The Vicar of Wakefield*

Part I

Modern Bride once conducted a survey and asked women: What was the most pleasurable aspect of planning your wedding? Their response? Shopping for their gown. While this may be true, it's been my observation that it's also a harrowing experience to choose *the most important dress* you will wear on *the most important day* of your life. This dress is symbolic of a past heritage and culture particular to each of us and of the day you begin to share your life with another.

Since the beginning of time, it's been customary for a woman to wear a very special garment on the day of her marriage. (The only one who may have missed out was Eve.) And while the traditional symbolism of this gown is forever in our consciousness, the dress must also be beautiful, elegant, and, in the nineties, combine the right mixture of sexuality and innocence (it must offend no one). At the same time, it must be the kind of dress that produces

audible "Ooohs and Ahhhs" as the bride makes her way, in a heavenly cloud of tulle, down the aisle.

This is your wedding gown, the dress you will wear when you give your love and commitment—forever—to the man you love. It's the only dress you will ever own that your future husband will be able to describe in dreamy detail ten, twenty, or even thirty years after you wear it. It is a dress that your mother and grandmother *have* to love. It is a dress that your friends and wedding guests *must* praise and admire. Is it any wonder that the search for this dress may be as taxing (and may take as long) as the one for the Holy Grail? But there is one major difference: The perfect wedding gown is attainable.

There are two major problems to overcome. The first relates to size. If you're larger or smaller than a size 10 you may experience difficulty when trying wedding gowns. Most traditional salons carry size 10 samples. A woman who is significantly smaller or larger is expected to get into a dress as best she can, then order one in her size and hope for the best. It can be a frustrating, depressing experience. (But it is an experience that can work to your benefit, if you know how.)

The second problem is money. Eighty percent of my clients work on a budget and most are paying for their own wedding. Many find, heart wrenchingly, that their budget and their dream dress are miles apart. They are unhappy. How many times have I heard from brides: "I want what I can't have." (But if you're savvy—you can!)

All of these factors have led me to dispute the *Modern Bride* survey. I've come to the conclusion that they exclusively polled bone-skinny women, the type who only consult Martha Stewart's book, *Weddings*, and who only shop at Vera Wang or Carolina Herrera. For these women, shopping for their gown must be the most pleasurable aspect of planning their wedding. But for others, I think it can be perplexing and tough. (It doesn't have to be.)

STEP 1: BEFORE YOU BEGIN—WHO DO YOU TRUST?

Many brides have been hurt by dishonest bridal shops. For this reason, it's important to know about unfair practices that exist within the industry and how you can protect yourself against them. If you fall victim to a shop that goes out of business and leaves you stranded, or you pay hundreds of dollars more for a gown than you should, or your gown doesn't come in on time, or you get ripped off, the emotional pain will be as devastating as the financial loss. Don't let yourself in for a traumatic experience. *Become an educated consumer.* Follow my guidelines. Be a winner—not a victim!

Rule 1: Shop only at reliable, honest stores that have been referred to you by recently married relatives, friends, or business associates.

THE BRIDAL GOWN INDUSTRY

The wedding gown business is a tough, competitive business. If you look at it from the retailer's perspective, however, you may gain an understanding of why unfair practices exist. I'm not here to justify these practices but to acquaint you with them. By learning how these practices may affect you (and how to avoid them), *you will save money!*

You might have noticed, for example, that many retailers remove the labels from their gowns. They do it for two reasons: One, they don't want you to shop price. And two, they want to stymie their competition. Most bridal gown manufacturers sell to every bridal shop on every corner. They don't protect the retailer. To combat this practice the retailer may tell customers that his merchandise is *exclusive.* Now if you believe that, and you find your dream gown in this particular shop, *it may prevent you from looking elsewhere.* I've had many clients walk into my store and say, "There's my gown. What's it doing here, and it's two hundred dollars cheaper?! I bought it at Suzy Jo's and they said it was an exclusive! Now what am I going to do?" Nothing (it's after the fact).

Rule 2: When you find your dream dress, shop other stores until you find the same one. Make sure the price is competitive and the gowns are identical. If you can't find your dress, look for gowns that the stores have in common. If the prices are competitive, you can bet your gown is competitively priced also. If you prefer one store to another (but the price is higher), talk to the owner. Many times he or she will match the price to get your business. Don't be afraid to ask and be persuasive.

Labels may also be removed if the store is selling copies of original dresses. In Miami and New York, for example, there are hundreds of sewing shops that make garments for retailers. Many times unscrupulous retailers will have an original copied. There's nothing wrong with this practice, provided the customer knows the gown is a copy and that the copy sells for significantly less than the original.

Rule 3: When you specifically ask a retailer for a designer gown (the same one you saw in a bridal magazine), it's essential to know that the gown *is* an original, not a copy.

WARNING: A shop that's in poor repair and has few samples may be in financial trouble. Make sure they carry the latest styles. (If they're going out of business [or thinking of it] it's unlikely that they'd stock new merchandise.) Be leery of a store that only offers last season's samples.

Rule 4: If a store can get you a dress they don't stock, they should be willing to offer you an incentive. After all, you could buy the dress from the store that has the sample. Ask the owner what they're going to do for you. Most times the retailer will beat the price or throw something in, such as the bustle or alterations.

WAREHOUSES AND OUTLETS

I have never seen such a blatant rip-off as these so-called warehouse/outlet operations and I'm going to give you my reasons why it's best to avoid them. When they first opened across the country, major manufacturers were dumping their unsold garments into their stores. Clients would walk into my shop and say, "I saw a Galina I love at an outlet and it's a steal." Retailers all over the country were up in arms. Every time a customer came in to tell us that a designer gown was in a warehouse or outlet, we'd call to complain (as did every other retailer in the country).

True, the gowns were discontinued, but the fact remained that prestigious designer gowns were being placed in warehouse and outlet stores. Retailers had their own discontinued samples to sell, and the warehouses and outlets were paying much less for their merchandise than we were. It caused havoc between the manufacturers and the retailers.

The problem was soon resolved and the manufacturers quit unloading their gowns. But the problem soon became a different one. Many warehouses and outlets copy designer gowns and manufacture them on their own, and many sell them for about the same price as the originals. Buying a poorly made copy when you could buy an original (for about the same price) is not smart.

I've shopped many warehouse- and outlet-type operations and am always jolted by their prices. I've seen many silk gowns, for example, that were poor quality but sold for as much as $1,399. At a traditional bridal shop you can get a delectable Demetrios for less money, and a Marisa for about the same price. Many offered Italian-satin gowns (matte satin, actually polyester), for as much as $999. Why would you pay top dollar for a copy when you can buy the real thing, like a beautiful, silk Jasmine or a fabulous Galina Bouquet creation, for less?

Many of these outlets and warehouses featured poor quality traditional gowns that sold for as much as Mori Lee gowns, and in my opinion, no one beats Mori Lee for quality or price. Why would you pay $600 for a poor quality, lightweight satin gown when you can buy a heavy, rich Mori Lee? It doesn't make sense.

I attribute much of the huge success of these stores to what I call the *warehouse or outlet phenomenon*. Tag a business with the words "discount," "warehouse," or "outlet" and people *assume* that they'll get the best prices. In this industry, that's not always the case.

The Other Type of Warehouse or Outlet Store

This type of operation buys directly from the manufacturer (just like a retailer). The difference: They mark up their gowns as much as 400 percent, only to mark them back down to the actual suggested retail price. *Savings to the bride: $0.*

Rule 5: Do not buy your gown from a warehouse/outlet operation. Shop them to compare the quality and price of their merchandise to merchandise found in traditional bridal stores. *Why buy a warehouse or outlet gown when you can get the real thing for close to the same price, or less?*

Consignment Shops

It's my opinion that consignment shops aren't to be trusted. And it's not the consignment shops I don't trust; it's the brides. If a bride tells a consignment shop that her dress cost $1,200 (but she really paid $800), who are they to doubt her? *The fradulent factor* (as I call it) comes into play when she wants to sell it for $800. Most consignment shops split with their clients, 50/50. In this case, the bride would get $400 and so would the consignment shop. Consignment shops also require that gowns be clean and in good repair. But dry cleaning is expensive and most likely will add another $100 to the price of their gowns.

Recently I altered a consignment-shop gown for a bride. I had the same gown in stock. She paid fifty dollars less for her secondhand gown. Another example: A bride came into my store to have her consignment-shop gown altered. She bought it on sale for $150. The skirt had one side shorter than the other and the side seams didn't match (obviously someone else had tried to alter or redesign the dress). The gown could not be fixed and the dress was not returnable; she bought it on sale.

Many brides put their gowns in consignment shops with the hopes of cleaning up. Not all do. There are honest ones. But it's up to you to find out if the gown is—or is not—a buy. Put on your Sherlock Holmes hat and do some sleuthing. Look inside the dress to find the manufacturer's label. Check to see if there's a style number. Call bridal shops to ascertain the price range of the manufacturer's gowns. If you get the style number, ask if the dress is still running. Look in last year's bridal magazines. If you find it, call bridal shops and ask if they carry it (or if they know the approximate price). Once you've obtained concrete information, you can determine if the dress in the consignment shop is such a deal!

Rule 6: Do your homework and you may find a real bridal bargain at a consignment shop, but be leery and cautious. *Secondhand dresses should sell for half the retail cost—no more.*

Gown Rentals

A woman once walked into my store to buy invitations. I asked if she had a gown and she told me that she was going to rent a Mon Cheri. I asked the price. It was one hundred dollars less than the retail price of the gown. She bought the gown from me and later sold it at a consignment shop. I think gown rental is a viable option, provided you do your homework. Read the contracts and the small print. Once again, you must determine if the gown you're going to rent is a bargain or not. You may be renting a gown for the same price that you could have bought it.

THE BRIDE'S REFERRAL SHEET

Ask recently married brides to rate the stores where they shopped. Ask each bride the following questions and ask them to grade each response, either:

A: Excellent   B: Above Average   C: Average   D: Poor

At the end of the sheet, total the number of As, Bs, Cs, and Ds. Visit only those stores with the highest ratings. Don't consider any shop that received less than a C rating. Cross it off your list.

Store Name:

	A	B	C	D
1. Were they pleasant and helpful?				
2. Did they show you the type(s) of wedding gown(s) you wanted to see?				
3. *Did they ask you to try different styles?*				
4. Were they pushy?				
5. Were they well stocked?				
6. Did they have the latest styles?				
7. Did they have a good selection in your price range?				
8. *Did they show you samples only in your price range?*				
9. *Was your gown delivered on time? And the bridesmaids' dresses?*				
10. Were the alterations professionally done?				
11. Did they have a good selection of headpieces and veils?				
12. *Were any extras included in the price or offered as an incentive for your business?*				
Total:				

THE DISCOUNTER

Some bridal shops discount gowns. Many are criticized because they don't offer full service, such as alterations, and because they may not stock the merchandise. It's up to you to make the decision to buy a gown from one of these salons. Once again, check references thoroughly. Make sure the store is reliable before you purchase. Speak to brides who have done business with them. Weigh the advantages and disadvantages before you buy.

STEP 2: THE HUNT BEGINS

REFERRALS

Get out your notebook and start by calling recently married relatives, friends, and business associates. Ask where they shopped for their gown and the following questions about each store. Copy the previous sheet and rate each store before you shop.

LET'S ANALYZE: *THE PIVOTAL POINTS

Questions 3, 8, 9, and 12 are *pivotal points*. These factors can mean the difference between success and failure—and saving money—when shopping for a gown. Let's examine them closely.

Question 3: *Did they ask you to try different styles?

You may think you know what you want, but it's critical to keep your options open and try all styles. I estimate that 40 percent of my clients purchase gowns that they had no intention of trying. The most important thing you can do for yourself is keep an open mind.

Question 8: Did they show you samples only in your price range?

This is a must! Don't fall in love with a dress you can't afford. Always check the price tag before you try on the gown. *If you get hooked on a gown you can't have, you'll be miserable.* By the same token, be honest with the salesperson. When they ask what your budget is, tell them. How many times have I heard, "I don't really have a budget." My reply, "Well then, let's start with five thousand dollar gowns." (This immediately elicits a different response.) "Oh no! I want to stay under a thousand." Be honest! It can only help you.

Question 9: *Was your gown delivered on time? And the bridesmaids' dresses?

Nothing can get your blood pressure soaring like a late wedding gown or bridesmaids' dresses! A store that doesn't deliver when they should (within three to four months of the order date) could be having financial difficulties. Be careful.

Question 12: *Were any extras included in the price or offered as an incentive for your business?

This can save you money. For example, I discount invitations—but only to those who buy their gown from me. Many stores may even include alterations. Find out what they offer but make sure the gown isn't excessively marked up to pay for the added extras. Make this determination by shopping other stores to ensure that the gown is competitively priced.

Step 3: Shop for Success

An Online Resource

The Knot, the number one wedding resource for brides, and its Bridal Gown Search, are available online and offer you a great, relaxing way to preview the latest styles in wedding gowns in the comfort of your own home. Sit down, boot up, tune in, and chill out, as over eight thousand glorious wedding gowns pass before your eyes in a searchable database. Get a feel for what you like and take notes. What better way to preview the latest styles and fashion trends? Use *The Knot* to your advantage; it's an excellent way to educate yourself. (For more information, see appendix I.)

Your Key to Success

The key to changing a sale dress into your dream gown is finding a talented, experienced seamstress. Many shops are criticized for high alteration costs and I'm one of them. But I learned my lesson the hard way. Years ago, I employed inexpensive seamstresses to keep the cost down. I got what I paid for. The workmanship was shoddy and I got complaints. To solve the problem I hired seamstresses who were also trained pattern makers; women who knew clothing design and structure. They could change gowns as well as do top-notch alterations. My problems were solved. I do not get complaints about workmanship.

There's no rule that states that a bridal shop must alter your gown. But it's up to you to find a skilled seamstress who can (preferably a pattern maker who also makes clothes), and who won't charge you an arm and a leg. These talented women are few and far between, but with a little effort, you should be able to locate one who meets your needs.

Many people get their clothes altered.

Ask your mother, business associates, or relatives for the names of seamstresses they would recommend. Then make appointments to interview them. Ask each one if she regularly alters wedding gowns or makes clothes. If she's not qualified, ask if she knows someone who is. When you find one who suits you, ask for references and check them. Look at samples of her work. Inspect the garments inside and outside. They should be so "clean" that you could turn them on the wrong side and wear them (if they've been properly finished).

One of the women who worked for me started a custom design and alteration business on the side. She worked out of her home, didn't have my overhead, and was much less expensive. She never advertised; people heard of her by word-of-mouth. This is the type of person you need to find to keep your costs down.

Rule 7: It's imperative that you find a qualified seamstress, one who makes clothes or has experience altering and changing wedding gowns, *before you begin to shop.* If you find the sale gown of your dreams, you may have to buy it on the spot. Don't be caught looking for a seamstress after the fact. *Be prepared.*

Start Early

The search for the perfect wedding gown must begin early. It must be diligent, targeted, and focused. Learning to strategically shop for your wedding gown can save you hundreds of dollars. It will take time and effort but the results will justify the means. Saving money is your prime concern, but just as crucial is finding an honest, reliable shop staffed with competent people who make you feel comfortable.

THE BRIDE'S GRADING REPORT

After visiting each store, answer each question and give each response a grade, either:

A: Excellent   B: Above Average   C: Average   D: Poor

Store: _____

	A	B	C	D
1. Was the staff helpful?				
2. Did they answer my questions?				
3. Were they pushy?				
4. Did the store have a pleasant ambiance?				
5. Did they have a good selection?				
6. Were they well stocked with the latest styles? (A store that isn't may be in financial trouble.)				
7. Did they offer incentives for me to shop there?				
8. Are alterations done in-house?				
9. Were gown prices competitive? (Look for the same gowns in other shops to ensure that the prices are competitive. *This is a must.*)				
10. When will the gown be delivered? (Be leery of a store who says six months or more. Most gowns are delivered within three to four months.)				
Total:				

Which store had the most number of As and Bs? Shop only at those stores with the highest ratings.

Note: Wedding gowns that are ordered are normally delivered within three months, although some take longer. If ordering, give yourself plenty of time to keep your stress level low.

Warning: Don't confuse yourself! Select the three highest rated bridal shops from your list of referrals. Choose only those that carry gowns in your price range. Make appointments and visit these stores, then rate them. Copy The Bride's Grading Report on the previous page, and take it with you when you shop.

COMPARING GRADING REPORTS

Compare the grading reports from all the stores where you shopped. Patronize only those with the highest ratings and those that make you feel the best, happiest, and most comfortable. If the store you prefer priced their gowns higher, speak with the owner. As I said, many times they will match the price.

If none of the stores please you, pick another (that has been referred to you) and start the process again. But don't confuse yourself. *The more dresses you try and the more stores you shop, the more unhappy and bewildered you'll become* (the dresses will all start to look alike). Stay focused and fill out a grading report for each shop. Keep your impressions unmuddled. Once you find the shop that makes you feel comfortable, has the style of gowns you love, and meets the above criteria, stick with it.

Part II: Shopping for Bargains

The sale rack in a bridal shop is your bonanza! Throughout the year, gowns are discontinued (the manufacturer stops making particular styles). The retailer has no choice but to put the gowns on sale. I also put gowns on sale because I get overstocked. Other bridal shops do the same thing. I have reduced $2,500 gowns, for example, to as low as $700. *When shopping for gowns, budget-conscious brides should look only at the sale racks.* Take advantage of this wonderful opportunity.

FABRIC AND THE DESIGNER—DETERMINING FACTORS

Fabric, more than any other factor, determines the price of a gown. Most brides ask why simple gowns cost more than elaborate beaded varieties. The answer is in the fabric. The other factor is the designer's status. A famous designer can demand more for his gowns than an up-and-comer.

Traditional beaded satin gowns are usually made of polyester. This accounts for their shiny white-white appearance. Most are also made in the Orient, where fabrics, laces, beads, and labor are cheap. These are the factors that make gowns affordable for most brides. Raw silk, the kind with the little lines and bumps (called slugs), has become popular and is affordable. Many companies are making raw silk gowns for under $1,000, including Ilissa, Regency, Jasmine, and Fink. Normally off-white in color (you don't find that polyester-white color in natural silk), these gowns have character.

Warning: There are many fakes, so be careful!

If a clerk says that the gown is raw silk or shantung (another name for raw silk), make sure it is by checking the fabric label inside the garment.

Most raw silk is affordable, but other types of silk are not. Silk satin, heavy and luxuriant and found only in exclusive gowns, is expensive, as is silk taffeta and damask, which looks like fine brocade. Find one of these dresses on sale and you may have struck pay dirt. In my opinion, there's nothing to compare. Chiffon is also becoming popular. Once again, determine if the gown is made of synthetic chiffon or silk chiffon. Always read the label.

Many women limit their search for the perfect gown by being inflexible. They will look exclusively at either long-sleeve or short-sleeve dresses. They shouldn't. Adding a sleeve or removing one or making a short sleeve from a long one is relatively easy to do. Try all the sale gowns and think of how you'd change it to make it exclusively yours.

This does not apply to changes that affect the design of the gown: modifying the length of the bodice, for example, making an off-the-shoulder dress into a traditional high-collared one, or turning a full-skirted ball gown into a body-hugging sheath. I am talking about easy changes that can be made simply.

Let me cite a few examples:

1. A straight, off-the-shoulder neckline can easily be turned into a *sweetheart* neckline (one that looks like the top of a heart) with the snip of the scissors.
2. A more formal gown can be made less so by cutting off the train.
3. Hem lace can be added to make a plain skirt more decorative (although this may get expensive).
4. Add a triangular panel of lace to a rounded waistline and it transforms itself into the popular basque waistline (that looks like a V extending from the center of the waistline).
5. Bows and rosettes can be made and added to the back bodice of an unadorned gown or removed from a gown to make it more simple and elegant.
6. The illusion or lace top and sleeves of many traditional gowns can be removed completely (and simply) to make them strapless.

The moral of the story: Look carefully at sale gowns and use your imagination to create your dream dress.

The Importance of Flexibility

Your Size and Sample Size—Turning Lemons into Lemonade

Most stores carry sample size 10s. This makes it difficult for brides who are smaller or larger to picture what a gown will look like in their size. It requires a good imagination. But there are ways around this dilemma.

A caring shop will take the time and make the effort to help a bride who is not sample size. She must get into the gown as best she can so that she can see it (and herself) to the gown's (and her) best advantage. A very small woman will need to have the gown pinned to her. A larger woman can try the gown, although it won't zip. If her arms won't fit into the sleeves, it's best to hold the sleeves up against the arms.

Rule 8: Use the warehouses and outlets to your advantage. *They have hanging stock in all sizes.* Try on different styles and see what looks best on you. Then shop traditional bridal stores to find the *original dress* of your dreams. Or, do what one of my clients, Carol, did.

A Funny Thing Happened to Carol . . .

I once had a client named Carol. She ordered a gown six months before her wedding. About six weeks before the event, she came for her first fitting. She had gained forty pounds (she wasn't pregnant) and the dress wouldn't zip by many inches. She cried uncontrollably. My seamstress-pattern maker came to the rescue.

She added two panels of white satin on either side of the zipper and appliqued it with lace. She gusseted the arms (added triangular pieces of fabric to the underside of the sleeves). The gown looked like it had never been touched and fit Carol perfectly.

A Money-Saving Miracle

After that incident, I got to thinking: Why can't sample-size dresses be made larger, or smaller? They can. All you have to do is find the seamstress who's skilled enough to do it. Brides buy samples because they're a bargain. We've turned 10s into 4s and 10s into 16s—and you'd never know they'd been altered. Polyester satin gowns are the easiest to do. The fabrics and laces are easy to match. Just visit your local fabric store.

Seamstresses who regularly alter, change, or make wedding gowns will also have fabrics and laces on hand. So do most bridal shops. You might ask the store where you bought the gown to sell you some satin and lace. They should be glad to oblige.

You may also ask the shop to order the fabric and lace you need. If that fails (let's say the gown is silk and has been discontinued), cut the train shorter and use that fabric to make the necessary changes. Match laces as closely as possible. No one will notice if the lace is a little different. Just make sure that the sequins match (colored or clear), that the lace is the same type (Alençon or Guipuré, for example), and that the patterns in the lace are similar.

Accessories—Hidden Costs That Spell $$$$

Slips, bras, shoes, garters, and jewelry can add up to hundreds of dollars, yet many brides forget to calculate their cost. Don't be one of them! Budget for all accessories.

The best way to save money on undergarments is to wait for a sale at a lingerie shop or a department store. Off-the-shoulder gowns, for example, may require bustieres (expensive, long-line bras). Many brides, however, no matter what their style of gown, choose to wear them because they're slimming. If you're thin and small busted, on the other hand, you may decide to have cups sewn into your gown. They're a comfortable alternative to a stiff bra or a bustiere and they're inexpensive. If your gown requires a crinoline (a full slip), borrow one. They come in many different sizes, from not-so-full, to very full. It depends on the look you want. (Make sure to take the same slip to every fitting.)

Costume jewelry can also be costly. If you don't have your own, borrow what you need. Try them on with your gown at your fitting. Make sure they match the look of your dress.

THE WEDDING GOWN BUDGET

	Budgeted Price or Estimated Price	Actual Price	The Difference (Plus or Minus)
Gown:			
Extra charges:			
oversize:			
extra long:			
rush cut:			
fabric or trim:			
Alterations:			
Accessories:			
Bra or bustiere:			
Slip:			
Jewelry:			
Garter:			
Shoes:			
Headpiece/Veil(s):			
Subtotal:			
Tax:			
Total:			
Analysis:			

1. If you're under budget—stay there! Good for you.
2. If you're way over budget, look for a different dress.
3. If you're over budget—*but have to have this gown*—remove guests from your list until you make up the difference.
4. Make up your mind to stick with your budget at all costs. Make the necessary changes—*now!*

Shoes are another story. I think it's essential to bite the bullet and buy good ones. Nothing will make you more miserable than aching feet. Break them in beforehand. Cover them with socks (so they won't get dirty) and wear them around the house. To save money, buy plain ones and decorate them with a little beaded lace (put on with a hot-glue gun or some Beacon Fabri Tac glue) that matches your gown. Or make lovely little bows and stitch them on. The difference in price between plain and decorated shoes can be twenty dollars or more. Do the decorating yourself.

If your gown is silk, it's best to buy plain silk shoes. Silk shoes, like silk gowns, are off-white. Most times, it's unnecessary to dye them. This saves money. Also, they may be worn again. After the wedding, dye them black or brown, for example.

SAMPLE WEDDING GOWN BUDGET

On the previous page is a sample wedding gown budget. Make a few copies and take them to the bridal shop(s) with you. When you find a dress you're interested in, fill in the budget and analyze the costs. Determine if the dress is, or isn't, for you. Also, while looking at gowns, get a feel for the price of headpieces and veils. Budget for them.

PRECAUTIONS

MEASURING TO SAVE MONEY

Every prospective bride has heard rumors about stores that purposely measure their clients incorrectly to make money by charging for excessive alterations. Unfortunately, many of these tales are true. Don't let this happen to you. Brides who are uneducated allow themselves to be duped! Be an educated consumer and follow these rules. Do not order a gown from any shop that does not follow this procedure. If you do, you're asking for trouble.

1. Be measured in underwear. Use a vinyl tape (cloth stretches). Measure around the fullest part of the bust, with arms at the sides. Pull the tape so that it's not loose or tight. Get a true measurement.
2. Measure the waist the same way (normally at the belly button).
3. Measure the hips at the fullest part. If the top of the thigh is fuller, measure there.
4. Write the measurements down.
5. *Ask to see the manufacturer's size chart for the particular gown you're ordering.*

Each manufacturer has their own size chart. Compare your measurements to those on the chart and select the size that most closely matches your measurements. If you're in-between sizes, go up a size. It's easier to take a gown in than to let it out. Also, if ordering a full-skirted gown, it's not necessary to consider the hip measurement. Full skirts cover all hip sizes.

Warning: Don't be influenced by the sample dress you tried on. The more they're tried on, the more they stretch. Base your decision on your measurements, only.

Rule 9: If a store doesn't measure you correctly or refuses to show you the manufacturer's size chart for the gown you're ordering—*go elsewhere.*

Extra Charges

If you're tall—over five feet seven inches—you should order *extra length* (the dress is cut longer than average). You will pay more for extra length, but if you're tall, it's essential. You will also pay more if you order the dress in a larger size—size 18 and over (although some manufacturers charge more for a size 16). The cost varies with each manufacturer. Make sure the charges are listed on your receipt.

ORDER IN TIME TO SAVE MONEY

Want to throw money down the drain? Then wait till the last minute to order your gown. Manufacturers require at least three months for delivery, some more. If you want a gown in less time, they will charge the retailer a rush-cut fee of 10 percent or more over the cost. This fee is then passed on to the consumer.

ALTERATIONS

Ninety-nine percent of the time, wedding gowns need alterations. These alterations, usually done by the store, may be expensive. The trick is to find a talented seamstress who will do it for less. When your dress is delivered, have the store give you a written estimate of alteration costs. Then review this estimate with your seamstress. If she saves you money, and you've researched her credentials thoroughly and checked her references, then hire her.

Get all details in writing. Include number of fittings and alterations charges, charges for extra fabric, etc., and the date that you'll pick up the gown. Make sure that she's able to steam or press your

gown when the alterations are completed. If not, it's up to you to find a reliable dry cleaner to do the job. Get an estimate of their costs in writing. Figure that cost into your budget and don't forget to add applicable sales tax.

PROTECTING YOUR INVESTMENT

Follow these guidelines to protect your investment:

1. *Always use a credit card.* You're more likely to recoup your losses if the store should go out of business.
2. *Make sure your receipt contains the following information:*
   - Manufacturer's name
   - Style number
   - Size
   - Color
   - Extra-length charges (if any)
   - Oversize charges (if any)
   - Extras that may be included: a free bustle or alterations
   - Where the dress is advertised (*Bride's,* April/May, page 265)
3. *Give yourself enough time.* Try to order at least six months in advance. Some manufacturers, Milady and Marisa for example, sometimes run longer than a three-month delivery.

   If there's a problem (the gown is delivered in the wrong color or size, for example) it may be returned *provided there's enough time to get a replacement.* And at all costs, order early to *avoid rush-cut fees.*
4. *Get a ship date.* After an order is placed by the store the manufacturer will respond with the *ship date.* This is the approximate date the dress will be delivered. The store then checks to see if the right style number, color, and size have been ordered. (At this point, there's time to correct mistakes.) Wait about two weeks, then call the store

and ask for the ship date. A store that can't give you the information either hasn't ordered the dress, or hasn't heard back from the manufacturer. Either way there's a problem. Keep on them until you get the ship date. It's your guarantee that the gown has been ordered.

5. *Develop a good rapport with the store.* Be pleasant and make sure they get to know you. As a store owner, I can tell you that I'm much more inclined to go out of my way for a kind, decent, rational bride than for an overbearing, demanding one.

WHAT IF SOMETHING GOES WRONG?

Things can go wrong. Here are some examples:

1. *The dress isn't in on time.* If your gown doesn't come in on time (and it's two weeks before the wedding), have the store provide you with another. It may not be the same one you ordered, however, unless you agree to take the sample. If you do, *it should cost much less.* Always make the store take the responsibility for the error, no matter whose fault it is—theirs or the manufacturer's—but try to be understanding. Mistakes happen even in the best of stores.

2. *The dress comes in the wrong size or in the wrong color.* I once ordered a gown in a size 4 instead of a size 14. It was an honest error. The bride, however, had ordered her gown in plenty of time, and when I explained my problem to the manufacturer he got me another dress in a few weeks. That's why it's so important to order your gown with time to spare. Allow for all contingencies. The same holds true if the gown is delivered in the wrong color. It can always be returned if there's time.

3. *The store won't give you a ship date.* It's four weeks since you've ordered your gown and the store doesn't have a ship date? Cancel the order. Write a certified letter to your credit card company with a certified copy to the bridal store. Purchase the gown elsewhere.

4. *The store goes out of business.* If your deposit was placed on a credit card, you should be able to recoup your losses. If you didn't, you're out of luck, other than to file a claim in small claims court. File fast, hopefully before the store files for bankruptcy protection.

IN CONCLUSION . . .

Shopping for a wedding gown—to save money—can be fun and enjoyable if you go about it in the right way. I've shown you that it's possible to find the gown of your dreams and stay within your budget. Study, take notes, shop hard, get everything in writing, and give yourself plenty of time. Then you'll be just like the brides in the *Modern Bride* survey: *Shopping for your gown* will *be the most pleasurable aspect of planning your wedding!*

Part III: Bridesmaids' Dresses

DON'T LET 'EM GET YOU DOWN

How many times have you said to yourself when asked to be a bridesmaid, "Oh, *no*! Not another horrendous dress!" As much as you like the dear bride, the thought of spending hundreds of dollars on something you'll never wear again isn't the most pleasant. Well, the tables have turned. *You're the bride*. What are you going to do?

YOUR CHOICES

Most bridesmaid dress manufacturers who make dresses that are wearable to functions other than weddings are expensive. Besides, 99 percent of the time, the dresses have to be altered, an additional cost to your maids. Then there's oversize and extra-length charges (if a maid is extra heavy or extra tall) and undergarments, shoes, jewelry . . . The list—and money—is endless.

WHAT SHOULD YOU DO?

• *Have them made?* In my opinion, this is not a viable solution. It's too stressful, time-consuming, and hectic. Besides, in all my years in this business, I've only seen one bride happy with the results. Skip the trauma and let them buy the dresses.

• *Buy them at a department store?* Recently, I was in an upscale department store in the local mall. I was shocked by both the quality and the availability of the dresses. The dresses hung on racks in all colors, all sizes, looked terrific, and the *prices were less than comparable bridesmaids' dresses!* (Not only that, they could be cut down and worn again.) What's wrong with this option? Get your maids' sizes and start looking. If a size isn't available, ask the store if they can get it for you. And remember, you can always return merchandise at a department store— and watch for sales!

• *Let the maids select their own dresses?* Yes, provided you lay the ground rules. Specify dress length, sleeve length, amount of glitz permissible, and type of fabric. And the most important factor: *color*. One shade of black, for example, can look different from another because of the dye lot. If you decide to go this route, send your maids a color swatch and tell them to match it as closely as possible.

YOU MAKE THE CHOICE

Don't let your maids make you crazy. You're the bride, you make the decision as to what they should wear based on what you think is best. If they're not choosing their own dress, try to select a style that's flattering to all. Take along your maid of honor or your mom to help make the decision. (Don't take four women into a bridal salon to make the selection; you'll get nothing but frustrated.)

IF YOU ORDER

Order your maids' dresses a week or two after you order your wedding gown (about five to six months ahead of the wedding date). The dress you choose must complement your gown. For that reason, maids' dresses are always ordered after the bride's.

If you wait until the last minute, you may have to pay a *rush-cut fee*—an additional fee to get the dresses delivered sooner than the normal twelve-week delivery date. Don't let your maids in for this extra expenditure. *Order early.* This is also a safeguard. If the dresses are delivered in the wrong color, there will be plenty of time to return them for replacements.

An Alternative

If you order dresses, there might be a pleasant alternative for your maids. Many of my clients give their bridal party the option of selecting *their own style of dress*—provided they order from the same manufacturer, in the same length, color, and fabric. Because these brides were understanding and flexible, their maids had a choice! A heavier woman might select a dress with a short, cap sleeve, for example, while another might select a tank top. It makes everyone happy and everyone looks great— and similar. What a wonderful compromise.

Get It in Writing

Get all details in writing, no matter where you purchase your dresses. Sizes, colors, style numbers must all be listed, along with additional charges. Make sure the deposit paid is noted on the receipt.

Precautions

When ordering dresses, it's essential that you get the correct sizes. Follow the instructions in this chapter for the wedding gown. Measure maids the same way. Do not order from any store that will not show you the manufacturer's size chart. Call a couple of weeks after purchase to confirm the order and to get the *ship date* from the store. Follow up on a regular basis.

Chapter Seventeen

THE HEADPIECE AND VEIL

Garland your hair with marjoram,
Soft-scented; veil your face and come
Smiling down to us, saffron shoes
On milk-white feet.

—Catullus, c. 60 B.C.

SAVING MONEY

WANT TO SAVE A HUNDRED DOLLARS OR EVEN TWO OR MORE?

Make your own headpiece and veils. It's easy, fun, and *very* economical. Look in bridal magazines to get a feel for what you want. Cut the photos out and put them in your notebook.

THE PERFECT HAIRSTYLE

Once you get your dress, decide on how you want to wear your hair. Find a hairdresser who's willing to experiment with you and work with him or her to find the perfect "do," one that flatters your face to perfection.

Tip: Once your hair is styled, take a good look in the mirror. Do you notice the hair first or your face? If you notice the hair, it's not the style for you.

Once you determine a hairstyle, choose a headpiece. Not the other way around. Your headpiece must complement your hairstyle, which complements your face, which complements your gown, and *creates a total picture. That's what counts.* Take the pictures of headpieces and veils from your notebook. Are they in sync with your dress and hairstyle? If not, throw them away and begin to look at photos that resemble your dress and models who feature a hairstyle like yours.

If You Purchase Your Headpiece and Veil

Try on your dress, then select a headpiece and veil to match. The laces must look alike (or be similar). The color of the sequins must match and the veil color must be the same as the gown. If your headpiece and veil are included in the price of your dress, chances are that you're paying an inflated price for the gown. Sometimes package deals aren't what they seem. Shop around to ensure you're getting the best price.

Making It

Go to a craft store, fabric store, or outlet and purchase some hat frames: headbands, tiaras, Juliet caps—whatever you'd like. They are inexpensive. Then go home to experiment with them and your hairstyle. (Return the ones you don't use.) If the frame is too wide, cut it to the right size with some wire clippers or scissors or bend it to make it smaller. If it's too big for your head, cut the back wire in half and put the ends back together, overlapping them to make the frame smaller. Once the frame fits, tightly tape the ends together using cloth tape in white or ivory or glue it. Once you find the shape that suits you—and it fits your head—you're ready to begin.

Matching the Dress

If there's lace on your dress and you'd like a lace headpiece, ask the store to order a quarter-yard of lace. (Ask what the cost is before you purchase. Some laces are extremely expensive.) If the lace is too costly, skip it. Buy lace that's close in design at a fabric shop. If you've bought a sample dress, ask the store to call the manufacturer and request lace. If it's not available, buy some that's close in design. You may also use silk flowers. Buy them at a craft store in the color and varieties you prefer. If you choose, you may also decorate with faux pearls and rhinestones or little satin roses or bows (all are available at craft stores in the decorating or silk-flower departments).

To Start

It's easy to make a veil. First, buy tulle from a fabric outlet in either white or ivory. It's downright cheap. To make a *cathedral* veil (long), you'll need four yards of tulle. A *fingertip* veil (medium length) requires a yard and a half, and a *shoulder-length* veil a yard. A *blusher*, the veil that covers the face, requires about a yard of tulle. You may have only one veil, or one of each, or a combination of veils. I often do two-tone veils. Some gowns are a combination of white and ivory, so I mix and match the tulle. It's a gorgeous, soft, elegant look. It's all up to you and what you prefer.

To properly measure the length of the veil(s), put your hat frame on your head. With a tape measure, have a friend measure the length from the hat frame (where the veil will be attached) to the length you want the veil. If it's cathedral length, measure 12 inches past the train. (The veil will pull shorter as you walk.) If measuring for the blusher, remember that it attaches at the back of the hat frame—not the front. It covers the headpiece when the bride walks up the aisle. At some point during the ceremony, the blusher will be flipped back, exposing the headpiece.

Cutting the Veil(s)

Step 1: Tulle comes on a bolt (and it's doubled twice). To begin, put it on a large table and unfold it once (it will still be doubled). Cut it lengthwise to the length you desire. On the table, the folded end will be on one side, the cut end on the other.

Step 2: Round off the tulle at one end by cutting (rounding) the tulle from the fold to the open end (it will look like a half-circle when cut). Take the tulle from the table and unfold it at the top (the uncut end). With your hands, gather the top together until the width is four or five inches, or the size of your comb, barette, or headpiece.

Step 3: With your sewing machine, or by hand, sew the gathered top of the tulle together.

Step 4: Sew the gathered end of the tulle onto a comb, or glue on a piece of Velcro. (If using Velcro, sew or glue the opposite piece of Velcro onto the gathered end of the tulle, whichever you prefer.)

The veil is done! Make as many as you'd like! We put our veils on combs so that they're easily removable. You may sew on as many veils as you want (to one comb). To make the veil(s) removable from the headpice, glue or sew on a piece of Velcro to the back of the headpiece. Then sew or glue on the corresponding piece of Velcro to the veil(s). It's up to you.

MAKING A BLUSHER

Step 1: The blusher is measured from the back of the headpiece to the front of the bodice. It stops in the middle of the bustline.

Step 2: To make, follow the above steps in "Cutting the Veil(s)." Once you've rounded the tulle unfold it. From the long side (opposite the side with the rounded ends), gather the tulle in your hands until it bunches, and follow Steps 3 and 4.

DECORATING THE VEILS

After the veil(s) is finished, it's time to decorate it (if you want). You may glue sequins or pearls to the veil(s). You may also choose to glue sequins or pearls onto your pouff (more about this later). It's easy. Or, you may even trim the veil with ribbon in a color that matches your dress, in any width you'd like.

To sew on ribbon, you need a sewing machine and minimal skill. (If you don't sew, ask a friend or family member who does.) Sew the ribbon to the tulle, about an inch from the edge. Then trim the tulle with scissors. It's simple. *Do not put a trim on a blusher.* It cuts the dress with a horizontal line. A blusher should be subtle. In the same vein, it's not wise to put pearls or sequins on a blusher. They'll make you look like you have measles.

To do something different, decorate the veil(s) with silk-flower petals. I recently did one that was a knockout! I bought silk roses at an outlet and then pulled them apart, petal by petal. The petals were in all sizes. (I cut the ends off the petals, the part that was attached to the stem.) Then, with my Beacon Fabric Tac glue, I glued them all over the lower half of the cathedral veil. The dress I was matching was a simple silk gown. The only adornment: roses around the neckline. I made the headpiece from silk roses and this veil was the perfect touch. It was elegant and easy to make. By the same token, if you had a dress that featured bows, you might glue small bows all over the back veil(s). Once again, let your imagination soar!

MAKING A POUFF

Some brides want a pouff (a cloudlike piece of tulle that frames the face and attaches to the back wire of a hat frame or headpiece). It also serves another purpose; it hides the back wire or the back of the headpiece. You may make a pouff large or small. It's all a matter of taste.

To Make

Steps 1 and 2: On a table, lay out a piece of tulle (don't unfold). Cut a piece two feet wide and unfold it completely. Fold both ends, width-wise, into the center, then fold both ends, length-wise into the center, overlapping the edges slightly.

Step 3: Pin the piece together at the center, from the top to the bottom.

Step 4: With your sewing machine, using a loop stitch, or by hand, sew down the center seam.

Steps 5 and 6: Remove the pouff from the sewing machine by cutting the thread or by cutting the thread from your needle if sewn by hand. With one hand hold the pouff and with the other hand pull the thread, as you push against the pouff. This motion will cause the pouff to gather. You should gather the pouff until it reaches the length of the back wire or back frame of your headpiece.

Step 7: The pouff is then sewn to the back wire or to the back of the headpiece.

Note: Always remember to pull the folds of the pouff apart with your fingers. It gives it a wonderful, soft look. Spray with clear, non-yellowing hair spray to hold the pouff in shape.

ATTACHING THE VEIL(S)

If your veil(s) is on a comb, it is simply inserted into the hair under the pouff and as close to the back wire (or back) of the headpiece as possible. The comb will be disguised by the pouff. To make the veil detachable, use Velcro. After sewing on the pouff, glue a piece of Velcro against the back wire or the back of the headpiece (underneath the pouff), and glue a corresponding piece on the veil. Once again, the pouff will hide the Velcro.

MAKING THE HEADPIECE

If you choose to make a plain fabric headpiece, studded, for example, with rhinestones, pearls, sequins, or silk flowers, it's necessary to cover a hat frame with fabric. Buy fabric that closely matches your dress at a fabric store or outlet and make sure the color is close. Cut pieces to fit the hat frame and glue on with Beacon Fabric Tac. (If the seams look unfinished, cover them by gluing on a narrow strip of ribbon in the same color. It works wonders!) Next, put a dot of glue on a piece of paper. With tweezers, dip the rhinestones, pearls, silk flowers, or sequins into the glue and place them on the fabric in a decorative pattern. It's that easy.

If you'd prefer a lace headpiece, it's not always necessary to cover the frame. Cut out small pieces of lace. Glue the lace onto the frame. If you'd like the piece to have dimension, glue cotton balls onto the frame—some big, some not so big—in strategic places. Then cover the cotton tufts with lace. It will give the piece a 3-D effect. You might then add small satin roses or small bows, for example. Let your imagination run wild.

MAKING A CROWN

Steps 1 and 2: Cut a round hat frame (available at fabric and craft stores) to the desired size to fit your head. Cut with wire clippers and glue back together.

Step 3: Glue on whatever you desire: flowers, lace, sequins, pearls.

Steps 4 and 5: Buy premade button loops (available at fabric and craft outlets), and glue onto the back of the headpiece or on the sides—wherever you choose. The comb (or bobby pins) will fit through the loops and will hold the headpiece securely in place.

MAKING A HEADBAND

You may buy a satin headband that needs no covering or a foam one that needs to be covered. If you must cover the band, do it with ribbon. Glue one end of the ribbon to one end of the headband and wrap the ribbon around it from one end to the other, overlapping and gluing as you go. Then decorate any way you choose, with lace, flowers, pearls, or sequins. Button loops are added to the headband (as they were to the crown), and it's made secure by using either a comb or bobby pins. I advise putting the veil(s) on a separate comb.

MAKING A TIARA FROM A WIRE FRAME

Most hat frames are round and are made from either buckram or wire. Either way, they are designed to fit easily on the head, but if the piece is too large, it will have to be cut down. Cut the back wire with wire clippers, fit it to the size of your head and tape the two ends back together with white or ivory fabric tape; make sure it's very secure.

Starting with a wire hat frame, glue lace directly to it. Next, glue silk flowers on top, and later a few silk leaves. (You may decide to first cover the frame with fabric or ribbon.) The tiara is finished.

ATTACHING THE VEIL(S)

A veil(s) may be stitched directly to the back wire (if you don't want to remove it). Sew the veil(s) by hand to the entire length of the wire so that it's covered. It's easy. If you can stitch a hem that's come undone, you can sew a veil to a hat frame wire.

If you prefer to remove your veils for the reception, your hair should be styled so that it covers the back wire. The veils can then be sewn onto a separate comb, and the comb placed in your hair. Or, you can cover the back wire with a little lace. Underneath the lace, glue on a narrow strip of Velcro. Sew or glue the corresponding piece of Velcro to your veils, and stick the veils onto the headpiece. After the ceremony, simply remove the veils. You may also decide to cover the back wire with a pouff. Simply sew it on. Underneath, glue on a narrow piece of Velcro (for disposable veils), or sew your veil(s) onto the wire and then sew on the pouff. The choice is yours.

USING A COMB

You may design your headpiece using a simple comb, which is placed on the back of the head. Cut a hat frame (buckram) to the desired dimensions; for example, an oval shape that is two by four inches. Sew it onto your comb, then cover with fabric, lace, or silk flowers—whatever your heart desires. Glue Velcro to the buckram to attach a veil(s), or sew directly onto the buckram. Or, you may sew the veils onto a separate comb. If you do, put the veils on first. Then put the comb (with the headpiece) on top.

Bows also make beautiful headpieces. Make a bow from fabric that matches your dress. Glue on pearls or whatever. Sew the bow onto a comb. Underneath the bow attach Velcro, or sew your veils on permanently.

To Save Money—Make Your Headpiece and Veil

There's no excuse not to make your headpiece and veil(s). You can experiment to your heart's content and make a picture-perfect piece that will make your friends green with envy (to match all those green dollars you saved)! (For more information about making your own veil, get my video, *Heart-stopping Headpieces and Veils: Make Yours and $ave*, see appendix I.)

Chapter Eighteen

THE WEDDING CAKE

Everyone ... has an Aunt Emma with an oven, but would you let her make your wedding cake?

—Don Sheff, president, New York Institute of Photography

When I interviewed Don Sheff for my first book, *For the Bride*, I held this truth, his statement, to be self-evident. It was undisputed fact. I'm not one for baking and I would never consider the idea of making a birthday cake let alone a *wedding cake*. But after years of planning weddings and researching this book, I began to have second thoughts about Aunt Emma. . . .

ALL CAKES ARE NOT CREATED EQUAL

• What makes for a great cake?

• Why do prices vary so much?

• I don't care about the cake—no one ever eats it.

• My caterer suggests serving a terrific dessert after dinner, so any dumpy cake will do.

• We're going to cut the cake at the beginning of the reception because the caterer needs time to slice it and serve it.

Daily, these comments flow from the mouths of my clients and they make me wonder: *What in the world has given wedding cakes such a bad rap?*

Take a few minutes to sit back and examine the role of the wedding cake throughout history. Think of the melt-in-your-mouth taste of a fantastic mocha cream or a rich, luscious, fruit-filled carrot cake. Imagine the elegance of a white wedding cake, five tiers high, iced in a basket weave of French vanilla buttercream, topped with fresh, dew-laden flowers that fall casually down its sides. How can anyone slough off the significance, beauty, and taste of this wonderful cake? There's none other like it! It's a once-in-a-lifetime experience.

When in Rome . . .

The Ancient Romans began the tradition of wedding cake. During the ceremony, the bride and groom were fed morsels broken from a wheat biscuit or roll. The remainder was crumbled over the bride's head as a symbol of fertility. The concept caught on, passed through the centuries, and was adopted by the various cultures of the civilized world. By the time the custom reached Elizabethan England, the wheat cake, a symbol of sharing and fertility, had become more than just tradition. The Elizabethans stacked the rolls high and placed them on their reception tables as centerpieces, for all their guests to admire and enjoy.

But it took those effervescent, pastry-loving French to envision that these simple, primitive centerpieces, concocted from wheat biscuits, could be held together with sugar frosting. (This was the forerunner of the tiered wedding cake.) But *oh* what the French did with those rolls!

The coarse wheat rolls evolved into succulent, fine-textured, cream-filled puffs. These too were stacked high, but were held together by the sticky sweetness of caramel. Later, the heavenly wispiness of spun sugar was used to decorate these sumptuous shiny golden pastries. In France, a bride and groom may still request the *croquembouche* (literal translation: crunchy mouthful) for their wedding cake, a remnant of seventeenth-century tradition. The wedding cake embodies a sense of history, of happiness and gaiety, fertility, plenty, and good luck. *It is tradition*. Give it the respect it deserves.

No One Ever Eats It: A Double-Edged Dilemma

A wedding cake is a dichotomy. Supposedly, few people eat it, but what would a wedding be without one? It is tradition. Yet it's expensive and costs hundreds, even thousands of dollars. So the question is: Why would anyone in their right mind spend good money on something that no one eats? When I began researching this chapter, it became evident to me that a wedding cake means one thing (any way you cut it): A waste of hard-earned dollars! Be smart. It doesn't have to be.

Don't Be Duped! Here's How to Save Money

Don't let a caterer talk you into serving dessert with dinner. *You've paid for a wedding cake (even if it's part of your packaged deal.)* Its purpose is to be seen, admired, *and eaten*. You may have spent hundreds, or even thousands of dollars on this traditional cake. *It is dessert!* While it's true that the wedding cake is cut and served long after dinner is over (which is why your caterer will insist that you serve an *additional* dessert with dinner), an additional dessert is redundant and will cost you more money.

If your catering contract includes an expensive dessert like cherries jubilee (that you're paying for), cancel it! Or, if your cake—and an additional dessert—are part of your packaged deal, cancel the dessert and put those dollars elsewhere! Spend the money on your honeymoon, or *upgrade your cake*. Instead of *their* dessert, end the meal with a light sorbet, for example, or strawberries dipped in chocolate (one per guest). If that proves too costly, put a good plate of chocolate mints on the table. The repast should always end with something sweet.

You are throwing money down the drain if you purchase a wedding cake and then serve an opulent dessert with dinner. Who's going to have room to eat cake an hour or so later, no matter how good it is? By the same token, you throw money away if you purchase an inedible, tasteless "dumpy" cake. *Who would want to eat it?*

Make your cake the pièce de résistance it should be. End the meal with light fare and save the cake for later, when everyone can enjoy it and savor it. Make it as delectable inside as it looks outside. I guarantee you: *They will eat cake, and you will have put your hard-earned dollars to good use!*

Your Cake Is the Last Hurrah

I've seen numerous postings on the Internet about cutting the cake at the beginning of the reception. Why waste good money on a beautiful cake, only to have it ravaged at the beginning of the party? *The cake is the focal point of the reception, to be looked at and admired.* It should be cut at the end of the evening, no matter what the caterer tells you.

Be Aware: Cake-Cutting Fees

After reading this chapter you may decide to make your own cake, or you may decide to hire a private premium baker. Many establishments, however, charge a cake-cutting fee if you serve a cake other than theirs. (A fee is charged, per person, to cut and serve the cake.) This can get expensive, and it's outrageous! You've already paid a fortune to have your reception at their establishment. Why should you have to pay extra to have your cake cut? You shouldn't. Be a tough negotiator and get the charge waived. You should not have to pay for cake cutting!

To solve the problem with the least amount of contention, tell the caterer that your aunt, uncle, etc. is a professional baker who is providing the cake as their wedding gift to you. He or she would be greatly insulted and hurt if you served anyone's cake but theirs. You'll be surprised at how quickly this revelation may solve your problem.

Your Contract: What It Should Include

- *The date, time, and place of the affair.*
- *The time the cake is to be delivered.*
- *The specific size of the cake; how many it's*

to feed; the number of layers and design. For example: one, four-tier, chocolate, double-fudge cake with raspberry filling. The first layer:

twelve-inch round; the second: ten-inch round; the third: eight-inch round; and the fourth: six-inch round. The first two layers are not separated. Lifters (that look like small, white Grecian columns) are placed between the second and third layers, and the third and top layer. No decorations are placed between layers. The icing is white buttercream in a basket-weave design. The cake will feed 150 people.

- *The cake topper:* whose responsibility it is to provide it and what it consists of, and its design, if the baker is providing it. For example, the cake topper will be made up of white and pale pink marzipan roses, about six inches tall.
- *The person (or company) responsible for assembling and decorating and what the decorating is to include.* For example, fresh white and pink roses in a cascade, from top to bottom. Base to be covered in greens, dotted with pink and white roses and baby's breath.
- *Waiver of cake-cutting fees (if applicable).*
- *Total cost of the cake, including delivery and set-up fees (if any), applicable sales tax, deposit paid, and when the balance is due.*
- *Cancellation and refund policy.* The contract should contain a clause stating that the deposit is transferable if you have to cancel for any reason, provided you reserve another cake with the vendor within a year of the cancellation of the contract. (Both parties should initial the change.)

THE GROOM'S CAKE

Early American wedding cakes were fruit-cakes, part of a tradition that the Pilgrims brought with them to America. It wasn't until the advent of white flour, baking powder, and baking soda in the 1800s that white wedding cake as we know it became the norm. The tradition of fruitcake, however, has withstood the test of time (and is still popular in many parts of our country), and is the cake that later became known as the *groom's cake*. At the reception, it was cut, boxed, and given to the guests as a favor. Legend has it that single guests who placed the boxed cake under their pillows would dream of their intended. Hence, it became known as *dreaming bread*. Traditionally, the groom's cake is placed beside the bride's and today it may come in any flavor or shape that the groom desires (after all, it's *his* cake).

When I interviewed Sylvia Weinstock, that prestigious baker of celebrity cakes, she showed me one of her groom's cakes. It was a life-size golf cart, constructed entirely of cake, even the wheels! It was an incredible engineering feat. And *wow!* What a cake!

A WORD ABOUT CAKE TOPPERS

I don't advise using anything valuable on the top of a cake—your grandmother's antique crystal figurine or an expensive Precious Moments porcelain. If the cake table is bumped, off flies the cake topper. Also, too often they're stolen. Use fresh flowers on top of the cake or an inexpensive piece of porcelain. *Don't put anything atop a cake that you will worry about!*

A Five-Part Plan for Success: Here Are Your Options

Premise: I will serve my wedding cake as dessert.
Statement of Fact: The cake must be divine and delicious.
Goal: To serve an elegant, delectable cake—*economically!*

But How?

The following tips are essential elements in creating the wedding cake of your dreams. Discuss each of them with your baker.

1. Know Your Cake, Inside and Out

Whether you've hired your own baker or your cake is part of your packaged deal, meet personally with the baker who will create your cake. Here are some tips for success from Sylvia Weinstock:

- The size of the cake should relate to the size of the room. Tall ceilings, for example, require a tall cake.
- The size of the cake should relate to the size of the bride and groom. If they're small people, the cake should not overpower them. If they're tall, the cake should be also.
- The cake should relate to the ambiance of its surroundings. If it's positioned in a formal, ornate room, the cake should be formal and ornate, too. If it's outdoors, surrounded by light and beautiful, colorful flowers, the cake should also be airy and vibrant.
- Relate the color of the cake to the color of the room, not the bridal party colors. Let's say your colors are hot pink and white and the walls of your reception room are paisley, green, and purple. Would you want a fuchsia and white wedding cake? When in doubt, go white.

- *Get everything in writing.* The most common complaint I hear from brides, after the fact, is that their cake wasn't designed to their specifications. Put everything in writing and leave nothing to chance.

2. Know Your Ingredients, or A Rose By Any Other Name Will Not Smell as Sweet

What makes for a great cake? *The ingredients.* That's the reason supermarket cakes are considerably cheaper than those made by private, premium bakers like Sylvia Weinstock.

Most supermarkets use prepared mixes. Add a little water and *voila!* you've got a wedding cake. Not so with premium bakers: butter, the finest cake flour, fresh eggs, and imported chocolate are the stuff of their cakes. These bakers really do put *your* money where *your* mouth is!

Ask the baker what type of ingredients he or she uses. If they utilize the prepackaged variety, either for the cake or the frosting, it's my advice to go elsewhere. You want a baker who mixes their own cake using fresh butter, eggs, milk, and cream. And one who creates their own icing using the finest ingredients. The taste of a premixed cake covered in prepackaged frosting (that's spiked with preservatives) is not worth their time or effort, or the money you're spending. *You want a real cake with real frosting!* Make your demands known.

3. Decorating Spells M-O-N-E-Y!

Bakers charge to decorate cakes. The more sugar roses, for example, the higher the cost. For that reason, *don't have it decorated.* Tell the baker to ice the cake with a smooth buttercream frosting and let your family, friends, or florist do the rest. All the baker needs to do is deliver and assemble the cake—well in advance of the reception (see "Decorating: What You Must Know," this chapter).

If the florist is decorating the cake, have him or her make a cake crown of fresh flowers for the top. Once the cake is assembled, he or she can put fresh flowers between the layers or around the layers. Fresh flowers and greens can then be put artistically around the base. (See "Warning: Fresh Flowers," this chapter.)

4. WHEN THE CAKE IS PART OF THE PACKAGE

When the catering facility or caterer includes the cake, it may be necessary to pay an additional fee to upgrade it. However, since you're no longer serving *their* dessert, they should be glad to exchange it for an upgrade to your cake. If you want extensive decorating, however, you may still have to pay an additional fee.

5. THE ULTIMATE MONEY SAVER: LET'S TALK DOLLARS AND SENSE

What I'm going to say may shock you, but it will save you money and you just may have some fun. Since quality ingredients are the key to a great cake, and these ingredients are used only by premium, costly bakers, *why not make your own?* Don't slam this book down in disgust! Think about it.

BAKE YOUR OWN CAKE EASILY, ELEGANTLY, ECONOMICALLY

It's easy to make a cake. I'm going to teach you how. In fact, I'm going to include recipes from some of the best bakers in this country (appendix II). Also included are tips for successful baking and decorating! (For information on my video, *Wedding Cake Concepts: Making Yours Easily, Elegantly, Economically,* see appendix I.) Just Think: The cake can be made and frozen in advance, frosted a day or two before, and kept in the refrigerator until it's time to take it to the reception site, where it's decorated.

It's my suggestion to bake the cake at the home of a relative or friend who is willing to store it, frost it, deliver it, and decorate it. This can be their wedding present to you. Or, if you have an Aunt Emma or a friend who's a great baker and would like to contribute the cake as a wedding gift, let them. Or, if you know of someone who would like to do it as a gift to you but can't afford the ingredients, buy the goods and let them make it.

You don't have to make a round-tier wedding cake. It could be a square-tier wedding cake. Or a combination of round and square. It doesn't even have to be tiered. You may decide to feature many different cakes, on different cake platters, all different heights, surrounded and topped by fresh flowers (bought at the supermarket). Look at the photos in this chapter. They should give you some terrific ideas.

THE TIMETABLE: MAKING THE CAKE, SYRUP, AND FROSTING

Wedding cakes can be made up to two months in advance and frozen (although for the best taste, make the cake as close to the wedding date as possible). Some cake recipes call for a dousing of *syrup,* a simple-to-make concoction that keeps cakes fresher and moister. Syrup can be made a few weeks in advance and kept in the refrigerator. Buttercream frosting can be made months in advance and frozen.

TASTE FIRST—EXPERIMENT!

Most cake recipes divide the batter. One part of the recipe may include instructions for making a two-layer ten-inch cake, the other part for a two-layer six-inch cake and a two-layer eight-inch cake. To experiment, make a two-layer ten-inch cake. Make one-third of the syrup recipe (if called for), and one-half of the frosting recipe (so that you'll have plenty to work with). By trial and error, you'll not only find the cake of your dreams, *you'll be gaining experience*.

Note: Light cakes, like lemon, are great to serve after a heavy meal or a late-evening reception. Dense cakes, like chocolate or carrot, are terrific for a cocktail–hors d'oeuvre reception, where lighter food has been served. Once you know what you want, you can hand the recipe and the decorating over to that special family member or friend who's making your cake (if you're not doing it yourself). Make sure you practice together beforehand.

Note: If baking for one hundred guests, you could make a lemon wedding cake for fifty and a chocolate groom's cake for fifty. Serve them both when the wedding cake is cut. After all, variety is the spice of life.

DECORATING: WHAT YOU MUST KNOW

By baking and decorating your own cake, you'll have the opportunity of producing a quality, luxuriant cake for *much less* than the cost of a premium baker (and for *much less* than

a supermarket cake!). And just think how proud you'll be.

I'm going to teach you how to decorate simply, easily, and elegantly, without buying pastry bags with fluted tips and all the other paraphernalia that professional bakers use for decorating. It's money wasted, time consuming, and the techniques professionals' employ would literally take you years to learn.

Professional baker Ron Ben-Israel (whose wedding cakes have been featured in many national magazines including *Modern Bride*, *New York Magazine*, and *Martha Stewart's Living*) says, "To avoid disappointment and heartbreak, don't try to duplicate techniques that take years to master. Elegance is an understatement. It's better to aim toward clean lines."

In this book, I'm featuring Ron's recipe for a wonderful European Genoise wedding cake (with white-chocolate buttercream frosting. *Yum!*). He is an up-and-coming star—and his cakes taste as celestial as they look! (For more information about Ron Ben-Israel, see appendix I and II.)

To keep things simple, all you'll need to decorate a cake, with the *Debbie Method*, is a long rounded metal spatula for applying frosting, cardboard cake rounds, and an inexpensive Tupperware turntable. You'll also need decorative items like ribbons, pearls, or fresh or dried flowers to put on or around the cake. Let your imagination take flight!

Look at the photos of cakes in this chapter. Neither took over forty-five minutes to decorate. I went to craft stores and picked up ribbons and faux pearls, three inexpensive porcelain pieces, and cheap stackable candy jars. I shopped at a Christmas outlet for items to decorate the holiday cake.

The cakes are frosted smooth. There are no fancy swirls, trims, or roses made with icing. That's not for us. I used stackable candy jars, in some instances, to hold single layers at varying heights rather than tier the cake, which is

TWO "DEBBIE DECORATED" CAKES

For the Holiday Cake:
Ribbon is cut for each layer, using the cake pans as a guide. It's pressed into the frosting, around the bottom of each layer (it sticks to the frosting). Artificial greens are put around the base, and candles are used for a romantic effect. A gold poinsettia is put on top.

For an Elegant Cake:
Inexpensive, stackable candy jars are filled with faux pearls and make for interesting cake stands. Faux pearls are pressed into the smooth frosting, and small, gold-sprayed, affordable porcelain pieces are placed on top. Fresh greens are put around the base and are adorned with the pearls.

more difficult. And I decorated *around* the cake, rather than decorating the cake itself. This is the easiest way to get a professional, elegant look in the least amount of time with the least amount of hassle.

Practice by buying a couple of cheap frosted layer cakes in varying sizes from the supermarket. Whack off all the do-dads and stick the cakes in the freezer until the frosting hardens. Frost over them with canned frosting if necessary to get a smooth surface. Then buy ribbons, pearls, etc., and experiment to your heart's content. To practice tiering the layers, follow the instructions in this chapter. (Or, you can do a trial run of your actual cake. *Practice makes perfect.*)

Once you've designed the wedding cake of your dreams, take pictures of it. *These photos will be the decorating blueprint that's followed on the day of the reception.* Be sure to practice with that artsy relative or friend who will be doing the decorating on the *big* day. Make a *decorating kit* ahead of time that includes everything they'll need to take to the reception to assemble and trim the cake, and don't forget the photos.

The Basic Rules of Good Baking

It's not hard to bake a good cake. But it's important that you adhere to the rules. *Cake baking is an exact science so follow the recipe to the letter.* Baking a cake is not like making soup. You can't add more salt while it's cooking to enhance the flavor.

INGREDIENTS

All ingredients should be fresh, including spices and flavorings. If your condiments are a year old or are not fragrant, throw them away. Flour, baking powder, and baking soda should also be fresh. Use only pure extracts, no imitation flavorings. *All ingredients should be room temperature when baking.*

For the purpose of making a wedding cake—the most important cake you'll ever make—*you are not going to substitute ingredients.* You're not going to use Cool Whip in place of whipped cream, for example, or margarine for butter. This is one time when you're going to throw calories to the wind!

When the recipe calls for:

- butter, use only unsalted butter
- milk and cream, use whole milk and whipping cream (preferably pasteurized cream, *not* ultra-pasteurized. It can be found at organic-food stores or health-food stores)
- cream cheese, use only regular cream cheese
- eggs, use only large eggs
- sugar, use only white granulated sugar or preferably, superfine sugar
- brown sugar, use only regular light or dark brown sugar
- flour, use only cake flour, *not* self-rising

Put sugars (white and brown), flour, and cornstarch in tightly sealed containers to protect them from humidity. Store them at room temperature.

Buy nuts in health food stores or organic food stores. Place them in freezer bags and freeze. Dried fruits should also be purchased in health-food stores or organic-food stores. To plump them, cover with cold water and boil for a few minutes. Cool them completely before using them in a recipe.

BAKING TOOLS AND MEASURING TECHNIQUES

I don't advise investing money in equipment that you'll probably never use again. But some tools are a necessity and can be used in your kitchen forever.

- *Electric mixer*, preferably the five-quart variety (which comes on a stand). If you don't have one, borrow one from your mom or a relative. (Any good electric handheld mixer will do for mixing cake batter or buttercream frosting, but the five-quart variety makes it easier.)
- *Individual measuring cups* (preferably Foley or Tupperware) should be used for dry ingredients. *Note the difference in measuring technique* (depending on the recipe's requirements).

To Measure Correctly

If the recipe states 1 cup sifted flour, place a solid measuring cup (unbroken rim, no spout) on a piece of wax paper (to catch excess). Sift flour into the cup, allowing it to mound over the top. *Do not touch or tap the cup*. Level off by running a knife blade or spatula across the rim of the cup.

If, on the other hand, the recipe calls for 1 cup flour, sifted, stir the flour with a spoon to aerate. Dip your cup into the flour and fill the cup. Level off by running a knife blade or spatula across the rim of the cup. Then sift the flour.

To measure brown sugar, pack it firmly into the measuring cup. Level off with the straight edge of a knife or a spatula.

- *Glass measuring cups* (preferably Pyrex or Oven Basics) are used for measuring liquid ingredients. When measuring quantities of one cup or less, use a one-cup measure. For quantities of two cups or more, use a four-cup measure.
- *Measuring spoons* (preferably Foley or Tupperware) should be used for measuring both dry and liquid ingredients. Dip the spoon into the dry ingredient and level off with the straight edge of a knife. Measure liquids by filling to the top. Never measure over the mixing bowl.
- *Metal spatula(s)*, used for cake decorating, can be found in most kitchen stores.
- *Cardboard cake rounds, squares, or rectangles* are made by cutting corrugated cardboard into the same size as the cake layers. Turn the cake pan(s) over and cut the cardboard to fit the bottom of the pan(s). These can also be bought, precut, in most cooking stores.
- A *Tupperware turntable*, the kind you put under your sink to hold all your cleaning supplies, is perfect for icing your cake.
- *Dowel rods*, either 3/4-inch plastic, or 1/2-inch wooden, found at hardware stores, are used to tier cakes. You need about fifteen.
- A *small craft saw* is used to cut plastic dowel rods. *Pruning shears* are used to cut wooden dowel rods.
- *Baking pans*: Whatever type of baking pans you buy, make sure they're heavy metal. Lightweight aluminum pans, for example, don't bake evenly, but heavier ones do. Buy pans that have a dull finish; they absorb heat better.

Note: All cake pans must be lined with wax paper, buttered, and floured before they're filled with batter. Turn the pan upside down and cut a piece of wax paper to fit the base. Then turn the pan right-side up and put the wax paper in the bottom. Next, butter the bottom and sides of the pan and dust with flour. Invert the pan and knock out excess flour.

Note: It's wise to invest in Magi-Cake Strips. They're metallic strips that are wrapped around cake pans. They prevent the cakes from cooking too fast around the rim and help to keep the cakes level, which makes for easier decorating.

• *Cake platters:* Large, heavy duty plastic platters (that look like cut glass) can be found at party-supply stores and even some supermarkets.

• *Cake racks:* These are metal racks used for cooling cakes. They're open and allow air to circulate. (I improvise by using the racks from my toaster oven and microwave.)

LOGISTICS AND MORE

If making more than one cake (or many layers), it's important to keep storage, logistics, and help in mind. You may need to incorporate the services of two relatives or friends who live close to the reception site and can make, store, frost, deliver, and decorate the cakes for you. Make plans accordingly.

THE OVEN: THE MOST IMPORTANT FACTOR TO GUARANTEE SUCCESS

Rose Levy Beranbaum, cake expert extraordinaire and author of *The Cake Bible*, says that you must test the oven temperature before baking your cake. *Your oven's temperature must be accurate to ensure a successful cake.* Mrs. Beranbaum says that most ovens are off by twenty-five degrees—some as much as forty degrees. That's why it's critical to determine your oven's accuracy.

Rose suggests that you bake a nine-by-one-and-a-half-inch yellow cake to test the oven. (The boxed variety is fine.) If the oven is too hot, the cake will be rounded and test done before twenty-five minutes of baking time. Rose suggests decreasing the temperature by twenty-five degrees. If the cake sinks, however, and takes longer than thirty-five minutes to bake, the oven is not hot enough; raise the temperature by twenty-five degrees. Either way, bake another test cake. *The perfect cake should have an even golden brown crust and be gently rounded or flat. Its texture should be fine, not coarse.*

To Properly Bake a Cake

Cakes must be baked as close to the center of the oven as possible. And, the cake pans must be placed so that plenty of air circulates around them. Don't crowd them. Jane Stacey, a prominent baker who's featured in Martha Stewart's book, *Weddings,* says to bake large layers (twelve inches or greater) one at a time. But, she says, you may bake smaller layers together, on one rack in the center of the oven, *as long as there's plenty of room between the cakes and they're not close to the oven's walls.*

Bake one or two layers at a time (depending on their size), cool completely, and then freeze if you desire. Do a couple more the next day, or next weekend. Relax and enjoy the experience.

To test for doneness, insert a toothpick into the center of the cake; it should come out clean. The cake should also spring back when you touch it in the center. *Cakes under ten inches should not pull away from the sides of the pan until they're removed from the oven.* (This rule, however, does not apply to Genoise, a light, airy European sponge-type cake, which will pull away from the sides of the pan no matter what size it is.)

When the Cake Is Done

Remove it from the oven and cool it on racks for about ten minutes. Run a spatula around the sides and invert the cake on a rack sprayed with nonstick cooking spray. Reinvert the cake so it's right-side up. Let it cool completely before frosting or freezing.

STORING AND FREEZING WEDDING CAKE (DEFROSTING, TOO)

You, or a friend or relative, should make the cake(s) in advance. Once the layers are done, cool completely and freeze each layer by wrapping it in a few sheets of plastic wrap and a few sheets of heavy-duty aluminum foil. Next place it in a freezer bag. (If the cake is too large for a freezer bag, use extra layers of plastic wrap and foil.) To thaw, move the wrapped layers to the refrigerator and let them stand overnight.

A day or two before the wedding remove the top crust and brush the defrosted cake(s) with syrup (if used). Frost the cake(s) and put it back in the refrigerator. (For information on proper frosting techniques, see appendix II.) For the best flavor, a butter cake should be taken out of the refrigerator approximately six hours before serving. Schedule yourself accordingly.

IF YOU'RE SCARED OF BUTTERCREAM—OR SHORT ON TIME

Rose Levy Beranbaum suggests buying prepared buttercream, if you don't want to chance making your own or if time is of the essence. She says it's easy to use, but there's nothing like the real thing. Rose also told me that many times couples make their wedding cake using the recipes in her book (*The Cake Bible*— a must read!). They even send her pictures of the finished product. She's amazed by the beauty of these cakes—made by novices! And, here's a bit of Cordon Rose wisdom for you: "If

you can't make a wedding cake together, think twice about getting married. It's the ultimate acid test!"

IF THE CAKE IS TIERED

A day or two before the reception, ice the layers and put the dowel rods into each tier (see appendix II). Refrigerate each cake tier in a box. Cover loosely with heavy-duty aluminum foil and seal the boxes. The cakes are now ready to be assembled.

On the day of the wedding, take the tiers to the reception site where you will assemble and decorate them. Take a little extra icing and your metal spatula to fix mistakes. Follow the instructions in this chapter and appendix II and give yourself plenty of time.

WARNING: FRESH FLOWERS

Many bakers warn about using fresh flowers on cake since they're treated with insecticides. I advise rinsing the flowers under cool water and letting them dry beforehand, but take note that flowers are grown with insecticides and are *not* edible. *Don't let the flowers penetrate the icing; rest them on top. Be sure to remove all flowers from the cake before it's cut and served.*

TRANSPORTING WEDDING CAKE

Use corrugated cardboard boxes to make cake boxes. Cut them a couple of inches larger than the cake and a couple of inches deeper. (Use a razor-blade knife.) Leave one side open to easily place the cake in the box without touching the sides. Next, put double-edged tape on the bottom of each cake layer (on the cardboard round) and place each layer in a box. The cake should not move. Close and tape the open side of the box. Cover each box with a

layer of cardboard and tape it shut.

Rose suggests putting the layers in the trunk of your car if the weather is cool. She also says to put a damp terry-cloth towel beneath the boxes, which will prevent them from moving. (I would do this no matter how you transport them.)

Warning: When transporting cake, make sure that the vehicle is *cold*. Turn on the air-conditioning well in advance of putting the cake in your car and leave it on. Leave the cake(s) in the refrigerator until they're ready to transport. Buttercream frosting will melt if not kept in cool temperatures.

About the Cakes in this Book and Your Guest List

Most of the recipes in this book are for three-tier cakes. I wouldn't advise that you go higher if you're a beginner. In fact, unless you've practiced, I don't suggest tiering the cake. Look at the example in this chapter. I think our cake is elegant, sophisticated, and beautiful—and it's not tiered! But the decision is yours to make.

The recipes featured in appendix II will feed thirty to one hundred people. When you read a recipe, use your ingenuity. Jane Stacey's wonderful half-sheet cake, which feeds twenty-five to thirty people, can easily be adjusted to serve one hundred. All you have to do is triple the recipe and make three cakes. You may then decide to cut them square and tier them, or put them on different size stands in varying heights and really make their look interesting. It's all up to you.

For those entertaining more than one hundred guests, you may make a separate sheet cake (or a separate, two-layer eight- or nine-inch tier). Either cake will feed about twenty-five to thirty and are made with the same batter, filling, and frosting, but are kept in the kitchen. When the wedding cake is brought to the kitchen to be sliced and served, the sheet cake (or eight- or nine-inch tier) is cut and served too. No one will be the wiser. (If you had 125 guests, for example, you would make one wedding cake for one hundred, and one additional sheet cake or eight- or nine-inch tier.)

And, One Year Later . . .

While it's tradition that the bride and groom freeze the top of their wedding cake for their first-year anniversary, most top professional bakers don't advise it. Many suggest a fruit cake for the top layer, which freezes very well, or you may say, "Oh, what the heck, I'll freeze it anyhow." If that's your attitude, do it this way.

Wrap the cake in a few layers of plastic wrap, then in a few layers of aluminum foil. Place the cake in three freezer bags, one on top of the other, sealing each one. Remove it from the freezer the day before and put it in the refrigerator. Let it come to room temperature before serving. Hopefully, the cake will taste almost as good as new.

In Conclusion . . .

I never anticipated when beginning this chapter that it would evolve into a how-to chapter about baking. *But I firmly believe that you can* *easily make your own delectable, quality cake. You can also make one that's more beautiful than the supermarket variety or even one from a premium baker (for a lot less money!)*. The key is to practice, take your time, and have fun. Turn the cake over to a responsible relative or friend who can *calmly* and *efficiently* handle the last-minute details of transporting, assembling, and decorating. When it comes to your wedding cake, these are the most important details of all. Bon appetit! (See appendix II, for our experts' delicious recipes and instructions on how to frost, tier, assemble, and transport a cake.)

Chapter Nineteen

FORMAL WEAR

Old fashions please me best.   —Shakespeare, *The Taming of the Shrew*

WHAT TO WEAR AND WHEN

TUXES AND TAILS

In the United States, weddings and tuxes and tails appear to go together like love and marriage. They shouldn't. Recently, I received a question from a bride, who said her father insisted that the male members of the bridal party wear tuxes for her semiformal morning wedding. She was against it. She was right.

Tuxes aren't for every wedding. Strollers and cutaways (that resemble tails) are suitable for morning affairs. Tuxes are for late afternoon and evening, and tails are *only* for the most formal evening celebrations. But there are other alternatives.

THE PLAIN BLUE SUIT

For a semiformal affair, like an afternoon wedding, there's nothing wrong with a plain navy blue suit with a white shirt and matching or contrasting tie. It's perfectly appropriate and the look is sophisticated and sharp. Add a boutonniere and the outfit is complete.

THE WHITE DINNER JACKET

For semiformal or formal weddings in tropical climates and in summer, it's perfectly appropriate for men to wear white dinner jackets, white shirts, black cummerbunds and ties, and black pants. It's a crisp, fashionable look and it's elegant. It's also different!

TO SAVE MONEY

Robert Haber, owner of Tuxedo Junction in Boca Raton, Florida, says that you can save money by sticking with the standard black tuxedo. They are inexpensive and the look is classic. You can't beat it.

If you want to follow fashion trends—a frock coat or those hot, decorated vests, cummerbunds and ties—you're going to pay a lot more. It's not necessary. A classic look is always best. (The same rule applies to the traditional white dinner jacket, stroller, or cutaway. They are also inexpensive.)

Robert suggests doing business with a vendor who will give a free tux to the groom (once he books his bridal party). He also suggests doing business with a small independent vendor to ensure that you get the best service. In his opinion, the large chain stores spend more on promotion than on the service they give their clients. He also points out that the independent vendor is competitively priced.

TIPS FOR SUCCESS

Ask these questions when interviewing a vendor:

1. Do you have stock on the premises?
2. Do you have a tailor on the premises?
3. May we try on the formal wear when we come to pick it up?

A vendor must answer Yes to these three key questions or you may experience trouble. Most tuxedo stores order their merchandise from a central source, which may be miles away. If the order comes in wrong, you're out of luck, unless they also carry some stock on the premises. It's a must.

A tailor on the premises solves the problem of last minute crises; a hem or a sleeve that's too long can be remedied in a few short minutes if there's a tailor on board to solve the problem. And, of course, it's essential that all members of the bridal party try on their formal wear when they pick it up. That will ensure that their outfit is complete and the fit is correct. A shop that answers yes to the above questions is a shop that cares about you! When it comes to formal wear, your peace of mind comes first.

PRECAUTIONARY MEASURES

Always get tuxedo insurance (offered by vendors). Weddings can get wild and if you ruin rented formal wear, you'll pay for it, unless you have insurance. Tuxedos cost hundreds of dollars.

Be Aware — Prom Time

If your wedding falls near prom time, be sure to reserve your formal wear at least three to four months in advance. And follow-up regularly with the vendor.

Get It in Writing

When you order tuxes or formal wear, get the specifics in writing: the date of the affair, the exact style ordered, the color, what's included (shirt, studs, etc.), the price, and deposit paid.

And Finally — Don't Take Chances

Shop with a reliable, independent vendor who's been in business a good while and who's interested in you. He wants you as a customer. To him, service is paramount.

And in terms of saving money, Shakespeare, in his infinite wisdom, hit the nail on the head: "Old fashions suit me best."

Chapter Twenty

RENTED TRANSPORTATION

Daisy, Daisy give me your answer, do!
I'm half crazy, all for the love of you!
It won't be a stylish marriage,
I can't afford a carriage,
But you'll look sweet upon the seat
Of a bicycle built for two.

—Henry Dacre, "Daisy Bell," 1892

Part I: Types of Transportation

LIMOUSINES

Limos can save you a ton of money—*because you don't need them!* Why spend hundreds of dollars on a limo (or two), when there are so many other options?

Reserve early if your wedding and prom season coincide. No matter what type of rented transportation you have in mind, reserve it early if your wedding and prom season run concurrently. Leave a deposit and specify the reserved date and times on your receipt (along with the deposit amount and the balance due). Be sure the cancellation policy is specified in the contract and that your deposit is transferable.

THE FANCY FAMILY CAR

Everyone has a relative or friend (who will be invited to the wedding) with a fancy car. Ask if you may borrow the car, and ask the son or daughter of a friend or relative to do the honor of driving (for a few extra bucks). Let him pick you up and escort you and your mom and dad to the ceremony. Afterward, he may escort you and your groom to the reception. (Have their date or spouse hop a ride with a relative or friend.) It's not necessary for your bridal party to ride in a limo. They can take their own cars.

Tip: Get your "chauffeur" a snazzy cap—white or black. Decorate it with a felt band, inscribed with yours and the groom's name and the wedding date (in pink or gold glitter, for example, using a glitter pen).

And don't forget a bottle of the bubbly (if permitted by state law. Check it out!) and two glasses. Buy a bottle of champagne and put it in the refrigerator. Get an ice bucket and two glasses. When your chauffeur comes to pick you up, have a friend or relative fill the bucket with ice. Put the champagne in the bucket and put it in the car (don't forget the glasses). Let it chill during the ceremony. Afterward, on your way to the reception, drink to love, life, and good health!

RENT A CAR OR TWO

Call your local car-rental agency and rent a luxury car for twenty-four hours or the weekend, depending on their rates. Shop well to compare prices and to get the best deal.

Once again, have the son or daughter of a friend or relative play chauffeur and drive you and your parents to the ceremony, and you and your groom to the reception. Make arrangements for them to return the car to the agency. (Be sure that the person(s) driving the car is present at the time the vehicle is rented.)

Many brides have told me of the advantages of a rental car. Not only do they have the use of a beautiful automobile, they save money! Besides, they have an extra car to pick up guests at the airport or to run errands. (Be sure the contract specifies unlimited mileage.)

Tip: It may be wise to purchase complete insurance coverage from the rental agency, even if you're covered by your own policy. Check with your insurance company before renting. Also, if you have an American Express credit card, use it. Many of the cards offered by American Express will pick up the additional insurance—for free! Call American Express for details.

THE MINIBUS, TROLLEY CAR, AND LIMO-COACHES

Many brides are hiring minibuses, trolley cars, and limo-coaches to escort them and their entire bridal party to the festivities. Once again, the cost is less than hiring single limos because you can transport more people with fewer vehicles. And these cars are fun! (If considering one of these options, heed the following tips and criteria.)

Part II: For the Limo-Addicted

If you just *have to have* a limo, here are some tips to ensure that you get the best deal:

• When you call, don't say you're considering a limo for your wedding. Merely ask what their hourly rate is. When they tell you, ask if that's their best price. Once they quote their best price, have them fax it to you.

• Rent a larger limousine that will accommodate more people, eliminating the need to rent two limos (or a minibus, etc.).

• Ask to see the cars beforehand. This is a must. An old or unkempt car is a signal to look elsewhere. (Once you find a car, make a note of the license plate number to ensure that the same car is delivered on the wedding day.)

• Make sure the vendor and the drivers are licensed and insured.

• Ask what your liability is, and the company's. It's advisable to hire a company who's insured with the ICC (Interstate Commerce

Commission). This information must appear in your contract.

- Ask for referrals.
- Ask if someone is available at all times to take phone calls in case there's a problem. This is essential.
- Put style of dress of the driver in the contract.
- Put deposit and balance due on a credit card.
- Make sure the cancellation policy is listed in the contract.
- The deposit must be transferable. (Put it in your contract.)

Black Means Savings

Most wedding and prom limos are white, but black cars are attracting many brides and grooms. It's a dramatic and elegant color. If you call a company and their white vehicles are reserved, ask for a black one—*and a discount.*

Be Aware: Packages

Many limousine companies offer packages to entice brides and grooms. Some offer champagne, hors d'oeuvres, a sign printed (for the limo's bumper) with the bride's and groom's names and wedding date. Others offer interior decorations. When shopping, *compare prices.* Chances are you'll be paying for these added extras. Do you really need them? (Or can you provide them yourself?)

Tipping—A Must

Most limo drivers live on tips. For that reason (and for the best service), it's wise to give the driver a few dollars *beforehand.* Let him know that if he does a good job, there will be another tip, after his services are completed.

Chapter Twenty-one

PARTING WORDS

Girls, close the doors now. Our part
Is over. And you, happy pair,
God bless you. Practice your nimble youth
In the gods' undying gift.

—Catullus, c. 60 B.C.

THINGS FAMILY AND FRIENDS DO FOR YOU!

SHOWERS

Bridal showers have changed! The days of silly games and umbrella cakes are long past. A shower's solitary goal is no longer to provide the poor little unprepared bride with her pots and pans. Now, they're *wow*!

According to the census, most couples cohabit before marriage. Many of my clients say, for example, "I don't want a traditional shower. Mike and I are building a house and we want a lawn mower or weed trimmer," or, "We want to go to Europe," or, "We want to build a fantastic patio," or "We want a barbecue." Fine, no problem! Inform your maid of honor that you want an *exceptional* shower (exceptional in kind, not one that breaks the bank). Why, you may even want to invite the guys! Times have changed.

Whether it be money for a honeymoon or implements or furnishings for your yard or pa-

tio, *why have a traditional shower if your home is established?* It's a waste of time and your guests' effort and money. Besides, who wants to spend the weeks before a wedding returning gifts?

REGISTRIES AND SHOWERS

People who attend showers are there to impart their best wishes (and to give small gifts) to the bride. Weddings are too expensive today to expect people to go gift crazy. A wedding gift is more than enough. Asking or expecting them to give expensive shower gifts is being presumptuous. For that reason, you should not enclose registry information with shower invitations. The implication: Bring the gift I *want*. Guests invited to a shower should have the option of choosing the gift of their choice, based upon your shower type and what they can afford.

One of my clients insisted on putting her

registry information directly on her shower invitation. I protested strongly, but to no avail. Had I received her invitation, I would not have attended her shower, nor would I have sent a gift. Invitations and gifts do not go hand in hand.

USE YOUR INVITATION TO YOUR ADVANTAGE

Guests will undoubtedly call the host: "What's a patio shower?" She will then inform them of the shower's purpose (and suggest what they should bring, tactfully). Your invitation must relate pertinent shower information to your guests. (It will also ensure that you get the right stuff!) For example:

Ms. Cindy Smith
requests the pleasure of your company
at a Patio Bridal Shower
in honor of
Ms. Bonnie Simpson
on Friday, the first of May

BRIDAL REGISTRIES

REGISTRIES AND WEDDINGS

When it comes to bridal registries, you can be tactfully pushy. Register at all stores, from the expensive to the inexpensive. Offer your guests a selection of gifts in all price ranges. Tell friends and families where you're registered. *Spread the word, through the grapevine, only.* Never include registry information with a wedding invitation.

HOW ABOUT A HOUSE REGISTRY?

Never give money to a vendor to establish a registry of any kind (like a Honeymoon registry). If the vendor goes out of business, you're out of luck and out of money. Don't ask for trouble.

But when the government gets involved, that's a different story! The Federal Housing Authority (FHA) has introduced a program called *The FHA Bridal Registry.* Their brochure sums it up: "Something Old, Something New, Something with a Yard and 2 or 3 Bedrooms." It works like this. A couple registers at a lending institution approved by the FHA. Their guests make contributions (as gifts) toward their new home. The advantage is tremendous. Before the advent of this program, lenders didn't know whether a couple's down payment was gift money or a personal loan, making the money suspect. Now they know and they're encouraging this program.

If you think a home is too expensive, or that you'll never be able to save enough to buy one, think again. The FHA makes it easier than you think. Here's what the brochure says: ". . . You don't have to have perfect credit and you can use gifts of cash for your down payment. And with an FHA loan, that down payment may be as low as a few months' rent: just $900 for a $30,000 home, $2,500 for a $60,000 home or $4,000 for a $90,000 home." Just think, buying a home is less expensive than getting married! (For more information, see appendix I.)

Money, Common Sense, and Etiquette

Weddings and Cash and Gifts

Never ask for cash or include any mention of cash on invitations to any wedding festivities. I'm constantly amazed by people who ask how they can tactfully include this information. You can't! If you want cash, spread the news through the grapevine. If you receive an unsuitable gift, make a note of what it was (for the thank you note) and return it to the store. Ask for cash or a credit or make an exchange.

Thank You Notes

Send thank you notes within three weeks of receiving any gift. Make them personal. Do not send notes that have a preprinted thank you message. It's up to you to tell your families and friends, in writing, how much you appreciate what they've done for you.

Thank You Gifts

Hosts receive gifts. If your maid of honor threw you a lovely shower, you might send flowers or a plant in appreciation. If your parents hosted your wedding, they should receive a lovely memento, not only because of the money they spent, but because of the time and effort and love they put into your wedding to make it wonderful for you!

The Final Countdown to Success

We've all heard stories about the officiant or caterer who had the date wrong and missed the wedding. What a disaster! There's no excuse, however, for this to happen to you. Use your common sense—and use follow-up!

The week before the wedding, call the vendors and service personnel. Have all contracts and receipts in order and ask for the balances due, if they haven't been paid, ask them the date, place, and time of the affair (and when they're to be there). *Let them furnish you with this information.* In that way, you'll know if they have their facts straight. Do the calls yourself (or let your fiancé call). Speak only to the person in charge.

Don't forget to pick up your wedding rings (if you haven't done so already) and be sure your marriage license is valid.

About Gown Preservation

Make sure that your gown is truly preserved and not just cleaned and put in a box. Gowns that are preserved are specially treated, come with a warning (they must be dry cleaned before worn), and come with a warranty.

THE FINAL CHECKLIST

The Week Before Call:	Date Called:
The officiant	
The ceremony organist, musicians, vocalists, etc.	
Reception entertainment	
Catering director (or caterer)	
Party rental store (if applicable)	
Cake baker (or bakery)	
Bridal shop	
Formal wear shop	
Photographer	
Videographer	
Florist	
Hairdresser, makeup artist, nail technician	
Limousine company (or car rental agency)	
Travel agent (if applicable).	

And Don't Forget:

Get all contracts in order from vendors and your receipts.
   (Call for the balances due.)

Pick up wedding rings.

Check your marriage license. Is it valid?

Verify all travel documents.

PRESERVING YOUR BRIDAL BOUQUET

Professional preservation of bridal bouquets is expensive. If you'd like to try to preserve yours, put the bouquet in a brown paper bag, seal it, and put it on the bottom shelf of the refrigerator. (Don't make the refrigerator colder than normal.) Leave the bouquet for three weeks, remove from the bag, than hang it in a cool dry room. There's no guarantee that this method is foolproof; different flowers take well to drying, others don't.

AND FINALLY . . .

Don't go over budget. Plan wisely and well. Pursue elegance in your own terms, within the confines of good taste, and have a beautiful, tasteful wedding and a wonderful, loving life.

All the best,

Deb McCoy

APPENDIX I

Wedding-Planning Videos
by Deborah McCoy

1. *The Chuppa: Creating an Heirloom*
2. *Show-stopping Centerpieces (Aren't Costly)*
3. *Tempting Tables: Yours for the Making*
4. *Making Irresistible Invitations (Inexpensively and Elegantly)*
5. *Wedding Cake Concepts: Make Yours Easily, Elegantly, Economically*
6. *Heart-stopping Headpieces and Veils: Make Yours and $ave*

Phone: 561-367-0201
Website: http://www.arcvideo.com

Bridal Registry

The Knot's Registry
AOL keyword: knot
Phone: 888-WED-KNOT

Buy a House Bridal Registry

The FHA (Federal Housing Authority)
Phone: 1-800-CALLFHA
Website: http://www.hud.gov

Cakes

Ron Ben-Israel
130 West 25th Street
New York, New York 10001
Phone: 212-627-2418
E-mail: cakemaster@weddingcakes.com
Website: http://www.weddingcakes.com

Jane Stacey
Sante Fe, New Mexico
Phone: 505-473-1243

Sweet Tiers
8779 Southeast Federal Highway
Hobe Sound, Florida 33455
Phone: 561-546-8822

Sylvia Weinstock
273 Church Street
New York, New York 10013
Phone: 212-925-6698

Cake-Baking Supplies

New York Cake and Baking Distributor
(For prepared buttercream frosting and more)
56 West 22nd Street
New York, New York 10010
Phone: 212-675-2253

Entertainment

Kenny Mondo's Professional Disc Jockeys
P.O. Box 210933
Royal Palm Beach, Florida 33421-0933
Phone: 561-790-5555

Samantha Farr & Secret Formula Entertainers, Inc.
3475 Sheridan Street, Suite 212
Hollywood, Florida 33021
Phone: 954-989-7206
E-mail: GSFarr@aol.com

Michael Rose Orchestra & Entertainment
Boca Raton, Palm Beach, and Stuart, Florida
Phone: 561-219-1000

Favors

Edible Elegance (Matchbox-Chox)
199 West Palmetto Park Road, #4
Boca Raton, Florida 33432
Phone: 561-392-1417
E-mail: deb@debmccoy.com

Health

National Tay-Sachs & Allied Diseases Association
2001 Beacon Street, Suite 204
Brookline, Massachusetts 02146
Phone: 617-277-4463 or 800-90-NTSAD

Honeymoon and Travel Information

Aloha Travel Auction
(available online through *The Knot*)
The Knot: Weddings for the Real World
Website: http://www.theknot.com
or AOL keyword: knot

Atrium Travel
301 Yamato Road
Boca Raton, Florida 33431
Phone: 561-994-4333

Travel Is Fun
7760 Southwest 88th Street
Miami, Florida 33156
Phone: 305-271-0010

Travel Cancellation Insurance

Access America, a division of:
World Access Service Corporation
6600 West Broad Street
Richmond, Virginia 23230
Phone: 800-284-8300

Interfaith Marriage Information

The Rabbinic Center for Research and Counseling
128 East Dudley Avenue
Westfield, New Jersey 07090
Phone: 908-233-0419 or 908-233-2288

Invitations

INVENTING ELEGANCE (Computer Generated)
For Software: Deb McCoy
199 West Palmetto Park Road, #4
Boca Raton, Florida 33432
Phone: 561-392-1417
E-mail: deb@debmccoy.com

Jewelry

About Pawnbrokers

National Pawnbrokers Association
World Trade Center
P.O. Box 420028
Dallas, Texas 75342-0028
Phone: 214-745-4746
E-mail: natpawn@ix.netcom.com

Ask an Expert

Jay Feder Jewelers
910 16th Street
Denver, Colorado 80202
Phone: 800-841-7283

Diamond Grading Laboratories

The GIA (Gemological Institute of America)
World Headquarters and Robert Mouawad Campus
5345 Armada Drive
Carlsbad, California 92008
Phone: 760-603-4000

In New York:
580 Fifth Avenue
New York, New York 10036
Phone: 212-944-5900

European Gemological Laboratory (EGL)
550 South Hill Street, Suite 1595
Los Angeles, California 90013
Phone: 213-622-2387

Diamond Insurance

Jewelers Mutual Insurance Co.
P.O. Box 468
Neenah, Wisconsin 54957-0468
Phone: 888-884-2424

Gemprint (protection for your gems)
10 Lower Spadina Avenue, Suite 203
Toronto, Ontario, Canada M5V 2Z2
416-260-8380

To Purchase a Loupe

For the Bride
199 West Palmetto Park Road, #4
Boca Raton, Florida 33432
Phone: 561-392-1417
E-mail: deb@debmccoy.com

Online Resource

The Knot
The Knot: Weddings for the Real World
Website: http://www.theknot.com
or AOL keyword: knot

Photography

Clay Blackmore
Robert Isacson
7825 Tuckerman Lane, Suite 212
Potomac, Maryland 20854
Phone: 301-765-0000
E-mail: claynco@aol.com
Website: http://www.blackmore-isacson.com

Denis Reggie
75 14th Street, Northeast
Atlanta, Georgia 30309
Phone: 404-873-8080
E-mail: dreggie@reggienet.com
The Knot on AOL, keyword: knot
The Knot on the Web: http://www.theknot.com
Wedding Photographers Network: accessed
through *The Knot*

Roberts Photographics, Inc.
Tim Roberts and Jack Jones
6560 West Rogers Circle, Suite 24
Boca Raton, Florida 33487
Phone: 561-241-1127
E-mail: troberts@roberts-photo.com
Website: http://www.roberts-photo.com

Monte Zucker
464 East MacEwen Drive
Osprey, Florida 34229
Phone: 914-918-0904
E-mail: MZPhotog@aol.com
Website: http://www.montezucker.com

Premarital Agreements

The American Academy of Matrimonial Lawyers
150 North Michigan Avenue, Suite 2040
Chicago, Illinois 60601
Phone: 312-263-6477

Premarital Nonreligious Counseling

PAIRS International Inc.
1152 North University Drive
Pembroke Pines, Florida 33024
Phone: 800-PAIRS-4-U
Website: http://www.pairs.com

PREPARE
For more information, send a self-addressed
stamped envelope:
P.O. Box 190
Minneapolis, Minnesota 55440-0190

Videography

ARC *Video Productions*
199 West Palmetto Park Road, Suite 5
Boca Raton, Florida 33432
561-367-0201
Website: http://www.arcvideo.com

Mr. Roy Chapman, Chairman
WEVA International (*Wedding & Event*
Videographers Association)
8499 South Tamiami Trail, #208
Sarasota, Florida 34238
E-mail: info@WEVA.com
Phone: 800-501-WEVA
Direct dial: 941-923-5334

Wedding Cancellation Insurance

Weddingsurance
R.V. Nuccio & Associates
P.O. Box 307
Fawnskin, California 92333
Phone: 800-ENGAGED (800-364-2433)

Wedding Consulting Services

Association of Bridal Consultants
200 Chestnutland Road
New Milford, Connecticut 06776-2521
Phone: 860-355-0464

Deborah McCoy, For the Bride
P.O. Box 1407
Boca Raton, Florida 33429
Phone: 561-392-1417
E-mail: deb@debmccoy.com
Website: http://www.debmccoy.com

Wedding Gowns Online

Deborah McCoy, For the Bride,
www.debmccoy.com

The Knot on the Web: http://www.theknot.com
AOL keyword: knot

Wedding Music

The American Guild of Organists
475 Riverside Drive, Suite 1260
New York, New York 10115
Phone: 212-870-2310
Order line: 800-AGO-5115

For Church or Temple Weddings:
Tapes: *Wedding Processionals & Recessionals*
Vocal Solos for Weddings
Book: *The Bridal Guide*
Pamphlets: *Guide for Hiring Church & Temple*
Musicians
Handbook of Church Music for Weddings
1800 North Hermitage Avenue
Chicago, Illinois 60622-1101
773-486-8970

The Wedding Album
Produced by RCA
800-221-8180

APPENDIX II

CAKES FROM THE EXPERTS

Note: The following recipes are provided by top professional bakers. Each has their own particular method of baking their cakes (which may differ from the general baking information in "The Wedding Cake" chapter). When using their recipe, follow their directions to the letter. (Tiering, frosting, and transporting information is at the end of this chapter.)

Rose Levy Beranbaum's White Wedding Cake With Neoclassic Buttercream Frosting

(With or Without Liqueur)
(adapted from *The Cake Bible*)

The cake is three tiers: 6 inches, 8 inches, and 10 inches
(two layers per tier), and will feed approximately 100 people

Note: Do not measure egg whites by the tablespoon. The tablespoon measure is given only as a guide. For accuracy, use a glass measuring cup; the fluid ounces (fl. oz.) are marked on the side. Beat the egg whites very lightly with a fork to break them up for easier measuring. (One large egg contains approximately 2 TABLESPOONS of white.)

Recipe for Two, Six-Inch Layers:

Ingredients (*at room temperature*):	Amount:
LARGE Egg Whites	3 fl oz. (6 TABLESPOONS)
Milk	2/3 cup
Vanilla	1 1/2 teaspoons
Sifted Cake Flour	2 cups
Sugar	1 cup
Baking Powder	1 TABLESPOON
Salt	1/2 teaspoon
Unsalted Butter, softened	8 TABLESPOONS (1 stick)

Recipe for Two, Eight-Inch Layers:

Ingredients (*at room temperature*):	Amount:
LARGE Egg Whites	5 1/4 fl. oz. (2/3 cup)
Milk	1 cup + 3 TABLESPOONS
Vanilla	2 2/3 teaspoons
Sifted Cake Flour	3 1/2 cups
Sugar	1 3/4 cups
Baking Powder	1 TABLESPOON + 2 1/4 teaspoons
Salt	3/4 teaspoon + 1/8 teaspoon
Unsalted Butter, softened	14 TABLESPOONS (1 stick + 6 TABLESPOONS)

Recipe for Two, Ten-Inch Layers:

Ingredients (*at room temperature*):	Amount:
LARGE Egg Whites	7 1/2 fl. oz. (1 cup minus 1 TABLESPOON)
Milk	1 2/3 cups
Vanilla	3 3/4 teaspoons
Sifted Cake Flour	5 cups
Sugar	2 1/2 cups
Baking Powder	2 TABLESPOONS + 1/2 teaspoon
Salt	1 1/4 teaspoons
Unsalted Butter, softened	20 TABLESPOONS (2 1/2 sticks)

Cakes may be made and frozen up to two months in advance. Make two layers at a time. Preheat oven to 350 degrees. Grease the pans, line the bottom with wax paper, grease again, then flour, invert and tap out excess. (To bake very even cakes use Magi-Cake Strips.)

TO MAKE:

In a medium bowl, combine the egg whites, 1/4 of the milk, and the vanilla and set aside.

In a large mixing bowl, combine all dry ingredients and mix on low speed for one minute to blend. Add butter (make sure it's *soft*, but not so soft it's losing its shape) and the remaining milk. Mix on low speed until all the ingredients are moistened. Then beat on medium speed, 1 1/2 minutes to aerate. Scrape down the sides. Gradually beat in the egg mixture in three batches. Beat for 20 seconds after each addition to blend. Scrape down the sides. Divide the batter evenly between the two cake pans. Put the two pans in the oven (on a rack placed in the center) so that air can circulate around them. Do not let them touch each other or the oven walls.

Bake the 6-inch layers: 25–35 minutes
Bake the 8-inch layers: 30–40 minutes
Bake the 10-inch layers: 30–40 minutes

Or until a tester (toothpick) placed in the center comes out clean. (Cakes under 10 inches should not pull away from the sides of the pan until they're removed from the oven.)

Cool in their pans on racks for 10 minutes. Loosen the sides with a spatula and invert onto racks sprayed with nonstick cooking spray. Reinvert immediately (to prevent splitting) and let cool completely.

If you frost the cakes after baking, allow them to cool completely. Remove the top crust with a serrated knife. Brush each six-inch layer with 2 TABLESPOONS of syrup (each side). Use a pastry brush. Brush each eight-inch layer with 3 TABLESPOONS syrup (each side). For each 10-inch layer, brush on 5 TABLESPOONS syrup (each side). Allow the cakes 15 minutes to absorb the syrup before frosting. If you freeze the cakes, brush them with syrup after the cakes are completely defrosted and before you frost them.

❧

Rose Levy Beranbaum's White Sheet Cake With Neoclassic Buttercream Frosting

(13″ × 9″)

(With or Without Liqueur)

This cake will feed approximately thirty people (adequately)
Makes one layer

Ingredients (*at room temperature*):	Amount:
LARGE EGG WHITES	6 fl. oz. (³/4 cup) (12 TABLESPOONS)
Milk	1¹/3 cups
Vanilla	1 TABLESPOON
Sifted cake flour	4 cups
Sugar	2 cups
Baking powder	1 TABLESPOON + 2 teaspoons
Salt	1 teaspoon
Unsalted butter, softened	16 TABLESPOONS (2 sticks)

Preheat the oven to 350 degrees. Grease a 13″ × 9″ pan, line the bottom with wax paper, grease again, and flour. (For a very even cake, use Magi-cake Strips). Mix the batter according to the directions for the three-tiered cake. Pour the batter into the cake pan. Bake in the oven for 35 to 45 minutes. (The cake will pull slightly from the sides of the pan.) Cool the cake in the pan on a rack for 20 minutes. Loosen the sides with a spatula and invert onto a greased wire rack. Reinvert to prevent splitting. Cool completely. Remove the top crust and brush the cake evenly (on both sides) with ¹/2 cup of syrup before frosting.

Rose Levy Beranbaum's Syrup Recipe

Makes 1 cup syrup

Storing: One month, refrigerated in an airtight container.

Ingredients (at room temperature):	Amount:
Sugar	6 TABLESPOONS
Water	2/3 liquid cup (use glass measure)
Liqueur (of your choice)	3 TABLESPOONS

In a saucepan with a tight-fitting lid, bring the sugar and water to a rolling boil. Stir constantly. Cover and remove from the heat. Cool completely. Transfer to a liquid measuring cup and add the liqueur. If the mixture has evaporated slightly, add enough water to equal one cup. (If multiplying this recipe for a larger quantity, add water to equal the appropriate amount.)

Rose Levy Beranbaum's Neoclassic Buttercream Frosting and Filling

(With or Without Liqueur)

Makes 10 cups to fill and frost a three-tiered wedding cake (one 6-inch, one 8-inch, and one 10-inch tier)

Storing: Six hours, room temperature. One week, refrigerated. Eight months, frozen.

Ingredients (at room temperature):	Amount:
LARGE Egg Yolks	15 (1 cup + 1 1/2 TABLESPOONS)
Sugar	1 3/4 cups + 2 TABLESPOONS
*Corn Syrup	1 1/4 cups
Unsalted butter, softened	5 cups
**Liqueur (of your choice)	1/3 cup to 2/3 cup

*Spray your measuring cup with cooking spray before measuring the corn syrup.

**If you'd prefer only the filling to be flavored with liqueur, use 2 1/2 cups of the frosting for the filling. Flavor with 1 1/2 TABLESPOONS to 2 1/2 TABLESPOONS liqueur.

TO MAKE:

Have ready near your stove a 2-cup, heat-proof glass measuring cup.

In an electric mixer bowl, beat the yolks until light in color. In a medium-size, nonstick sauce pan, combine the sugar and corn syrup and heat, stirring until the sugar dissolves and syrup comes to a rolling boil (the entire surface will be covered with large bubbles). Transfer the mixture at once to the glass measuring cup to stop the cooking. Beat the syrup into the egg yolks in a steady stream. Start by pouring a small amount of syrup over the yolks with the mixer turned off. (*Don't allow the syrup to fall on the beaters.*) Immediately beat at high speed for 5 seconds. Stop the mixer, add a large amount of syrup. Beat for 5 seconds. Continue with remaining syrup. For the last addition, use a rubber scraper to remove syrup clinging to the glass cup. Beat until completely cool.

Gradually beat in the butter and liqueur (if you'd prefer).

Once completed, place in an airtight bowl. Always bring the frosting to room temperature before using. Rebeat if necessary to restore texture. Frost according to directions later in this chapter.

❧

Rose Levy Beranbaum's Neoclassic Buttercream Filling and Frosting

(For the one-layer, 13″ × 9″ sheet cake, makes 5 cups)

Ingredients (at room temperature):	Amount:
LARGE egg yolks	8 (5¼ fl. oz.)
Sugar	¾ cup + 3 TABLESPOONS
*Corn Syrup	5 fl. oz. (½ cup + 2 TABLESPOONS)
Unsalted butter, softened	2½ cups
**Liqueur (of your choice)	2½–5 TABLESPOONS

Note: You may cut the cake in half, length-wise, with a serrated knife and use part of the frosting as a filling. Flavor it with liqueur if you'd like.

*Spray the measuring cup with cooking spray before measuring corn syrup.

**If you'd prefer *only* the filling to be flavored with liqueur, use 1¼ cups of the frosting for the fill-

ing. Flavor with 2 teaspoons to 1 TABLESPOON liqueur.

Make according to the instructions for the buttercream filling and frosting for the three-tiered cake. Frost according to directions later in this chapter.

❧

Ron Ben-Israel's Lemon Genoise Wedding Cake—With Optional Raspberries—and White Chocolate Buttercream Frosting

A very light, moist European cake, 3 tiers (2 layers each tier);
one 12-inch tier; one 9-inch tier; one 6-inch tier
(The 12-inch and 9-inch tiers will feed approximately 75 to 80.)*
(The top tier can be saved for your first anniversary.)

*One 2-layer, 12-inch round tier will feed 50 adequately. One 2-layer, nine-inch round tier will feed 30 adequately. Make either an extra 9-inch or 12-inch round tier and keep it in the kitchen for extra guests, if necessary.

Storing: Ron advises that you don't freeze Genoise—although you may. (He never freezes any of his cakes!) This cake, however, will store

well in the refrigerator, with the addition of syrup and icing, for at least three days. (And, you may freeze it and the buttercream if you choose [more about this later].)

An aesthetic tip: Ron says that two-layer cakes smack of home baking. He suggests cutting each layer in half, horizontally, and filling each layer with frosting that you stud with raspberries. (Each tier, therefore, will have four cake layers and three layers of filling! Seven layers! *Très elegant!*)

About Ron's Recipes: Genoise and buttercream use the same technique. Both call for heating the eggs and sugar over hot water and then whipping the mixture to achieve a high and stable foam. The other ingredients are then gently folded in. The result: A very light and airy cake with creamy, melt-in-your-mouth frosting!

Ron's Recipe for Two 6-Inch Layers

Ingredients:	Amount:
Vegetable oil	3 TABLESPOONS
Pure lemon extract	1¼ teaspoons
Pure vanilla extract	½ teaspoon
LARGE whole eggs	4 (or 7 fl. oz.) (or 3/4 cup + 2 teaspoons)
Granulated sugar	½ cup
Sifted cake flour	½ cup
Corn starch	7 TABLESPOONS
Grated lemon zest	1 TABLESPOON

BEFORE YOU MIX: INSTRUCTIONS FOR ALL LAYERS:

Preheat the oven to 350 degrees. Grease and flour the pans. (Ron says it's not necessary to use wax paper when baking Genoise.)

TO MAKE:

Mix flour and cornstarch together. Set aside. Add the vanilla and lemon extracts to the oil. Set aside. Place the eggs, sugar, and lemon zest in a metallic mixing bowl set over a pot of simmering water. Stir constantly until the sugar has melted completely and the mixture is warm and thin. (This releases the oil in the zest and intensifies the flavor.) Remove from the heat and with an electric mixer (use the whisk attachment, if you have it), whip on high for about five minutes, until the egg mixture has tripled in volume (and the beaters leave marks in the stable and shiny foam). Sift half the flour mixture over the whipped eggs. Fold to blend. Then sift the other half over the whipped eggs. Fold well to blend. Add the oil that's been mixed with the extracts. Fold until just blended. Fill pans 2/3 full. For very even cakes, use Magi-Cake strips.

BAKING INSTRUCTIONS (FOR ALL LAYERS):

Bake two 6-inch layers together: 20–25 minutes
Bake two 9-inch layers together: 25–35 minutes
Bake each 12-inch layer separately: 30–40 minutes

Note: Avoid opening the oven door. Wait until the allotted baking time is up. Open the door and look at the cake(s). If it doesn't appear done, re-close the door and check again in five minutes.

Genoise will shrink slightly from the sides of the pan and will be golden brown. Invert the cakes immediately onto racks to cool. (After they're completely cool, refrigerate for a few hours. This makes them easier to handle and to split into additional layers, if desired.)

If freezing, wrap the cakes in a few layers of freezer wrap. Place them back in their pans for protection. Stack them in the refrigerator with large cardboard circles in between to prevent them from being crushed.

Ron's Recipe for Two 9-Inch Layers

Ingredients:	Amount:
Vegetable oil	6 TABLESPOONS
Pure Lemon Extract	2^1/$_2$ teaspoons
Pure Vanilla Extract	1 teaspoon
LARGE whole eggs	8 (or 14 fl. oz.) (or 1^3/$_4$ cups)
Granulated sugar	1 cup
Sifted cake flour	1 cup
Corn starch	^{3}/$_4$ cup
Grated lemon zest	2 TABLESPOONS

Preheat the oven to 350 degrees. Follow the directions for making the 6-inch layers. Bake for 25 to 35 minutes.

Ron's Recipe for One 12-Inch Layer

Twelve-inch layers must be baked one at a time, so Ron says you must mix the batter for each layer separately. *You must make two recipes to produce two layers* (for one twelve-inch tier). This recipe will produce more batter than necessary to fill one pan. *Fill the pan only ^{2}/$_3$ full.*

Ingredients:	Amount:
Vegetable oil	6 TABLESPOONS
Pure Lemon Extract	2^1/$_2$ teaspoons
Pure Vanilla Extract	1 teaspoon
LARGE whole eggs	8 (or 14 fl. oz.) (or 1^3/$_4$ cups)
Granulated sugar	1 cup
Sifted cake flour	1 cup
Corn starch	^{3}/$_4$ cup
Grated lemon zest	2 TABLESPOONS

Preheat the oven to 350 degrees. Follow the directions for making six-inch layers. Fill the pan ^{2}/$_3$ full. Bake each twelve-inch layer for 30 to 40 minutes.

∽

Ron Ben-Israel's Lemon Syrup

Makes three cups, enough for a three-tiered cake

Storing: One month in an airtight container, refrigerated.

Ingredients:	Amount:
Granulated sugar	1 cup
Water	2 cups
Fresh lemon juice	^{1}/$_2$ cup

Bring the water and sugar to a boil in a medium saucepan, stirring constantly. Add the lemon juice and cover. Remove from the heat and let cool completely.

Before frosting, cut the top off the cakes with a serrated knife. Sprinkle both sides evenly with syrup. (Ron uses a new, clean hair-coloring bottle.) If the cake is frozen, allow it to thaw completely before removing the top and sprinkling with syrup.

Ron Ben-Israel's White Chocolate Buttercream Frosting

This frosting is based on Swiss meringue, which is used in European bakeries, but Ron's is faster and easier to make! (It's necessary to make two recipes, separately, to provide enough frosting for Ron's three-tiered cake.)

Storing: One week refrigerated. One month frozen.

Ingredients:	*Amount:*
LARGE egg whites (pasteurized)	8 (1 cup)
Granulated sugar	1^1/$_2$ cups
Unsalted butter, softened	1^1/$_2$ pounds (6 sticks)
White chocolate, melted gently and cooled	^{3}/$_4$ pound (12 oz.)

Beat the butter until smooth and creamy. Set aside. (Make sure the room is cool and that the butter remains cool.) Put the egg whites and sugar in a very clean, grease-free metal mixing bowl set over a pan of simmering water. Stir constantly, until the mixture is warm to the touch. Remove from the heat. Beat with an electric mixer on high until the egg whites are cool and hold peaks (they should be shiny). With the electric mixer on low speed, add the butter slowly until blended. Add the chocolate and beat until blended. Mix on high speed to lighten the mixture. Rebeat as you frost the cake to maintain a smooth texture.

Note: If you freeze the buttercream, bring it to room temperature before using it to prevent curdling. Make sure the mixing bowl and beaters are also at room temperature. On a cold day, run the mixing bowl and beaters under hot tap water before proceeding. If the mixture begins to curdle while mixing, stop the mixer and suspend the bowl over hot water for a few seconds. Rebeat to maintain texture.

Assembling the Wedding Cake

Five Days Before the Wedding

Make the cakes. If the cakes are made and frozen, move them to the refrigerator to defrost overnight. Make sure they're completely thawed before sprinkling with syrup and frosting.

Make the lemon syrup, if you haven't already.

Four Days Before the Wedding

Make chocolate buttercream frosting. Keep it in the refrigerator. If you made it and froze it, move it to the refrigerator to defrost overnight.

Three Days Before the Wedding

Cut the top off the cakes with a serrated knife. Sprinkle both sides evenly with syrup. If you'd like, cut each cake layer into two layers with a serrated knife. Starting with the bottom 12-inch layer, spread the frosting in a thick, even layer over the top surface. Stud with raspberries (if you choose). Place the second part of the layer on top of the first. Continue layering and filling the layers until the 12-inch tier is complete. Cover and refrigerate until the filling is firm. Continue the process with the 9-inch and 6-inch tiers.

Frost the tiers according to directions in this chapter. If tiering the cake, follow the directions in this chapter.

Box and cover the cakes (see the directions later in this chapter).

Two Days Before the Wedding (and the Day Before)

Relax and enjoy yourself!

❧

Jane Stacey's Vanilla Wedding Cake with Whipped Cream Filling and Swiss Meringue Buttercream Frosting

This recipe makes one 2-layer, half-sheet cake ($17'' \times 11'' \times 1^1/2''$) that will feed about 25–30 people.

What You'll Need:

> 1 recipe Orange Simple Syrup
> 1 recipe Vanilla Wedding Cake (to make one 2-layer cake)
> 1 recipe Whipped Cream Filling
> 1 recipe Swiss Meringue Buttercream Frosting

TO PREPARE IN ADVANCE

Jane specifies that for the best flavor, the cake should not be frozen. The simple syrup, however, will keep for three weeks, refrigerated, and can be made well in advance. The cake may be made four days in advance and refrigerated. The whipped cream filling needs to be made at the time the cake is assembled (three days in advance). The frosting can be made two days in advance (when you frost the cake). *Schedule yourself accordingly (if you're making the cake).*

Four days before, make the cake. Wrap it securely in a few layers of plastic wrap and place it in the refrigerator. Three days before, make the whipped cream filling and assemble the cake (according to the directions in this recipe). Wrap with plastic wrap. Two days before, make the frosting and frost the cake. Let it sit in the refrigerator, boxed and wrapped, until it's ready to transport.

Orange Simple Syrup

Storing: Up to three weeks, refrigerated.

Ingredients:	Amount:
Orange juice	2 cups
Granulated sugar	3/4 cup
Grand Marnier, Triple Sec, or other orange-flavored liqueur (optional)	2 TABLESPOONS

In a small pan, heat the orange juice and sugar over medium-high heat until it boils. Reduce the heat to medium and cook until all the sugar dissolves. Remove from the heat and let it cool. Add the liqueur, if desired. Transfer the syrup to a small container and store, covered, in the refrigerator until ready to use.

Vanilla Wedding Cake

Makes one 2-layer cake

Ingredients (at room temperature):	Amount:
LARGE eggs, separated	15
Granulated sugar	2 cups
All-purpose flour	1 1/2 cups
Cake flour	1 1/2 cups
Unsalted butter, melted and cooked until brown, then cooled	1/2 cup
Milk	3/4 cup
Pure vanilla extract, good quality (or seeds from one large vanilla bean)	2 teaspoons

BEFORE MAKING

Preheat the oven to 350 degrees. Grease and flour two jelly-roll pans or two half-sheet baking pans (17″ × 11″ × 1 1/2″).

MAKE AND BAKE

Sift together the cake flour and the all-purpose flour. With an electric mixer on high speed, whip the egg yolks, gradually adding 1 cup of sugar. Beat for 3 to 5 minutes until the mixture is thick, light, and no longer grainy. Transfer the yolk mixture to a large mixing bowl. Put the egg whites into a large mixing bowl and whip with an electric mixer on medium speed until they're light and frothy. Increase the speed to high. When the whites form soft peaks, gradually add 1 cup of sugar. Continue to beat until the whites form stiff peaks and are glossy. Transfer the whites to the bowl containing the yolks. With a large rubber spatula, fold the whipped whites into the yolk mixture until barely any streaks of white remain visible. DO NOT OVER MIX! Gently stir in the milk and the vanilla. Sift the flour mixture, in several batches, into the batter. Fold gently, thoroughly, and quickly as you sift in the flour. DO NOT OVER MIX! Quickly fold in the melted browned butter. Transfer the batter to the prepared pans, dividing it evenly. Bake in the center of the oven for about 25 minutes (one on the middle rack, one on the upper rack, and rotate halfway through the cooking time) or until the center of the cake tests clean with a skewer and the edges just begin to pull away from the sides of the pan.

Let the cakes cool in the pans on wire racks for approximately one hour. Loosen the cakes from the pans by running a spatula around the edges. To remove the cakes, invert each onto a large piece of cardboard which is cut larger than the size of the pan. (You may make them yourself or purchase them from a kitchen store.) Do not reinvert. The cakes are too fragile. Wrap with plastic wrap and place in the refrigerator.

Whipped Cream Filling

Storing: Up to one hour, refrigerated.

Ingredients:	Amount:
Heavy whipping cream	1$1/2$ cups
Granulated sugar	$1/4$ cup
Pure vanilla extract, good quality, or	2 TABLESPOONS
Grand Marnier, if preferred	

Using a chilled mixing bowl and beaters, beat the cream with an electric mixer on medium-high speed until soft peaks form. Add the sugar and vanilla (or liqueur). Increase the mixer speed to high. Whip the cream until it is stiff. Refrigerate until ready to use (up to one hour).

Swiss Meringue Buttercream

Ingredients (at room temperature):	Amount:
LARGE egg whites	1$1/2$ cups
Granulated sugar	3 cups
Unsalted butter (cold but not hard), cut into TABLESPOON-size pieces	2$1/4$ pounds (9 sticks)
Grand Marnier (optional)	3 TABLESPOONS

Over low heat, in a stainless-steel mixing bowl placed over a pan of simmering water, whisk together the egg whites and sugar. Heat the mixture, whisking frequently, until it is hot and no longer granular. Remove from the heat. With an electric mixer on high speed, whip the egg whites and sugar until stiff peaks form and the meringue is nearly at room temperature.

Reduce the mixer speed to medium. Add the butter, piece by piece, pausing occasionally as the mixture whips to allow the butter to become completely absorbed. Use a rubber spatula to scrape the sides and the bottom of the bowl.

When all the butter is added, return the mixer speed to high and mix just until the buttercream is creamy and thick.

Add Grand Marnier one TABLESPOON at a time (if using) until it's absorbed and the buttercream is light, creamy, and thick.

Assembling the Wedding Cake

Three Days Before the Wedding

With a long, serrated knife, trim the cakes of any dry edges or to make them more uniform. (Make sure the first layer and the second layer are about the same size.) Dip a pastry brush into the orange simple syrup and generously moisten the first layer but don't soak it! Spread the whipped cream filling in a thick, even layer over the surface of the cake. Slide your spatula under the second layer to loosen it and gently slide it on top of the first layer. Gently nudge it into place. Moisten the second layer with the orange simple syrup. Wrap the cake with plastic wrap and refrigerate until firm, at least one hour or overnight.

Two Days Before the Wedding

Frosting the cake:

Make the buttercream frosting. With a long metal spatula, apply a thin coat of buttercream first to the sides and then to the top of the cake to seal in crumbs. (This is called a crumb coat.) Refrigerate the cake until the frosting is firm (about one hour). Spread a second, thicker layer of buttercream over the sides of the cake and then the top. Make sure the surfaces are smooth and even. Refrigerate the cake until firm. Use a third coat of frosting to even out any irregular or uneven places. Dip the spatula in hot water and wipe dry. Run the warmed spatula over the surface of the chilled buttercream to smooth it. Refrigerate the cake, uncovered, for at least four hours (or longer) before transporting and serving.

Decorate according to directions (and ideas later in this chapter). Or let your imagination run wild!

Betty Baird's Orange Butter Cake

This delectable recipe will make a three-tiered cake (two layers per tier); one 12-inch tier, one 9-inch tier, one 6-inch tier. It will feed approximately 65 people. It's necessary to make two recipes to make one three-tiered cake. You will have enough batter remaining to make a small sheet cake, 13″ × 9″.

Ingredients (at room temperature):	Amount:
LARGE Egg Whites	10 1/2 (11 fl. oz.)
Whole Milk	2 1/4 cups
Pure Vanilla Extract	2 teaspoons
Pure Orange Extract	1 1/2 TABLESPOONS

Cake Flour, Sifted	7 cups
Sugar	3³/4 cups
Baking Powder	2¹/2 TABLESPOONS
Salt	1¹/2 teaspoons
Butter, unsalted, softened	1²/3 cups
Grated Orange rind	3 TABLESPOONS
Orange food coloring	(to color)

STEP ONE:

Preheat oven to 350 degrees. Grease and flour two 6-inch and two 9-inch pans. Make one recipe of batter.

Beat the egg whites slightly with a fork before measuring. Combine the egg whites with ¹/4 of the milk. Add extracts and mix until just blended. Put dry ingredients into a mixing bowl and using the whisk attachment on your mixer, mix on low speed to blend. Add the butter and remaining milk to the dry ingredients. Beat on medium speed until blended. Then beat for two minutes. Scrape down the sides of the bowl and gradually add egg-white mixture to the flour mixture in three stages. Beat at low speed for about 30 seconds after each addition. Fill the pans half full. Tap gently on the counter to remove air bubbles.

Bake the two 6-inch layers, in the center of the oven, for 25 to 35 minutes. The cakes will be done when a toothpick inserted into the center comes out clean. Cool on racks. Next, bake the two 9-inch layers in the center of the oven for 35 to 45 minutes, until a toothpick inserted into the center comes out clean. Cool on racks in pans.

The cakes may be frozen at this time.

STEP TWO:

Preheat the oven to 350 degrees and grease and flour two 12-inch pans and one 13" × 9" sheet-cake pan.

Follow the above recipe and instructions for mixing the batter.

Bake each 12-inch layer separately in the center of the oven for 40 to 50 minutes, until it pulls slightly from the sides of the pan and a toothpick inserted in the center comes out clean.

Bake the sheet cake in the center of the oven for 35 to 45 minutes, until it pulls slightly from the sides of the pan and a toothpick inserted in the center comes out clean.

The cakes may be frozen at this time.

Betty suggests using any good buttercream frosting with her cake. Why not one of the ones in this chapter?

How to Frost the Cake—Tips for Success

• Frost the cake a day or two before the wedding.

• If the cakes are just baked, make sure they're completely cool, even chilled before frosting. Put them in the refrigerator for twenty minutes beforehand.

• *Do not frost frozen cake.* Let the cake thaw completely before frosting. Make sure the syrup (if used) and buttercream frosting are at room temperature. Beat buttercream with a mixer before using. *This is a must!*

• Level each cake (two cakes = one layer). With a large, serrated knife, cut the top off each cake to make it level. To do this accurately, put the cake back in the pan. Use the rim as a guide and lop off the top with a serrated knife. If the cake is too low in the pan, lift it with cardboard rounds. Betty Baird, owner of Sweet Tiers in Hobe Sound,

Florida and baker of Burt Reynolds and Loni Anderson's wedding cake, gives this advice: Put the cake on your Tupperware turntable. Put your knife level with the top of the pan and spin the turntable. The top will lop off evenly.

• Put one layer, cut-side down, on two cardboard cake rounds that have been cut to fit and taped together. (Cardboard cake rounds are made by cutting cardboard to fit the size of the cake pan. Tape them together with Scotch tape in four places, equidistantly.) Put a dab of frosting on the taped rounds to prevent the cake from slipping.

• Cut pieces of wax paper and put them on a platter (to make a platter: cut three cardboard cake rounds larger than the cake, tape them together with Scotch tape, and cover with decorative aluminum foil) with the pieces extending over the edge, all the way around. Put the cake on the platter. (After the cake is iced, remove waxed-paper pieces and you have a clean platter.)

• Brush all crumbs from the cake before frosting. *Note:* Jane Stacey suggests first putting a thin layer of frosting on the cake (called the crumb coat). Once the cake is frosted, put it in the freezer until the frosting is hard. Remove the cake and put another layer of frosting on top. Betty Baird, however, says the crumb coat can be avoided by keeping plenty of frosting on the spatula. This places a barrier between the cake and the spatula, literally burying the crumbs as the frosting is applied. (Experiment and see which method is best for you.)

• Put about 1/4″ filling or frosting on top of the first layer. Level with a metal cake-decorating spatula. Then chill the cake in the refrigerator for about thirty minutes. Remove and put the top layer of the cake on the bottom layer.

• Put the cake on the Tupperware turntable. Spin the turntable while putting the frosting on the sides with your metal cake spatula. Hold the spatula parallel to the sides of the cake while it turns; keep it steady. This will give you a smooth finish. Practice until you get it right.

• Stop the turntable. Put the frosting on the top and smooth with the spatula. Redo the sides of the cake by spinning the turntable.

• After the cakes are frosted, put each tier in a cake box (get a few from the supermarket bakery or a cake supply store), cover loosely with aluminum foil, and tape them shut. Put the boxes in the refrigerator.

⌒

Tiering a Cake

It's fairly easy to tier a cake, once the layers are assembled. (For more information, see appendix I for my video, *Wedding Cake Concepts: Make One Easily, Elegantly, Economically.*)

Step 1: Start with the first tier of the cake. Using a cake pan that was used to make the layers of the second tier, invert it. Center the cake pan on top of the first tier, and press it lightly into the icing. Lift it off the cake.

Step 2: Put a 3/4-inch plastic dowel rod or a 1/2-inch wooden dowel rod into the center of the first tier of the cake; press it all the way in. (It should be higher than the top of the cake.) Make sure it's straight. If not, remove and reinsert near the middle, but not in the original spot.

Step 3: With a pencil, while the dowel rod is still in the cake, mark the dowel rod where it meets the icing. Remove the dowel rod.

Step 4: Cut the dowel rod at the mark with a small crafts saw. This is your prototype.

Step 5: Use it to measure and cut the others. You need six. One for the center, five others to be placed around it. Next, put one dowel rod into the center of the cake, and place the five other dowel rods into the cake in a circle around the center rod, about 2 1/2 inches from the edge of the cake. (Press the dowel rods all the way into the cake.)

Step 6: Frost the top of the cake smooth, covering the holes made by the dowel rods. You are now ready for the second tier.

Step 7: Prepare the second tier as you did the first. (The second tier should be on cardboard cake rounds, and frosted, and ready to go. Don't forget to put a dab of frosting on the cake rounds before frosting so that the cake won't slip.) Gently press an inverted cake pan (used to make the top layer of the top tier of the cake) into the icing on the top layer of the second tier.

Step 8: Prepare the dowel rods as you did for the first tier. Put the dowel rods in the second tier, one in the center, five around it. Frost the cake smooth to cover the holes. (See steps 2–6.)

Step 9: Sprinkle a layer of shredded coconut, about 1/3 cup, around the center of the first tier, about 1 1/2 inches from the edge. The coconut prevents the icing from lifting when the cake is taken apart to be cut. (Shredded coconut is found in supermarkets.)

Step 10: Use Betty Baird's "plop and drop" method to place the second tier on the first. Pick up the second tier and as your guide, look at the top of the first tier for the imprint of the cake pan. Gently position the second tier on top of the first, within the imprint, and let the cake drop. Use a spatula to smooth the surface afterward.

Step 11: The third tier is now ready to be put on the second (it should be on cardboard cake rounds, frosted, and ready to go). Sprinkle the top of the second tier with sprinkled coconut and then gently put the top tier on the second. Smooth the icing with a spatula.

The cake is tiered!

∽

Transporting the Cake

Do not tier the cake before transporting it to the reception site. After the tiers are frosted, put in the dowel rods, frost smooth, and sprinkle the bottom and second tiers with coconut. Put the tiers in boxes and cover. *Put them in the refrigerator and don't remove them until you're ready to transport them. Make sure the vehicle is cold and stays cold!* BUTTERCREAM FROSTING CAN MELT. Transport the cakes in the boxes and assemble and decorate at the reception site. Take along extra frosting and your spatula to fix mistakes.

NOTES

Chapter Four: The Double Budget and Tips for Successful Shopping and Saving Money

1. Center for Study of Responsive Law, *The Frugal Shopper Checklist Book* (Washington, DC: Center for Study of Responsive Law, 1995).

Chapter Seven: The Engagement Ring

1. Scarisbrick, Diana, *Symbols of Wealth, Power and Affection* (New York: Harry N. Abrams, Inc., 1993), 7.
2. Tober, Barbara, *The Bride* (New York: Harry N. Abrams, Inc., 1984), 97.
3. Scarisbrick, *Symbols of Wealth, Power and Affection*, 82.

4. Manchester, William, *The Death of a President* (New York: Harper & Row, 1967), 533.
5. Matlins, Antoinette, and Bonanno, A. C., *Jewelry & Gems* (S. Woodstock, VT: GemStone Press, 1989), xii–xiii.
6. Feder, Jay, *The Practical Guide to Buying Diamonds* (Denver: 4 Cs Press, 1986), 18.
7. Tiffany & Company, *How to Buy a Diamond* (New York: T&CO, 1992).
8. *The GIA Jeweler's Manual* (Santa Monica, CA: Gemological Institute of America, 1989), 31.

Chapter Nine: The Reception

1. Tober, Barbara, *The Bride* (New York: Harry N. Abrams, Inc., 1984), 121.

BIBLIOGRAPHY

Antin, Roger M., *Bride's*, New York: Conde Nast Publications, Inc.

Bartlett, John, *Familiar Quotations*, Boston: Little, Brown and Company, 1955.

Beranbaum, Rose Levy, *The Cake Bible*, New York: William Morrow and Company, Inc., 1988.

Book of Common Prayer, The

Bridal Guide, New York: Globe Communications.

Brody, Rosalie, *Emily Post Weddings*, New York: Simon & Schuster (in association with the Emily Post Institute, Inc.), 1963.

Bruton, Eric, F.G.A., *Diamonds*, Radnor, Pennsylvania: Chilton Book Company, 1978.

Center for Study of Responsive Law, *The Frugal Shopper Checklist Book*, Washington, D.C.: Center for Study of Responsive Law, 1995.

Champlin, Joseph, M., *Together For Life*, Notre Dame: Ave Maria Press, 1991.

Chapman, Roy, *Wedding & Event Videography*, Sarasota, Florida: Del Mar Communications, Inc.

Demetrios, *For the Bride*, New York: DJE Publications.

Diamant, Anita, *The New Jewish Wedding*, New York: Summit Books, 1985.

Editors, *Mrs. Beeton's Family Cookery*, London and Melbourne: Ward, Lock & Co., Limited, 1923.

Feder, Jay, *The Practical Guide to Buying Diamonds*, Denver: 4 Cs Press, 1986.

Feinberg, Steven L., *Crane's Wedding Blue Book*, New York: Simon & Schuster, 1993.

Gaal, Robert A.P., *Diamond Dictionary*, Santa Monica: Gemological Institute of America, 1977.

The Gemological Institute of America Editors, *The GIA Jeweler's Manual*, Santa Monica: The Gemological Institute of America, 1989.

Harvey, Gail, *Poems of Love*, New York: Gramercy Books, 1989.

Hawes, Elizabeth, *Martha Stewart Weddings*, New York: Clarkson N. Potter, Inc., 1987.

Limousine and Chauffeur, April, 1997

Malgieri, Nick, *How To Bake*, New York: HarperCollins, 1995.

Manchester, William, *The Death of a President*, New York: Harper & Row, 1967.

Matlins, Antoinette L., Antonio Bonanno, F.G.A., A.S.A., M.G.A., and Jane Crystal, *Engagement & Wedding Rings*, South Woodstock, VT: GemStone Press, 1990.

Matlins, Antoinette L. & Antonio Bonanno, F.G.A., P.G., M.G.A., *Jewelry & Gems: the Buying Guide*, South Woodstock, VT: GemStone Press, 1989.

McCoy, Deborah, *For the Bride*, New York: JE House Publishing, 1993.

McElveen-Hunter, Bonnie, *Elegant Bride*, Greensboro, North Carolina.

Miller, Anna M., *Gems and Jewelry Appraising*, New York: Van Nostrand Reinhold, 1988.

Modern Bride, New York: Bridal Group Publishers.

Morse, Sidney, *Household Discoveries and Mrs. Curtis's Cookbook*, Petersburg, N.Y.: The Success Company, 1914.

Nash, Ogden, *The Private Dining Room*, New York: Little, Brown and Co., 1952.

Newman, Renee, *The Diamond Ring Buying Guide*, Los Angeles: International Jewelry Publications, 1992.

Pagel-Theisen, Verena, G.G., F.G.A., *Diamond Grading ABC*, New York, Antwerp: Rubin & Son, 1990.

Pellaprat, Henri Paul, *The Great Book of French Cuisine*, New York: The World Publishing Company, 1971.

Primetime Live, Denver: Journal Graphics, Nov. 4, 1993, Transcript #322.

Routtenberg, Lilly S. & Ruth R. Seldin, *The Jewish Wedding Book*, New York: Schocken Books Inc., 1967.

Rubenstein, Helge, Ed. *The Oxford Book of Marriage*, Oxford, New York: Oxford University Press, 1992.

Sax, Richard, *Classic Home Desserts*, Shelburne, Vt.: Chapters Publishing Co., 1994.

Scarisbrick, Diana, *Rings, Symbols of Wealth, Power and Affection*, New York: Harry N. Abrams, Inc., 1993.

Tiffany & Co., *How to Buy a Diamond Brochure*, New York: T&CO., 1989.

Tober, Barbara, *The Bride*, New York: Harry N. Abrams, Inc., 1984.

Vows: The Bridal & Wedding Business Journal, Boulder, CO: Grimes and Associates, Inc.

Notes

Notes

Notes

Notes

Notes

Notes

Notes

Notes